Volume **1**

Essays from cHORIZON

PERSPECTIVES IN
WESTERN CIVILIZATION

WILLIAM L. LANGER, *Editor*
Coolidge Professor of History, Emeritus   *Harvard University*

AMERICAN HERITAGE PUBLISHING CO., INC.   *New York*
HARPER & ROW, PUBLISHERS, INCORPORATED   *New York, Evanston & London*

Perspectives in Western Civilization: Essays from Horizon   Volume 1

Copyright © 1972 by American Heritage Publishing Co., Inc.

Library of Congress Catalog Card Number: 79–185243

ISBN: 06–043841–X

INTRODUCTION

WILLIAM L. LANGER

I t is now roughly a century and a half since historical research and writing ceased to be the occupation of retired statesmen or gentlemen scholars. The rigorous, systematic training thenceforth given to professional students has improved the quality of historical literature immeasurably. But it has also increased the quantity of the product to the point where only the specialist can master even a restricted segment. The days when all cultured society awaited the next volume of Macaulay, Thiers, or Michelet have gone beyond recovery. No man is nowadays competent to write the whole history of a nation or a period on the basis of original research. At best he can draw together the vast specialized literature and supply his own interpretation of the synthesis.

With so extensive a knowledge of historical events it stands to reason that the textbooks used by students can never be more than the merest distillation of the data. Indeed, the material must be compressed to the point where it may become lifeless or at least colorless. Only a more detailed treatment can convey something of the flavor of past events.

It is exactly this function that the present selection of essays from *Horizon* magazine is intended to fulfill. These articles cover the gamut of European history, though not in any systematic way. One might say that they sample the events of the past, providing for selected topics the detail necessary for better appreciation and acquainting the student with problems and solutions that have of necessity to be omitted from a general text. These essays are all written by people of competence in their field. They are fully abreast of modern knowledge of their subjects and serve to put flesh on the bare bones of historical fact. Anyone with an interest in the past should enjoy the scope and variety of this collection, while the student should find it stimulating and provocative as well as informative.

CONTENTS

The retrieval of the Mycenaean civilization through the excavations of Schliemann, Evans, and Blegen, and the demonstration by Ventris from the Cretan and Peloponnesian clay tablets that the Mycenaeans used an archaic Greek script and were therefore true Greeks, must certainly be rated the triumph of classical archaeology. As the author of the present essay shows, it is all but certain that Homer in the Iliad *and the* Odyssey *was reciting legendary Mycenaean exploits. In one form or another these survived the long Dark Age of Greece (c. 1200–800* B.C.*), as did certain art forms and techniques. Evidently the Mycenaeans succeeded in building an advanced, well-organized, enterprising, and warlike society. The unfolding of the story by the late Sir Maurice Bowra makes fascinating reading, backed as it is by the authority of an eminent student of Greek literature and life.*

HOMER'S AGE OF HEROES

C. M. BOWRA

In the last hundred and fifty years, scholars have done an enormous amount of work on the Homeric poems in their desire to find out when and how they were composed and what truth, if any, lies behind their stories. At times the critically minded might well ask to what end all this work was leading. The bits of the puzzle did not seem to fit; there was fierce disagreement on most fundamental points. But slowly and quietly, despite many false starts, progress has been made. The bits are coming together, and we can see the general pattern. Archaeology has brought the Trojan War back from legend to history; the comparative study of oral epics has shown how Homer must really have worked; the discovery and decipherment of documents from the Greek past of 1200 B.C. have thrown unexpected lights into what seemed to be a lost world. The inspiration of a few men of genius and the solid support of many hard-working inquirers have changed the whole character of Homeric studies, and we can now relate Homer to his historical background and see how he worked and what he worked on.

The classical Greeks believed that at a period in the past, which

The reverence accorded Homer by the Greeks of the classical age is evident in this idealized marble portrayal of the bard.

9

our system of chronology would place from about 1400 to about 1200 B.C., their ancestors had been a race of supermen, of heroes, who were endowed physically and mentally beyond the common lot and who lived for action and the glory which it brings, especially through prowess in battle. Such a belief in a heroic past is to be found in many peoples, and for parallels we need look no further than the great Germanic migrations from the fourth to the sixth century A.D. or to the cycles of high adventure which the French connect with Charlemagne in the ninth century, or the Russians with Vladimir Monomakh of Kiev in the twelfth century, or the Yugoslavs with the fall of the old Serbian kingdom to the Turks at the Battle of Kosovo in 1389. With such beliefs the Greek tradition of a noble past has much in common, and like them, it found its expression in heroic, narrative song. From what must once have been a vast mass of songs, we have only the *Iliad* and the *Odyssey*, which the Greeks, without hesitation, ascribed to Homer. In all their pristine strength and splendor these epics stand at the dawn of European literature as its first and in some ways its most remarkable achievement.

The *Iliad* and the *Odyssey* survive in isolation. Of other poems resembling them we have only a few stray lines, and of Homer himself we know next to nothing. He says not a word about himself, offers no personal judgments, and hardly ever speaks, even in the first person. External traditions about him are late, contradictory, and untrustworthy. Where all is darkness it is not surprising that some scholars have decided that he did not exist or at least did not compose the two poems, and many alternatives have been sought to what is regarded as the uncritical gullibility of the Greeks about him. The case for some kind of multiple authorship has appealed to many whose standards of literary criticism come from books composed in conditions very unlike those of the Homeric poems and who are unable to understand that in the course of centuries literature has changed its habits. For some one hundred and fifty years the Homeric poems have been carved into pieces by minute analysis and explained variously as combinations of single short lays, or expansions of original, basic poems, or ingenious transformations of poems dealing with quite different subjects. Yet all this labor has led to no single point of agreement. Each analyst believes he has found the solution, but he has no disciples. Something seems to have gone wrong, and we can in fact see what it is.

The fundamental error of the analytical method is that it treats the Homeric poems as if, like modern books, they were written to be read. They belong to a different, much older art. They were not written but recited, not read but heard, and the difference accounts for the peculiarities which have troubled modern scholars but did not trouble the Greeks. Before the invention of writing, all poetry was recited or sung, and the practice still flourishes in many regions where not everyone is literate, or books are confined to limited, special fields like law and theology, or recitation is still enjoyed for its own sake as a dignified and agreeable pastime.

The oral poet works quite differently from the poet who writes. Recitation is his only means of making his work known, and his first duty is to keep his audience's attention at all costs. If he bores or confuses them, he loses their interest and, with it, his source of livelihood. His technique, which comes from generations of practiced bards, tells him what to do. Above all he must not allow his story to become too complicated; he must deal with one and only one thing at a time, with all the clarity and firmness of outline of which he is capable. This means that he sacrifices much that the writer of books thinks indispensable. In oral art the moment a theme has done its task it is dismissed without ado, and no attempt is made to tidy the loose threads. The need to stress the special character of each dramatic occasion may lead to inconsistencies with what is said elsewhere. A long poem, whose performance may last for several days, may be loose in construction just because each episode must be complete in itself. A passage which performs one task in one place may be repeated word for word in another place to perform a slightly different task. The audience does not know what it is to turn over pages to see if everything fits exactly, and it is content with the fleeting situation as the spoken word reveals it. Oral poetry has its own rules, which are well known to us from a large mass of poems collected from many parts of the world where the art is still vigorous and popular. It is by the standards of this art that Homer must be interpreted and judged.

Although the *Iliad* and the *Odyssey* were composed for recitation and show all its familiar marks, each has its own mastering design and its own kind of unity. In the *Iliad* the whole poem hangs upon the wrath of Achilles, and though other episodes are introduced on a generous scale to make it indeed a tale of Troy, it is the wrath which gives a unity to the whole. The last book picks up the themes of the first and tells the end of the wrath with which all the action began.

The *Odyssey* is composed in three movements: the first tells of the anarchic condition of Ithaca in the absence of Odysseus, the second of his many adventures between his departure from Troy and his final arrival on Ithaca, the third of his vengeance on Penelope's suitors after his arrival. In each movement the characters are admirably consistent, lifelike, and even at times complex. The rich, elaborate, and traditional language shows no real variation between one section and another, and the poetical vision is sustained throughout. Devices, such as similes or the repetition of conventional themes for the arming of warriors or the conduct of sacrifices or putting boats to sea, are managed with admirable judgment and made to provide variety just when it is needed. Both the *Iliad* and the *Odyssey* are clearly artistic wholes, and such interpolations as they may contain do not disturb the main pattern.

It does not necessarily follow that both poems are the work of the same poet. There are certainly differences between them, in temper, in language, in pace, in construction, and in outlook, but these are less than between *Romeo and Juliet* and *The Tempest* or between *Comus* and *Samson Agonistes*. All considered, the *Odyssey* looks very like a later work by the author of the *Iliad* and may have been intended to be in some sense a sequel to it. The poems were probably composed between 750 and 700 B.C., since such a date fits the latest datable details in them. They belong to a period from which almost no other literature survives, and their origin was certainly in Ionia on the eastern coast of the Aegean Sea. There is no reason to think that their author's name was not Homer.

Between the events of which Homer tells and the lifetime of the poet himself there is a gap of some five hundred years. Another three centuries separate Homer from the classical Greeks of the Golden Age. These later Greeks believed that the main events of his poems were historically true, but of the poet's lost world they knew almost nothing—far less than we do today. It remained for modern research, moving on three main lines of discovery, to unearth an advanced civilization which corresponds in many respects to that of which Homer sang.

The first move came from archaeology, when in 1870 a retired German businessman, Heinrich Schliemann, who was obsessed by a passionate love of Homer, drove a deep trench into the traditional site of Troy near the southeastern shore of the Dardanelles. Three years later, after digging through many levels, he found what he thought to be the city of Priam and its treasure. But what he identified as Homeric Troy was, in fact, a city which flourished at least a thousand years earlier than any possible city of Priam, and at the end of his life Schliemann knew that he had not discovered what he sought. It fell to his successors, and especially to the University of Cincinnati expedition led by Professor Carl W. Blegen, to identify, in a higher level at the same site, the ruins of the city which must indeed be the Homeric Troy. Schliemann also attacked sites on the Greek mainland, notably at Mycenae, where he uncovered a royal graveyard where the bodies lay intact in all their gold masks and ornaments. The work his inspired insight inaugurated has been continued ever since, and each year it has added to our knowledge of this rich and spectacular past.

The heroic age of which Homer sang has its historical counterpart in this Mycenaen civilization, which had its beginnings in Crete, notably at Knossos. About 1450 B.C. Knossos waned and Mycenae waxed, developing its own new movements in the fine arts and its own characteristic pattern of life. That it was fashioned for war is clear from the vast scale of its Cyclopean fortifications, from the rich variety of weapons found in its graves, from the many scenes of battle which its artists delighted to portray on gold or ivory or gems or pottery. Yet the Mycenaean world did not exist only for war. It made notable achievements in the fine arts, and its works and wares found markets in distant lands from the Adriatic to Syria. A power like this one was fully capable of maintaining a war such as that against Troy, and tradition may well be right in saying that the expedition was led by the king of Mycenae. But the Mycenaean civilization, which had many seats in the Peloponnesus and even northward as far as Thessaly, came to an abrupt and violent end about 1200 B.C., when its towns and citadels were destroyed and its material culture fell into rapid decay. The destroyers probably came from the northwest and, even if they were related racially to the Mycenaeans, were vastly inferior to them in culture. By 1200 the Dark Age of Greece begins.

A second, much less abundant source of information comes from Egyptian and Hittite records. The Egyptians were much troubled by the "Peoples of the Sea," and among these we may recognize two names which Homer uses for his Greeks—Achaeans and Danaans. The first took part in an attack against Egypt from the west about 1230 B.C. and were routed by Merneptah; the second peoples were among the confederates of a concerted invasion by land and sea about 1182 B.C. and were routed in the Nile Delta by Ramses III, who had reliefs of the battle carved on a pylon at his temple at Medinet Habu. The Hittite records, found in their ancient capital of Boghazköy, contain tantalizing references to the Ahhiyawans, who cannot be other than the Achaeans, and who played a

13

considerable part in Hittite foreign affairs in the fourteenth and thirteenth centuries, first as allies and later as raiders by land and sea. They were classed as a great power; and in one document in particular the king of Ahhiyawa is mentioned as being the equal of the kings of the Hittites, the Egyptians, and the Babylonians, only to have his name erased, as if in the interval he had forfeited his title to honor.

From the Egyptian and Hittite documents we get a clear enough picture of Achaeans, living probably on the Greek mainland but with outposts in Asia Minor and Cyprus, who through their ships pursued a policy of expansion toward the east and the southeast, aiming eventually at seizing land in Egypt. In such conditions an attack on Troy would have had its place; for Troy, which stood near the narrowest point of the crossing from Europe to Asia and seemed to have been a tributary of the Hittites, would have had to be captured before Asia Minor could be invaded from the north-west. For the Achaeans such a policy would have been almost a necessity, and we can understand why the Trojan War took place. The Achaeans, who are known alike to Homer and to the Egyptians and Hittites, are evidently the same people as those known to archaeology as Mycenaeans.

Neither archaeology nor foreign records tells us much about the internal organization of Mycenaean society, or indeed whether its members were authentic Greeks. For this information we must rely on the clay documents found in Mycenaean sites, first at Knossos and later in great quantities at Pylos in the southwestern corner of the Peloponnesus. These were deciphered in 1952 by a young English architect, Michael Ventris, who proved beyond doubt that they contain an archaic form of Greek. In one of the great tragedies of historical scholarship, Ventris was killed in 1956 in a road accident, but his epoch-making discovery had been made, and he left a rich legacy for others to develop.

The Mycenaean script, which is adapted from an earlier script current in Crete, whose reported decipherment has raised much controversy, is a syllabary, and its eighty-seven signs stand either for vowels or for consonants followed by vowels. Such a syllabary is far less efficient than an alphabet and contains many ambiguities owing to its lack of sufficient signs. This probably did not matter to its original users, who must have been officials who kept records only for certain purposes and were well acquainted with what the signs meant by convention. The documents are for the most part inventories of possessions, offerings to gods, documents on land

tenure, military orders, and lists of men and women allotted to
certain tasks. They contain not a trace of anything that can be
called literature and have more than a touch of the précis in their
manner. But their value is incalculable. They prove that the Mycenaeans were Greeks; that they had a highly organized system of
government, were certainly quite as rich as Homer believed, worshiped some of the gods known to him, and had names very like
those which he gives to Greeks and Trojans—including both
Achilles and Hector, though neither of these has any claim to be
Homer's original.

From these three sources we get, quite independently of Homer
or other Greek source, a well-established notion to the Mycenaean
world, of its wealth, its fine arts, its expanding and aggressive policies, and its ability to wage war. From it we may turn to the site of
Troy and specifically to the level known as VIIa, a rebuilding of
the city after the earthquake of circa 1280 B.C. This level keeps the
old walls and gates, but has otherwise been refashioned for the
needs of war. Empty spaces have been filled with houses; food supplies were kept in earthenware vessels dug into the floor; internal
communications were improved by paved roads. About 1240 this
city was destroyed by fire, and layers of ashes, calcined stones,
burned bricks (to say nothing of corpses in the main streets and
under the walls) tell the same story. This was the Troy of which
Homer knew, and its destruction was the work of invading Achaeans. It does not matter that it can have been no more than a fortress, covering some five acres. What matters is that it guarded the
way into Asia, and the Achaeans captured and destroyed it. It was
the last great event in their heroic legend. Story told that its capture cost the Achaeans dear, and that afterward disaster fell upon
them. Within fifty years their great cities and fortresses of the
mainland suffered the same fate as Troy, and the Mycenaean
world came to an end. A few survivors escaped by sea to Ionia and
brought with them the songs of their homeland and the memories
of its heroic deeds.

It is of this heroic age that Homer tells, directly in the *Iliad* and
less directly in the *Odyssey*. His information about it was extensive
and surprising. He knew that Troy had been besieged and taken by
an Achaean confederacy under the king of Mycenae, that among
the Trojan allies were people who looked like Hittites, that Achaeans like Bellerophon had been active in an earlier generation in
Asia Minor, that they did not hesitate to raid Egypt. He also knew
more surprising details which meant nothing to his own age and

15

A fifth-century Greek artist depicted Achilles (left) as a heroic figure in shining armor. The Mycenaeans' view of themselves, as seen on the Warrier Vase (opposite), was rather less flattering.

can only be memories of the Mycenaean world. He consistently speaks of bronze weapons, and though he knows about iron, he does not mention that it was used for war. The helmets of his warriors have plumes and horns like those on the Warrior Vase from Mycenae. His Ajax carries a shield "like a tower," which was normal in the fourteenth century but went out of use soon afterward. He speaks of such characteristic Mycenaean things as sword hilts riveted with silver or gold studs, of silver work inlaid with gold, of palaces with upper floors and rooms opening on vestibules and courtyards, of open precincts for the gods instead of temples. His shield of Achilles is made in a technique like that used in the inlaid dagger blades from Mycenae; he gives to Nestor a cup with images of doves on the rim, and such a cup, made of gold, has been found. When he tells of the slaughter of men and animals at a great man's funeral, he is confirmed by a tomb at Dendra. He knows about the towers and gates of Troy and, more surprisingly about the structure of its walls. Because of their unusual batter below the perpendicular ramparts, Patroclus is able to climb them up to the point where Apollo casts him down.

Homer knows of the gold of Mycenae, of the *temenos*, or special piece of land, allotted to princes and mentioned in Mycenaean documents, of thrones inlaid with ivory ornaments such as have been found in more than one place, of bronze greaves like those

17

found in Cyprus and the Peloponnesus. He has heard of even remoter objects and situations. When Odysseus goes out on night
operations, he wears a felt cap covered with boars' teeth; though
such caps were common before 1300 B.C., they went out of use
afterward. He gives an account of Egyptian Thebes which seems
to come from the fourteenth century, when Amenhotep III decorated temples with floors and doors of gold and silver and built
pylons which survive for Homer as a hundred gates. Homer's
knowledge of the Mycenaean age is extensive, and through it he
sets his story in a heroic past when men were wealthier and more
powerful than in his own day.

At the same time many of Homer's details come from ages later
than the Mycenaean. His dead are not buried but burned, a practice which seems to have started soon after the Trojan War. Though
he knows about Thebes, he believes Egypt is so far away that even
birds take a year to cross the sea from it. His warriors do not fight
from chariots, like the Mycenaeans, but use them simply as a
means of transport to places on·the battlefield where they dis-
mount and fight on foot. Instead of two horses his chariots usually
have four. From his own time or near it come descriptions of the
wealth of Apollo's shrine at Delphi, the Gorgon on the shield of
Agamemnon, the wheeled tripods of Hephaestus, the advance of
infantry in close line in battle, the structure of the brooch of
Odysseus with its two pins fitting into sheaths, the part played by
Phoenicians in the seafaring life of the *Odyssey*. Above all in his
similes, which bear no relation to the Mycenaean world, he draws
from his own observation and touches on many subjects which lay
outside his heroic theme but touched him intimately by their simple and varied appeal.

Why does Homer draw on the material of different centuries?
How does he know anything about the Mycenaean world? The
answers would be easy if we could believe that he inherited written
texts of Mycenaean poems and that he drew upon them for material before bringing it up to date to suit his contemporary audience at points where it might be unintelligible. However, though
the Mycenaeans used writing, there is no evidence that they used
it for poetry, and, more important, it is clear that when the Mycenaean civilization perished, its system of writing perished with it.
This is indeed an extraordinary, almost unparalleled phenomenon,
and it can be explained only by the hypothesis that the scribes
were a small class whose work the new conquerors did not understand and did not use. At any rate, on all the thousands of potsherds

The famous "Nestor's Cup" of hammered gold, discovered in the tombs of Mycenae. It is about six inches high.

which originated between circa 1200 and 750 B.C., when the new Phoenician alphabet was introduced into Greece, there is not a single inscribed letter, and we are forced to conclude that Homer cannot have learned about the past from any written records. He may conceivably have seen some Mycenaean objects preserved as heirlooms, and he almost certainly knew the site of Troy (though not Ithaca), but even this would not account for his knowledge of the Mycenaean world. How did he find it?

As so often with Homer, the answer comes from looking at other oral poets who tell of the past. They do not learn from books; their knowledge of the past, which is often impressive, comes from oral tradition. Such a tradition may last for centuries, and this is what happened in Greece. We cannot doubt that heroic songs existed in the Mycenaean age, and it is even possible that the magnificent meter of the hexameter had already been invented, since Mycenaean Greek, as we can see from the tablets, falls easily into it. Bards passed on to their successors not only names and stories, metrical devices and tricks of narrative but something much more substantial and useful—a large number of formulaic phrases covering most needs of the heroic story and ready for use when the poet needed them. Such formulas were indispensable to oral composition and were fashioned with much care through many centuries until, by Homer's time, they met almost every want in his story. Oral poets operate less with single words than with phrases, and these phrases have been polished and perfected by generations until they have a true distinction of their own. Some of these formulas in Homer are extremely ancient, and he himself may not quite have known their original meaning, but they belonged to the tradition in which he learned his craft, and for that reason he used them. He could and no doubt did supplement them with new phrases of his own making, but these old formulas were his link with the past, and it is through them that he knew so much about an age which was at least five hundred years before his own. Whenever we come across something indubitably ancient in the *Iliad* or the *Odyssey*, we may be sure that it came to Homer through a long succession of bards whose art can be traced back to Mycenaean times.

Homer seems to have supplemented this traditional knowledge with a knowledge of the actual site of Troy. His story in the *Iliad* makes hardly any mistake in geography; and though many of the points may seem unimportant, like the course of the Scamander, or the distance from the city to the Achaean camp, or the plants and bushes on the plain, they all indicate that he knew more about the battlefield than even his formulas can have given him. Indeed, even today, when we stand on the ruins of Troy and look over the plain, we feel that we can see why his masterpiece fits so well into the landscape. The Troy he saw was certainly in ruins, but he knew that it had been a great city, and he took advantage of his local knowledge to create such scenes as those of Andromache on the tower seeing the dead body of her husband dragged behind the chariot of Achilles or Priam going out at night across the plain to ransom the body of his dead son from the terrible man who has killed him. Among these ruins, which were old even in his time, Homer created again an ancient tale and gave to it a strength which it surely never had before.

Homer is not a historian, and he lived long before scientific history was invented. His re-creation of the past in poetry is not historical because it combines competing elements which come from some six centuries. No doubt, too, he made his own improvements on legends, and we have no right to presume that all he says is true. What he tells is what he himself believed because the Muse had told it to him. By the Muse he means the divine power of creative song which he knew in himself and rightly regarded as the daughter of Memory, because it was indeed a people's memory that had preserved so much for him. We do not know how he performed his songs. He himself makes bards sing to kings at their courts, and perhaps this is what he himself did, though it would not prevent him from singing also at religious festivals and public gatherings. Nor do we know how his poems were written down. It is most unlikely that his pupils memorized them and passed them by word of mouth to later generations, since for this there is no parallel in oral performance; indeed, it is alien to the methods of such composition. The easiest explanation is that since he himself was alive when the wonderful art of writing returned to the Greeks in the form of the Phoenician alphabet, he dictated his poems to someone who knew it and the written texts were guarded by professional bards who recited them to later generations. Yet he remains an oral poet who uses all the devices of this special craft and draws his art from a long tradition. His aim was more to delight than to instruct, but he believed that men delighted to hear of the glorious doings of men and that such doings, and the sufferings which they bring, find a reward and a consolation in song. To this task he gave his incomparable gifts. He learned the ancient formulas and used them as if they were fresh as the morning for his vision of the heroic generations who once belonged to his race and whose memory was treasured through all the changes and catastrophes of the intervening years.

*The abiding interest in the trial and death of Socrates derives largely
from the fact that the issue confronting the Athenians at that time has
confronted many governments ever since, even unto the present day.
Can a state or government, devoted though it may be to freedom, afford
to stretch respect for liberty to the point of tolerating teachings thought
subversive of the system desired and supported by the majority of its
citizens? In the last analysis, may this not be tantamount to signing
its own death warrant?*

*We know little of Socrates's trial beyond what is told us so movingly
by his pupils, notably by Plato. Socrates was charged with impiety,
which was regarded as a threat to the security of the state, and
furthermore with corrupting the young. Just what this latter charge had
reference to is hard to say, except that some of the young blades of
Athens appear to have interpreted what they heard from Socrates and
others as a license to unbridled self-expression, without reference to the
rights of others. The fact that a majority of the large jury considered
Socrates guilty suggests that his notions and teachings had long been
uncongenial and suspect to many of his fellow-citizens. The author
explores all angles of this challenging episode in a highly competent
review of the situation and the evidence.*

*Mr. Finley, Professor of Ancient History at Cambridge University,
is the author of several studies of the ancient world. A collection of his
essays, including the two in this volume, has been published under the
title* Aspects of Antiquity.

WAS SOCRATES GUILTY AS CHARGED?

M. I. FINLEY

This indictment and affidavit are sworn to by Meletus, the son
of Meletus of the deme Pitthos, against Socrates, the son of
Sophroniscus of the deme Alopece. Socrates is guilty of not believing in the gods in which the city believes, and of introducing other
new divinities. He is also guilty of corrupting the young. The
penalty proposed is death."

When Socrates, then seventy years old, was put on trial in his
native Athens in 399 B.C., the proceedings began with the clerk of
the court reading this indictment aloud to the large (but normal-
sized) jury of 501 men, all citizens in good standing over the age of

*"I am not going to alter my conduct," Socrates is said to have told his
accusers, "not even if I have to die a hundred deaths."*

23

thirty. The Athenian system of government was amateur in the strict sense of the word: there were no district attorneys, scarcely any police, and no professional lawyers. If a crime was committed, major or minor, some individual—acting in a private capacity—had to do something about it. He had to lay a charge before the proper official, as Meletus did, and then he had to attend the trial, mount the rostrum, and present his case to the jury. Meletus was supported by two other men, Lycon and Anytus. When they had taken their allotted time, controlled by a water clock, it was Socrates's turn. He denied the charges, defended his life's work and his ideas, and by direct interrogation challenged Meletus to produce the young men whose religious beliefs he had corrupted.

This took hours, while the jury sat on their wooden benches and the spectators stood about behind them. As soon as the speeches were finished, the verdict was given. Athenian juries, unlike their modern counterparts, had full control of the decision. They were judge and jury together, and there was no appeal from their verdict. Nor did they have an opportunity to discuss the case. They simply filed up one by one and dropped their ballots into an urn. The votes were counted in sight of everyone, and the result was announced immediately: guilty 281, not guilty 220.

When a defendant was convicted, the jury had next to fix the penalty, which they did by voting once more, this time on choices put to them by the accuser and the defendant. Meletus asked for the death penalty. In reply, Socrates made a series of counterproposals; for example, he suggested that he be voted one of the highest honors the state could confer, namely, maintenance at public expense in the Prytaneum for the rest of his life. Such a proposal was consistent with his refusal to accept any imputation of guilt, but it appeared so frivolous and offensive that, if the ancient evidence is to be trusted, eighty of the jurors now switched their votes, and the majority for capital punishment was a large one, 361 to 140. Socrates then went off to jail and everyone else went home, each juror receiving as pay for the day's work three obols, half a workman's normal wage. A month later Socrates drank the cup of hemlock, having refused his friends' efforts to persuade him to flee the country, and died quickly and painlessly.

This much about the trial of Socrates is clear and straightforward enough. But very little else is, and that is a pity. Socrates and Athenian democracy are both dead, but his trial remains alive as a great myth, and like all myths, it is believed—by those who believe it—to exemplify a universal truth. Here is the proof, it is

*In a canvas done in 1787 in the mannered classical style, Jacques
Louis David portrayed Socrates reaching for the cup of hemlock.*

said, of the tyranny of the majority, of the trampling of the voice
of reason and individual conscience by mass rule, of the common
man's hatred of the man of genius. Socrates may be dead, but the
issues are not. That is why it is still important to know what facts
lie behind the myth.

The prime, although not the only, source of the myth is an early
work of Plato's known as the *Apology*. (The Greek word *apologia*
means "defense"; it does not imply that a wrong has been done for
which the wrongdoer begs pardon.) This work appeared a few
years after the trial and pretends to be the actual text of Socrates's
two speeches to the jurors. It is necessary to say at once that it is
nothing of the kind. All the proceedings in Greek trials were oral.
There were no stenographers, and no official records were kept
other than the text of the indictment and the verdict. No one could
later report the speeches in full unless the speakers themselves had
written them out beforehand and preserved them. This Socrates
surely had not done. Instead, the *Apology* is a brilliantly dramatic
piece in which Plato's hand is visible in every paragraph. In addition, we have two other accounts of Socrates's trial, both by Xeno-   25

phon (still others were extant in antiquity but are now lost). These versions do not agree with each other, and in places they are quite contradictory.

Here before our eyes is the mythmaking process at work. These "apologies" could be written and circulated precisely because there was no authentic text of what Socrates really said. In fact, Plato himself hints elsewhere that, far from making the great speeches of the *Apology*, Socrates gave a bumbling performance. He was no orator but an arguer and conversationalist; what was very effective in small groups of disciples was of no use, and even harmed his case, in a set speech to a large, partly hostile, and inattentive audience. It is doubtful that this mattered much in the actual event: most Athenians had had thirty or forty years to make up their minds about Socrates, and no single speech was likely to have changed anyone's mind in 399 B.C., any more than today. But the death of Socrates mattered very much indeed to his disciples, so much so that they wrote the "apologies" which, in their view, Socrates *should* have made. That is to say, they took a stand on the issues, on the politics and morals of the Athenians—which they disliked violently—and on the teaching of Socrates and the meaning of his life. Plato's view of these things was not Xenophon's. Because Plato was by far the greater man and the more persuasive, his view prevails down to our own day. And yet, that is not necessarily proof that he was right.

Paradoxically, it is not what Socrates said which is so important, but what Meletus and Lycon and Anytus said, what they thought, what they were getting at, and what they feared. To begin with, who were they that they should initiate so vital an action? Unfortunately, we do not know anything of consequence about either Meletus or Lycon, but Anytus was a prominent and responsible political figure, with a career of considerable distinction and patriotic service behind him. His participation creates a strong presumption that the prosecution was a carefully thought-through step, not a merely frivolous or petty persecution.

And who were the jurors who decided that Socrates must die for what he taught? Every year in Athens there was drawn up a jury panel of 6,000 men, volunteers for the service. For each trial, the requisite number was selected from the panel by lot. Since in 399 B.C. there could not have been more than 20,000 men all told who were eligible to sit on juries, Socrates was tried and condemned by a sizable percentage of his fellow citizens. We know nothing about them individually, but granting that there may have been a disproportionate number of the very poor, who wanted the three obols; of the very old, who found jury duty an entertaining and exciting way to pass the time (at least that is what the comic playwright Aristophanes alleged in *Wasps*); and of the richer men, who could afford to give time to their civic duties, the 501 jurors were not a bad sampling of the citizenry. Judging from that sample, the conclusion is that the Athenians were divided about Socrates. More correctly, they were divided on the question of how dangerous he was, for many of those who were willing to acquit thought him either a fool or a bore, or both.

Obviously we cannot know what went on in the minds of individual jurors while they listened to Socrates and his accusers. We cannot say why each man voted as he did. But we do know a lot about their collective experience. The most important fact in their lives was the great war between Athens and Sparta, the Peloponnesian War, which began in 431 B.C. and did not end (though it was interrupted by periods of uneasy peace) until 404, five years before the trial. In 431 Athens was the greatest power in the Greek world, head of a very considerable empire, prosperous, and proud —proud of its position, of its culture, and, above all, of its democratic system. "The school of Hellas" it was called by Pericles, and Athenians believed and cherished that claim. By 404 everything was gone: the empire, the glory, and the democracy. In their place stood a Spartan garrison and a brutal, dictatorial junta (which came to be known as the Thirty Tyrants). The psychological blow was incalculable, and there was not a man on the jury in 399 who could have forgotten it.

Nor could they have forgotten the appalling losses of the war. Two great plagues struck the city almost at the beginning, and in the four years 430–426 they carried off about one-third of the population. In 415 Athens made an all-out effort in an invasion of Sicily. That ended in disaster in 413: perhaps half the effective fighting force was killed or missing. Finally, the Thirty Tyrants butchered another 1,500 men, drove many others into exile, and plundered wealthy foreigners for their own personal enrichment.

It is testimony to the vigor of Athenian society that the city recovered as rapidly and completely as it did. The Thirty Tyrants had a short life: they were driven out in 403 by the combined efforts of a handful of the exiles and the survivors at home. The traditional democracy was then re-established, not to be challenged again for a century. One of its first actions was to declare a general amnesty, and so powerful was the spirit of conciliation that both

27

Plato and Aristotle, of all people, praised the democratic leaders for it.

Nevertheless, it is a common view today that Socrates was tried and executed as an act of political vengeance by the restored democracy. It is true that Socrates was no friend of democracy as it was practiced in Athens. He criticized it freely and frequently, but on the other hand, he was deeply attached to Athens itself, fought in the hoplite ranks in several battles, and at least once in his life held office. There is nothing here to warrant the political vengeance theory, but there may be among his friends and disciples. One was Critias, the evil genius of the Thirty Tyrants, the most ruthless, brutal, and cynical of them all. Critias fell in the fighting that helped bring down the tyranny, and with him died Charmides, another of the Thirty. Charmides was uncle to Plato and well known as a disciple of Socrates. In these two men (and in others), we can understand easily enough how many jurors saw at work a poison which they traced back to the teaching of Socrates. Because of their bitter personal memories of the war and the tyranny, their votes may well have been turned, at least subconsciously, against a man who, they knew (and he himself never denied), had wrong ideas and even wronger disciples.

It is curious, however, that neither Plato nor Xenophon so much as hints at such a motivation behind the trial. How could they have missed this ready-made opportunity to demonstrate the wickedness of democratic rule? In a letter attributed to Plato, not only is the spirit of amnesty praised but, the writer continues, "By some chance, however, some of the men then in power brought my friend Socrates to trial." The writer of the letter—whether it was Plato himself or someone else in the Academy does not matter— was not so incompetent as to have said "by some chance" if he intended "for political reasons," and I suggest that he was fundamentally right, that political revenge will not do as an explanation, beyond its background role in the minds of some jurors. The simple fact is that the indictment accused Socrates of impiety and corruption of the young, and of nothing else. We live in an age which tends to be cynical about such matters: "It's all politics" is the usual comment. Maybe so, but the ancient Greeks took religion seriously on its own terms, and we must too, if we wish to understand the times.

To appreciate what an Athenian could have meant by "impiety" (the Greek word is *asebeia*), three facts must be kept in mind. One

is that Greek religion had become very complicated over the centuries, with a great variety of gods and heroes who had numerous and crisscrossing functions and roles. The second is that their religion had little of what we would call dogma about it, but was largely a matter of ritual and myth. And the third is that it was thoroughly enmeshed with the family and the state. Impiety was, therefore, a very loose notion: a man could be deemed impious for desecrating an altar, for revealing the secrets of a mystery cult, or merely for saying things which were considered blasphemous. But whatever form an act of impiety took, the fundamental point was that it was a public matter: impiety was an offense not only against the gods but also against the community, and therefore punishment was not left to the gods but taken in hand by the state.

Because of the looseness and vagueness of the concept, its definition rested with the jury in each case. They decided whether or not a particular act, if proved, was punishable under the law. This meant in practice that the frequency of such charges and trials in Athens depended largely on the state of public opinion at any given moment. And the period of the Peloponnesian War was a bad moment. A decree was passed almost at the outset forbidding, as impious, the study of astronomy, very likely as a reaction to the plague. The first victim, we are told, was the great philosopher-scientist from Asia Minor, Anaxagoras, the friend of Pericles; and there were others. There is further evidence of the upsurge of magic and superstition in Athens in this generation, such as the sudden popularity of the cult of Asclepius, the magical healer; or the appearance of imprecatory tablets (a kind of voodoo magic directed against a personal enemy); or the swarms of private soothsayers, diviners, and oracle-mongers whom Thucydides speaks of with such contempt. In 415 B.C. there was the famous double sacrilege, the profanation of the mysteries at Eleusis and the mutilation of the hermae, which drove Alcibiades into exile (and others to their deaths) and may in consequence have cost Athens the war. We cannot speak with certainty, but I have little doubt that in this affair Alcibiades was framed. A large number of men conspired to perpetrate these acts of impiety. There followed months of denunciations and investigations, as a result of which some men were executed and others exiled, and the repercussions were felt in Athens for years.

Against this background, Socrates was accused of a specific form of impiety; namely, that he disbelieved in the city's gods and introduced new ones. In Plato's *Apology* this is denied with great vigor, and there is sufficient and convincing proof that Socrates

29

was in fact a man of very deep piety, who scrupulously performed the sacrifices and other rites. Besides, it is hard to see why the introduction of new gods should have been an indictable offense when it had been happening right and left just at that time. Not only had Asclepius arrived—he was at least a *Greek* god—but there was also an influx of foreign deities, like the Phrygian Cybele and the Thracian Bendis, whose shrines were set up with official permission. No one accused Socrates of joining in their worship, but even if he had, there could have been no objection. All that was said against him on this charge was that he was constantly referring to his inner *daemon*, which talked to him regularly and prevented him from taking wrong courses of action. This was more than the voice of conscience: Socrates plainly believed that it was a *god* who spoke to him. But in a society in which soothsaying was a recognized profession, that is pretty thin ground for prosecution.

There remains, then, the last and most crucial element in the charge: corruption of the young. Plato's *Apology* stresses (and justifies) Socrates's role as a teacher and allows Socrates to admit that his disciples were the young men with leisure for study—in other words, the sons of the wealthiest citizens. (Some of these young men, it must be remembered, eventually became active partisans of the oligarchic coup in 411 and of the Thirty Tyrants in 404.) In Xenophon's *Apology* there is a dramatic moment when Socrates turns to Meletus in court and challenges him: Name one man whom I corrupted from piety to impiety. Meletus answers: I can name those whom you persuaded to follow your authority rather than their parents'. Yes, replies Socrates, but that was a matter of education, in which one *should* turn to experts and not to kinsmen. To whom does one go when one requires a physician or general? To parents and brothers, or to those most qualified by knowledge?

This interchange, fictitious though it may be, somehow strikes at the heart of the issue. Until some fifty years before the trial, there was no Greek schooling to speak of. Children were taught to read and write and figure by the servants who looked after them, usually old male slaves. Beyond that level, formal instruction was restricted to music and physical training. Men of the generation of Pericles and Sophocles learned everything else by living the life of active citizens: round the dinner table, at the theater during the great religious festivals, in the Agora, at meetings of the assembly —in short, from parents and elders, precisely as Meletus said they should.

Then, roughly in the middle of the fifth century, there came a revolution in education, especially at Athens. Professional teachers called Sophists appeared. They quickly attracted the young men of means to whom they gave higher education—in rhetoric, philosophy, and politics. A very good education it was, too, and at high fees. In the process they developed a startlingly new attitude among their disciples; namely, that morals, traditions, beliefs, and myths were not a fixed mass of doctrine to be handed on unchanged and without question from generation to generation, but that they were something to be analyzed and studied rationally and, if necessary, to be modified and rejected. Inevitably, these innovations were looked upon with great distaste and suspicion in many quarters. A kind of know-nothingism developed in reply. In one dialogue, the *Meno*, Plato satirizes this attitude with cold deliberation by making Anytus the spokesman of blind conservatism and traditionalism. "It is not the Sophists who are mad," he has Anytus say, "but rather the young men who pay out their money, and those responsible for them, who let them get into the Sophists' hands, are even worse. Worst of all are the cities who allow them in and do not expel them."

The role assigned to Anytus in this section of the *Meno* is a classic example of Plato's bitter irony. It cannot be taken at face value as a necessarily faithful statement of what Anytus thought and said. But there were many Athenians who did think and say such things. Some of this reaction can be explained in obvious terms: there were then, as there are in all ages, people who dislike anything newfangled, whether in education or politics or women's dress. But it would be a great mistake to think that this is a sufficient explanation. The age of Pericles and the Peloponnesian War which followed made up a period in which Athenian society—more correctly, a part of it—went through a radical transformation in its outlook, its psychology, and its manner of living. The Sophists contributed to this transformation although they did not create it. They symbolized, and made immediately visible, the emergence of a new intellectual class divorced in their thinking from the mass of the citizenry as never before in Athens. Sages like Solon were revered because they expressed in their sayings and their lives the ideals of society as a whole. The new sages did quite the opposite: they tore down the prevailing beliefs and the traditional values, especially in religion and morals.

One may speculate on how this conflict of values might have been resolved had the war not intervened. But the war did inter-

A Hellenistic sculpture of Plato.

vene. And the plague. Then it was no laughing matter when young
aristocrats organized a dining club called the *Kakodaimonistai* (literally, devil-worshipers), whose program was to mock at superstition. They tempted the gods, for example, by dining on unlucky
days; and once, just as the Sicilian expedition had been well
launched, the citizens of Athens awoke one morning to discover
that in the night the sacred hermae which kept guard over streets
and house entrances had been mutilated all over the city. There
was a limit to how much blasphemy the gods would tolerate: when
they had had enough, the whole city would suffer the consequences,
not just the individual blasphemers. And so corruption of the
young became, in the eyes of many, not a matter of abstract principle, but a practical danger to the city at a time when it was already beset with troubles.

But what has all this to do with Socrates? Of all the ironic aspects of Plato's Anytus scene in the *Meno*, none is more striking
than the way in which Socrates there urges that the Sophists are
the proper teachers of virtue. One of the main, serious themes in

32

many of Plato's dialogues is precisely the opposite, namely, that Socrates was bitterly and totally opposed to the Sophists, to their professionalism and their relativistic ethics in particular. Nevertheless, there was a link in the public mind. The classic exposition is the *Clouds* of Aristophanes, performed at the festival of the Greater Dionysia in March 423. The plot, if I may call it that, is the effort of old Strepsiades, a rich rustic, to cheat his creditors by having his son learn from Socrates the techniques necessary for this purpose. The Sophists, the old man has heard, are experts in making the worse case appear the better, and similar dishonest and immoral arts. In the course of the comedy, the Sophists are depicted as cranks, crackpots, and crooks, and the audience hears all the accusations which subsequently emerged, in a very unfunny context, in the trial of Socrates: that the Sophists destroy morals and religion, teaching that the sun is nothing but a golden stone, sneering at the old gods and introducing new ones, and corrupting the young by inculcating disrespect for parents and elders. In one rather long section, Aristophanes drops the buffoonery and burlesque and, in all earnestness and great detail, he praises the good old education of the gymnasium and the palaestra, with its stress on music, athletics, and decorous behavior. In the end, the Thinking Shop burned down and, as Professor E. R. Dodds rightly remarked, the audience was expected to enjoy the holocaust, and to "care little" if Socrates were burned in it.

It is easy to demonstrate that the picture of Socrates in *Clouds* is almost totally false. Aristophanes's Socrates is a conglomerate of the scientist-philosopher like Anaxagoras, of the Sophists, and of pure comic invention. Of the real Socrates there is little other than his poverty, and even that is caricatured. I have no idea how much Aristophanes knew, in a systematic way, about the teaching of Anaxagoras and Protagoras and Socrates. But whether he was expert or not, the line he took was that distinctions were irrelevant. The whole lot were corrupters of youth, and what did it matter if one corrupted with his astronomy and another with his ethics, or if one took pay and the other did not? There were several reasons why Socrates was the choice victim for the cruel burlesque of *Clouds*. He was the best known of the various intellectuals under attack. Most of the others were foreigners who came and went; whereas Socrates was a citizen, a native of Athens, who was always there, in the most public places. He was poor and ascetic, proud of his simple clothes and his bare feet. He was ugly, a serious point. Just imagine small boys gaping from a safe distance at Socrates, with his satyr-like face, talking and talking and talking. Small boys grew up to be members of Aristophanes's audiences, and to be jurors at the trial of Socrates. Aristophanes was surely playing on currently popular themes. Although he did not invent them, he intensified them, and he must bear a heavy responsibility, at a distance, for the eventual trial and execution of Socrates.

The distance from *Clouds*, however, was twenty-four years. The question still remains: Why was Socrates put on trial in 399? My answer is as unsensational as it could be, precisely the answer given in the letter attributed to Plato: Socrates was indicted by some chance. Anytus and Meletus and Lycon joined together for personal reasons, which we can only guess at. That they were able to do so is no problem: personal grievances have been the root cause of many trials, in Athens as elsewhere. That they *succeeded*, however, can be explained only by the long, complicated background I have been describing. It was this chance combination of history and personal factors that produced the great tragedy in 399. It was not inevitable that Socrates had to be tried and executed. But when he *was* accused in 399, it was immediately probable that the atmosphere which had been building up since 431 would destroy him.

And yet, had only thirty-one jurors voted the other way, Socrates would have been acquitted in spite of everything, so close was the margin. There was no lynch psychology; there are even no indications that public emotions were wildly aroused. No one was creating a martyr. That came afterwards. To the people close to Socrates, and to others who were deeply interested in philosophy, this was no mere personal tragedy but something very much deeper and more universal in its meaning. It was these men who, in the next generation or two, created the symbol and the myth. The actual indictment may have been a matter of chance. But what lay behind it was not; it was inherent in any society in which power lay in the hands of any group simply because it had wealth or numbers or some other purely external qualification. Only the virtuous —the philosophers—should govern; otherwise there could be only evil consequences. Democracy was a particularly sinister form of misrule, but for Plato the death of Socrates symbolized the evil of any open or free society, not just of a democratic one.

It was the nineteenth century, in particular, which abstracted one part from the myth created by Plato and seized on that side of it only—the dangers of mass rule. In truth, the fate of Socrates is a demonstration of the old axiom that eternal vigilance is the price of liberty. Freedom never sits so securely that it may not be harmed by its own upholders. In fifth-century Athens the elements of insecurity were both numerous and strong. There was the chronic poverty of resources, with its never-ending threat of famine; there was the long-drawn-out war with Sparta; there was the fact that freedom and democracy were, by definition, the privilege of a minority and excluded slaves and numerous noncitizens; and there was widespread superstition and irrationalism. There was also a technical weakness in the system. The juries had too much latitude, in the sense that they could not only decide on a man's guilt, but they could also define the crime he had committed. When impiety—and this is only an example—is a catch basin, no man is safe.

That much can be conceded to the myth in its modern version, but no more. The execution of Socrates is a fact, and it is one of several such facts which reveal that Athenian democracy was not a perfect instrument. It is equally a fact, which both ancient and modern spokesmen for the myth conveniently overlook, that the case of Socrates was isolated in its time. There could be no better witness to this than Plato. It was in Athens that he worked and taught, freely and safely, for most of his long life; and what he taught was hostile, down to its very roots, to much that Athenians believed and cherished. No one threatened him or stopped him. The Athenians are entitled to have their record judged whole for the two centuries in which they lived under a democracy, and not solely by their mistakes. So judged, it is an admirable record, an argument *for* a free society. Ironically both Plato and Xenophon (and some modern historians) idealized Sparta as against Athens. Sparta was the Greek closed society *par excellence*. There Socrates could never have *begun* to teach, or even to think.

Alexander the Great's exploits were, despite his early death, so
extraordinary that legends about him sprang up at once and flourished
throughout two thousand years. Yet there is relatively little trustworthy
information about his career. What we know beyond the peradventure
of doubt is that he was one of the greatest generals and conquerors of all
time, a commander who set new standards of strategic planning as well
as of tactical operations. But the very extent of his conquests has raised
the question whether he consciously aimed at a fusion of the Hellenic
and Persian cultures and the creation of a world empire based on
divine monarchy. This problem, as intriguing as it is important, was
explored by the late C. A. Robinson, Jr. on the basis of his deep
knowledge of the record. Mr. Robinson was Professor of Classics at
Brown University and the author of several studies of Alexander.

THE TWO WORLDS OF ALEXANDER

C. A. ROBINSON, JR.

Alexander passed across Asia like a flash, and since he never lost
a battle and was young, handsome, and personally dramatic,
he stirred the imagination of men as few have ever done. He was,
as Napoleon said, the greatest general who ever lived. But his real
significance, in the history of Western civilization, goes beyond his
military genius to his conception of a world state based on the
equality and co-operation of all peoples. This political vision, so
strangely found in a young and prideful conqueror, outlasted his
life and his empire to inspire men in every age from his day to ours.

So dazzling was Alexander's military conquest that for centuries
it almost obscured his real nature. In fact, medieval Europe and
the Orient of all periods completely forgot the true Alexander.
They knew only the Alexander of legend and romance, embedded
in an amazing body of literature that began to form soon after his
death and ultimately circulated, in eighty versions and in twenty-
four languages, from Iceland to Malaya.

Even today chieftains in remote parts of Turkestan claim descent
from Alexander, while their ordinary folk are said to be sprung

In a detail from a Roman mosaic (reproduced in full on pages 44–45)
Alexander leads his army into battle. On his armor is the head of
the mythical Medusa, whose face turned all who saw it to stone. 37

from his soldiers and their horses from Bucephalus. The early Christians portrayed Jesus in Alexander's likeness, the Jews looked upon Alexander as a propagandist of the Most High, and the Koran calls him Dulcarnain, the Lord of Two Horns. Alexander, or Iskander as he has generally been known to Asia, was supposed to have built a gate to exclude Gog and Magog, who were later equated with the Ten Tribes of Israel and then with barbarism itself. As geographical knowledge expanded, the mythical gate was moved from the Caucasus to the Great Wall of China and finally to the Arctic Circle. Still other stories brought the conqueror of the known civilized world to the Blue Nile and to Britain—and then, as if that were not enough, to the heavens and on to the Land of Darkness and even farther to the end of the world, where one finds the Well of Life.

The net of legend extended back to include Alexander's father, King Philip of Macedon, and his mother, Olympias, an Epirote princess of fiery, passionate nature. Ancient historians, for example, say that Philip met this imaginative and terrible woman when both were initiated into the mysteries of Samothrace. During religious celebrations, it seems, Olympias was always more deeply affected than other women and used to supply the reveling companies with great tame serpents, which would often lift their heads from out of the ivy or coil themselves about the garlands of the women, thus terrifying the men. At any rate, according to the story, she and Philip fell in love with each other on sight.

Some time after their marriage, the story continues, Philip dreamed that he was putting a seal upon his wife's womb; and the device of the seal, as he thought, was the figure of a lion. Some seers said that Philip should keep a closer watch upon his young wife, but Aristander, the best of all seers, maintained that the woman was pregnant, since no seal was put upon what was empty, and pregnant with a son whose nature would be bold and lionlike.

Moreover, it was commonly believed in antiquity that the temple of Artemis at Ephesus burned to the ground on the night of Alexander's birth. One witness made a remark frigid enough to extinguish the flames, to the effect that it was little wonder that the temple had burned because the goddess was busy bringing Alexander into the world. Since the ancient Greeks loved coincidences. it is probable that they moved the month of Alexander's birth back to midsummer (356 B.C.) in order that Philip, who had just taken a large Greek city, might receive three messages simultaneously: that Parmenio, his chief general, had conquered the

Illyrians in a great battle; that his race horse had won a victory at the Olympic games; and that Alexander III, as he was later called, had been born at Pella, the capital of Macedonia. The seers added to Philip's delight by saying that the son whose birth coincided with three victories would always be victorious.

Philip was a practical man and military genius with the savage appetites and passions of his mountaineer ancestors. For the sake of honor and renown, as his bitter Athenian opponent, the orator Demosthenes, declared, he was ready to let his eye be gouged out, his collarbone broken, his hand and his leg disabled. Personally ambitious, urbane, and friendly, Philip lacked moral scruples and was ready at any time to lie, to break a treaty, to buy friends, or to bribe statesmen. He seemed to feel that a diplomatic victory was as good as one on the battlefield, and he had the ability to lull states to a sense of security until the time arrived for striking the fatal blow. "Taken all in all," concluded a contemporary, "Europe has not yet produced such a man as Philip, the son of Amyntas."

It is a safe guess that Alexander inherited his military skill and cold rationalism from his father. But the son's own inner being, his mysticism and romanticism and impetuousness, came from his mother, Olympias. Perhaps from her, too, came the ability to kindle the imagination of multitudes by a single act—as when, desiring to rally the Greeks wholeheartedly to his cause at the outset of his expedition against the Persian Empire, he visited Troy and stirred in the breast of every Greek glorious memories and the picture of a new Trojan War against the Asiatic foe.

At the age of thirteen, Alexander had the philosopher Aristotle as a teacher, and during three impressionable years his keen mind became thoroughly Greek in character, while his romantic imagination developed a love for Homer and his supposed ancestors Heracles and Achilles. On his expedition to Asia, Alexander took along a text of the *Iliad*, which Aristotle had edited for him, and kept it with his dagger under his pillow at night. It seems clear that Aristotle implanted in the youth a love of learning of encyclopedic scope, with a special interest in scientific investigation and medicine. Moreover, Alexander learned from the philosopher that moderation is necessary in government—a virtue he was not likely to get from Olympias—and he also learned, or rather was taught, that all barbarians (i.e., non-Greeks) were slaves by nature, especially those of Asia.

Alexander's admiration for Greek culture was tempered by the simple, vital, active life of Macedonia. This was a narrow coastal strip, with a mountainous interior, along the Aegean Sea in northern Greece. Though the Macedonians were Greeks, the proud citizens of Old Greece southward despised them as a semicivilized people with a veneer of Greek culture.

These Macedonians, who were destined to remake the world, formed the first nation in European history. Rough and simple though they were, they looked upon themselves as one people, and not, in Greek fashion, as the citizens of this city or that. In the time of Philip and Alexander, the Greeks themselves were caught up in a deep crisis. Were they to continue to insist on the sovereignty of their city-state, or had the time come for a fundamental change in their thinking, for a reconciliation of autonomy with a wider union? A century earlier, in the days of Periclean Athens, they had reached a summit of civilization never before attained by the human race. Now—despite great men such as Praxiteles, Plato, and Aristotle, who lived amongst them—they were torn by fratricidal warfare, an economic depression, and the interference by the Great King of the predatory Persian Empire in their internal affairs. How much attention, therefore, should they pay to certain orators who were urging them to unite under the Macedonian monarchy in a war against Persia, the traditional foe?

The sharp division in Greek thought exactly suited Philip's personal ambitions. By 338 B.C. he found that Athens and Thebes were the only city-states remaining that would fight effectively on behalf of Greek freedom. Without much difficulty he defeated them at Chaeronea in a battle that ended forever the ability of Greek city-states to dominate the peninsula's politics. And then he called together at Corinth representatives of most of the states in Greece and joined them in a federation known as the League of Corinth.

The chief action of the League was to appoint Philip commander in chief of a Panhellenic war of revenge against Persia, to punish her for her invasion of Greece a century and a half earlier. Doubtless, Philip planned no more than an expedition against Asia Minor, for the empire of the Persians stretched 2,700 miles from the Hellespont (or Dardanelles) across Asia Minor through Syria, Palestine, and Egypt, and then eastward through Mesopotamia and Iran to India. It was a rich and mighty state, well-governed and able to dispose large armies of disciplined, courageous men. In Asia Minor alone there were 20,000 superb Persian cavalry; and of the various other troops, 20,000 obstinate Greek mercenaries formed the empire's chief hope as heavy infantry.

Philip delayed his departure two years, during which time he gave himself alternately to state business and carousals. Then, suddenly, he was murdered. At the age of twenty, Alexander fell heir to his kingdom, his army, his plan of the Asiatic expedition, and the command of the Corinthian League.

If Alexander is famous for incredible speed of action, he should also be known for his caution at almost every point in his career. Instead of rashly setting off for Asia in what could only have been another in a long line of interminable wars, this youth spent the next two years insuring that his lines of communication would not be cut while he was absent from Greece. This required long marches through trackless forests, over high mountain ranges, and across the Danube to what is today Bulgaria, Rumania, and eastern Yugoslavia, striking such fear into the hearts of the inhabitants that they did not stir during his absence.

The expedition against Asia, when at last it was ready to set out, had an air of permanence about it. Artists, poets, philosophers, and historians went along with Alexander, just as in later days they were to accompany Napoleon. There were also surveyors and engineers, geographers, hydrographers, geologists, botanists, and other scientists to study the phenomena of Asia and perhaps to send back to Aristotle specimens for further observation. One person deserves special mention: Aristotle's nephew, the historian Callisthenes. He was implicated in a plot against Alexander's life in Central Asia, was arrested and executed. Aristotle hated Alexander for this, and so powerful was Aristotle's influence that, when the generation that knew Alexander died out, not a favorable biography of him was written for three centuries. Instead there was created the familiar picture of the bloodthirsty, lucky despot, which it has been the task of modern scholarship to study and correct.

Alexander's army of Macedonians and Greek allies consisted of about 30,000 infantry and 5,000 cavalry. These troops rarely fought as a body, but even when only small contingents were engaged, Alexander combined the various arms. This practice, and especially the close union of light troops and cavalry with the phalanx, largely explains the invincibility of the Macedonian military machine. Moreover, Alexander invariably pursued the enemy with the aim of destroying him utterly, a policy which the Prussian strategist Von Clausewitz has termed "the strategy of defeat."

In a pitched battle, Alexander's army was likely to line up as follows: in the center, intended as a firm anchor, was the phalanx— 9,000 heavily armed infantrymen, formed in a mobile rectangle eight or more men in depth, with three feet between every two men. This demanded soldiers who were highly trained and disciplined, who would not huddle together for safety, but it also meant that rough ground or momentary shocks from the enemy would not disarrange the mass. To the right of the phalanx came Alexander and his magnificent Companion cavalry—the real striking arm—with lancers, javelin men, and archers thrown out to their right as flankers and skirmishers. To the left were other cavalry and light troops. Parmenio, the second in command, was in charge of the left wing. As an able and cautious tactician he was especially suited for this post, since in the oblique order of battle (the favorite also of Frederick the Great of Prussia) it was the duty of the left wing to hold firm, while Alexander, choosing the decisive moment, charged from the right and rolled the enemy in upon the spears of his slowly advancing infantry.

Alexander varied these arrangements as circumstances dictated. As for tactics, he once said that this was merely a matter of using his brains; his success, he added, was due to never putting anything off. His men worshiped him, and though obviously he was not a reckless adventurer, they had no doubt about his lucky star.

Alexander's organizing ability manifested itself in the siege train, which was far superior to anything of its kind elsewhere. There were siege towers, placed on rollers or wheels and covered with hides to protect them from fires; they might be over 150 feet high, with many stories, so that the top of any part of an enemy wall could be reached. Boarding bridges were used at Tyre for the first time in history. It was possible to undermine the enemy's walls by tunneling or to knock them down with battering rams, which had huge beams over 100 feet long with metallic heads. The besiegers themselves were protected by movable sheds, known in later days as tortoises. But the greatest military invention of antiquity, used for the first time at Tyre by Alexander, was the torsion catapult, which could fire huge arrows accurately for 200 yards as well as stones weighing fifty or sixty pounds. Alexander never employed catapults as field artillery in a pitched battle, but he used them in irregular warfare, in sieges, mounted on ships as at Tyre, and to clear a river's bank of the enemy.

Over this army, infused with a proud professional spirit, stood Alexander, commander in chief of the League of Corinth, and as king of Macedon responsible to no one but himself in military matters and (subject to certain checks of the army assembly) in civil affairs as well. By his side he had seven bodyguards, a staff of what we might describe as general officers, and also a group of eighty to one hundred influential officers, known simply as Companions. These men formed his council, as it were, and provided military and civil officers as needed.

The Grand Army was destined to march under Alexander many thousands of miles during eleven long years, often at terrific speed; it was not unusual for a contingent to cover forty or fifty miles a day with him for several days. Events frequently proved his bravery and self-discipline. He was often wounded—on the neck, head, shoulder, and in the thigh; in Turkestan, the fibula of his leg was broken; thrice he was wounded in Afghanistan; in India an arrow pierced his lung; and besides he suffered attacks of fever and dysentery. Every inch of the march was new, yet his reinforcements reached him regularly, over 60,000 in the first eight years alone. And every inch of the way he met opposition, save in Egypt. He fought four pitched battles: three with Persia, and another with an Indian rajah in the Punjab, where he encountered for the first time large numbers of terrifying elephants who barred his passage of a great river.

In addition to the disciplined armies of the ancient East, which greatly outnumbered his own, Alexander had also to fight fierce mountain tribes. There were deserts to overcome, and a long guerrilla warfare with its utterly strange tactics awaited him in eastern Iran. There were, too, strong cities to besiege, the island city of Tyre alone requiring seven months and all his tenacity.

Alexander's plan was probably to conquer as much of the Persian Empire as possible and hold on to it, but his every success opened up further vistas until the possession of the entire empire was his. The conquests confronted him with enormous problems of administration, for he now had an empire of his own that contained not only many different races but peoples in all stages of civilization. Greater still, since his ambitions developed in this direction, was the task of giving a sense of unity to a world state.

It was in the spring of 334 B.C. that Alexander, then twenty-two years of age, began the march. Many portents from heaven were reported; it was said, for example, that the wooden statue of Orpheus sweated profusely. Most people feared the sign, but Aristander, the reliable seer, bade Alexander be of good cheer and assured him that he was to perform deeds worthy of song and story that would cost poets and musicians much toil and sweat to celebrate. Thus, amid great excitement, the army set out for Asia under a leader who was destined never to return.

Darius III, the Great King of Persia, considered it beneath his

The Battle of Issus, fought in 333 B.C., *is shown in a damaged Roman mosaic discovered at Pompeii. The scene is a copy of a painting done*

dignity to bother personally with yet one more intruder from Greece. This he left to his satraps in Asia Minor; but when they were decisively defeated at the Granicus River, he began to bestir himself and collected an army of perhaps 100,000 men. Alexander was now at Tarsus, with all of Asia Minor successfully behind him. He knew that Darius and his vast host were somewhere in the broad Syrian plains: he feigned sickness, hoping to entice Darius into the narrow plain of Cilicia. This was the only time in his life that his intelligence service broke down, for it happened that either king tired of waiting for the other, and Alexander crossed the

by a contemporary of Alexander. The Macedonian king is at the left, mounted on Bucephalus; at right center, in his war chariot, is Darius.

Amanus Mountains in search of Darius the very night that Darius crossed the same range by a different pass in search of him.

Alexander found himself with his lines of communication cut, a hostile empire all around him, and Darius between him and home. Immediately he retraced his steps and at Issus overwhelmed the Persians. Darius, who was a coward as well as a despot, promptly fled and despite the rapid pursuit managed to escape.

On his return to camp that night, Alexander found that his men had picked out for him the tent of Darius, which was full to overflowing with gorgeous servitors and many treasures. Straightway, 45 then, according to Plutarch (the biographer of the first century A.D.), Alexander put off his armor and went to his bath, saying, "Let us go and wash off the sweat of battle in the bath of Darius." "No, indeed," said a Companion, "but rather in that of Alexander." And when he saw the basins and pitchers and tubs and caskets, all of gold and curiously wrought, while the apartment was marvelously fragrant with spices and unguents, he turned his eyes upon his Companions and said, "This, as it would seem, is to be a king."

Alexander never laid eyes on the wife of Darius, who was reputedly the most beautiful woman in Asia. Years later, though, he married one of her daughters. As for the other captive women, seeing that they were surpassingly stately and beautiful, he merely said jestingly that Persian women were torments to the eyes. According to the Royal Journal, or Diary—the "official" truth and as close to the real truth as we shall ever be able to come—Alexander never had a mistress. Moreover, he drank but rarely, and then it was generally a deliberate action, enabling him to associate freely with comrades from whom his new position was slowly isolating him. His self-restraint and moderation he ascribed to the belief that it was more kingly to conquer himself than others, though his temper always remained his worst enemy. Probably his boastfulness was annoying chiefly to his close associates.

Alexander had come to Asia with a fleet made up of Athenian ships and in part a hostage for Athens' good behavior during his absence. He quickly saw that it was no match for the Phoenician fleet of the Persians, and to avoid the loss of prestige that would follow upon defeat, he disbanded it. After Issus, however, when it might have been advantageous to continue the pursuit of Darius, Alexander realized that he could not leave the Phoenician coast in the hands of the enemy, with their own fleet free to raid Greece. He resolved, therefore, to take the home bases of their fleet and thus bring it over to his side.

It turned out exactly as he expected, though he could not have foreseen the difficulty of taking Tyre, a heavily fortified island half a mile offshore. By building his own fleet as well as a mole to the island, Alexander eventually took Tyre and totally destroyed it. It was a great crime, as great a one as his destruction of rebellious Thebes shortly before his departure from Greece. If, however, a man is to be judged by the standards of morality of his own day, we should add that the destruction of cities was common contemporary practice. Plutarch says that Alexander waged war according to usage and like a king; while Arrian—the second century

A.D. historian whose account is the best we have; since it drew from the soundest contemporary sources—remarks that Alexander was the only one of the ancient kings who, from nobility of character, repented the errors he had committed.

Egypt fell to Alexander without a blow, for she hated Persian misrule. On the coast he planned a great city, the first of the seventy-odd cities Alexander founded on his march. His purpose was to give the eastern Mediterranean a commercial and administrative center that might also act, if circumstances warranted, as a link between East and West. Meanwhile, it was essential to provide a commercial substitute for ruined Tyre. The site of Alexandria was chosen with consummate skill, for it was west of the westernmost mouth of the Nile and therefore, thanks to the currents of the Mediterranean, free from the river's silt.

While the army was laying out the city, Alexander and a few friends made a dramatic trip across the Libyan Desert to the oasis of Siwa, to see the oracle of Zeus Ammon, which in Greek eyes was second in importance only to Delphi. It was a youthful stunt, and Alexander, we must remember, was never anything but young. There was a purpose in it, too, as there generally was with Alexander. He had crossed the Danube a few years earlier to insure his communications. Now he wished to confirm that the desert actually existed and would serve as a natural boundary. Also he could bribe the priests to police the desert for him and, en route, accept the surrender of envoys from Cyrene to the west.

So great was the impression that Alexander made on men's minds that a story soon grew up that Alexander had gone to the oracle to ask about his birth, and that, in fact, he was greeted as the son of Zeus. The story has no foundation in history, and Alexander left Egypt without hearing it. He was intent on finding Darius.

The two kings met for the last time east of the Tigris River at Gaugamela, though the battle popularly takes its name from Arbela, a town nearby. Darius kept his men under arms the entire night before the battle, suspecting a surprise attack, a fact that not only lowered their vitality but added to their natural fear. Alexander, however, followed his usual custom and ordered his soldiers to take dinner and rest themselves. While his Macedonians slept, he himself passed the night in front of his tent with his seer Aristander, celebrating certain mysterious sacred rites and sacrificing to the god Fear. And it is said that the older of his Companions, and particularly Parmenio, when they saw the plain and mountains all lighted up with barbarian fires and heard the sound of voices arising from the enemy camp as if from a vast ocean, were astonished at their multitude and argued that it would be difficult to repel such a tide of war in broad daylight. They therefore came to Alexander's tent after he had finished his sacrifices, and on their behalf Parmenio urged him to make a night attack upon the Persians. But Alexander, realizing the hazards of a battle in the dark, gave them the celebrated reply, "I will not steal my victory."

It was October 1, 331 B.C. The Persian army did not even approach the 1,000,000 infantry and 40,000 cavalry of later legend, but it was larger than the one at Issus—so much larger than Alexander's, indeed, that it extended well beyond his flanks. Alexander's infantry still stood at 30,000 men; the cavalry perhaps had grown to 7,000. As the battle progressed, Darius was again seized with terror and was the first to turn and flee. He hoped to raise a rebellion in eastern Iran, but some months later he was murdered in the Parthian Desert by his cousin, a remarkable prince of Bactria named Bessus. Alexander gave the body a fitting burial.

It is not difficult to imagine Alexander's thoughts as he passed through the lands and capitals of the ancient East, Babylon, Susa, and Persepolis. The hereditary foe of Greece had been utterly defeated, and he was now the ruler of the largest empire the world had ever seen. When he took his seat for the first time under the golden canopy on the royal throne at Persepolis, his old friend, Demaratus of Corinth, burst into tears and declared that those Greeks were deprived of great pleasure who had died before seeing Alexander seated on the throne of Darius. Acting against Parmenio's advice, Alexander deliberately set fire to the palace, in order that the world might clearly understand that one regime had given way to another. Legend created from this the fanciful story of Thais, the Athenian courtesan who incited the banqueters to the act and thus punished the Persians for their evil deeds. But the cold fact was that the rule of the Persians had come to an end; so, too, had the war of revenge.

The death of Darius confirmed what the sword had already proclaimed, that Alexander was in fact the Great King of the former Persian Empire. Determined to hold and organize his conquests, he recognized the necessity of examining and possessing his state. He probably considered this a relatively easy task, though the flight of Bessus, Darius' murderer, to Bactria (northern Afghanistan) had its own implications. Bactria was an extensive and solid area of
Iranian rule, where the Indo-Europeans preserved much of their

early vigor and vitality; still, Alexander had no way of guessing that nationalism in eastern Iran would give him the longest and stiffest resistance in his career.

In the course of the march to Bactria and Sogdiana (Russian Turkestan) there occurred one of the great tragedies of Alexander's life. This was the conspiracy of Philotas. Philotas' family was ancient and proud and had fought nobly for Philip and Alexander. Parmenio, his father, had recently been brushed aside by Alexander and left at Ecbatana; two of his brothers had died during the expedition. Moreover, Alexander's endless marches into an utterly unknown world were preventing the conquerors from settling down to the enjoyment of their gains. Most important of all, perhaps, was the fact that in Macedonia the king was little better than the nobles, and yet here was Alexander grown powerful and aloof, often acting and thinking strangely. Had not the time come, thought Philotas, for the Macedonian nobles to take things into their own hands?

When the plot against Alexander was discovered, Philotas was brought before the army, as Macedonian law required. He confessed and was killed by the soldiers with their javelins. Alexander than sent orders to the generals at Ecbatana to put Parmenio to death also—an action, it has always been said, that marks the darkest moment in his life; in later eyes, it was plain murder. Yet an ancient Macedonian law decreed that relatives of a conspirator against the king must also die. The execution of Parmenio was judicial, although it is difficult to believe that Alexander, had he wished, could not have persuaded the army to a different action in the case of a man to whom he owed so much. Probably he decided to let the famous general pay the penalty of the law in order to break the Macedonian opposition to him.

Alexander had indeed been displaying dramatically strange ideas and actions ever since he first set foot in Asia. It is quite impossible, at this point in his career, to put a label on them and say what he had in mind, but the end result was one of the greatest revolutions in the history of thought. Alexander had acquired, it should be remembered, the Greek point of view toward barbarians (non-Greeks). Plato had held that all barbarians were enemies of the Greeks by nature; and Aristotle, as we have already remarked, said that all barbarians were slaves by nature, especially those of Asia. Now let us observe Alexander's extraordinary capacity for rapid growth along many lines.

Alexander had come to Asia Minor in a dual capacity, as king of

Macedon and commander in chief of the League of Corinth. Soon
he became the ally of the Greek cities along the Asia Minor coast,
the adopted son of a native queen, Ada of Caria, and the Great
King at least in the interior districts. This latter title became his in
actual fact not much later, and before his death he was also the
suzerain of Indian rajahs, and a god in both Greece and Egypt. In
working out his position in the state, his solution was to take over
the existing forms of government and to assume a different relation
to the various sections of the empire, much in the manner of the
British monarch of a later day. More extraordinary than his allowing the queen of a barbarian people to adopt him—to show that he
had come as *their* king, too—was his appointment of two barbarians as governors of provinces in Asia Minor. Then, he asserted
his independence of the Corinthian league by not punishing Darius'
captured Greek mercenaries, but adding them to his own army.
Finally, he began a significant improvement on the Persian administrative system by separating the military, civil, and financial
powers of the provincial governors. All this he did in eighteen
months, during which time he had also won two pitched battles
with the Persians and overcome various strong cities and mountain
tribes.

The conclusion of the war of revenge, which the burning of the
palace at Persepolis helped to signalize, meant also the end of
Alexander's reliance on his Greek allies. Not much later, therefore,
he dismissed them all and allowed those who wished (as most of
them did) to re-enlist in his imperial army. Was this an indication
of a rapidly growing personal dominion, or was it his way of showing the vast barbarian world that the Greeks were not to occupy a
privileged position, that all peoples were to be treated equally? A
clue may be found in Alexander's adoption of Persian dress for occasional wear at this time, though once again we have the hostile
gossip to the effect that Alexander was giving himself up more and
more to Oriental luxury and indeed, that he had a retinue of
concubines.

The actual question that Alexander was confronting was simply
whether he was to substitute Greek despotism for Oriental—that
is, whether it was to be the same old world, or whether a new state
could be formed along very different lines. We learn from Plutarch
that Alexander considered it his kingly business to mix all men as
in a loving cup. Alexander had been able to test Greek smugness
by contact with barbarians, on the battlefield and off, and experience had convinced him of the essential sameness of all people. It

was in Egypt, Plutarch continues, that Alexander accepted the teaching of the philosopher Psammon, that all mankind is under the kingship of God. Still more philosophical, Plutarch adds, was Alexander's own opinion that although God is indeed a common father of all mankind, still, He makes peculiarly His own the noblest and best of men.

To give concrete expression to these ideas, to create a common bond within his world state, was Alexander's hardest task. For the moment, at least, his founding of cities had to suffice. Usually these were not wholly new cities, as is generally supposed, but rather existing settlements to which he added old or wounded soldiers. They were located at strategic points and were intended to police the countryside and guard communications. But, of course, the soldiers were Greeks and Macedonians (the distinction between the two peoples was soon forgotten) and from these islands of Hellenism, or Greek culture, there spread a knowledge of Greek ways which, as Alexander hoped, helped to unite the peoples of his empire. The Hellenization of Hither Asia, as it turned out, was the most important specific result of Alexander's life.

These, then, were the chief "strange" ideas that Alexander had held up to the time of Parmenio's execution. It is little wonder that he should exclaim that Hephaestion was the only friend to understand and approve his plans of empire.

In the spring of 329 B.C. Alexander crossed the Hindu Kush into Bactria by the Khawak Pass. Almost at once his most important body of Greek cavalry, which had been under the executed Parmenio, rebelled and was sent home. The resentment of these men at the death of their beloved commander and their subsequent dismissal presented Alexander with the greatest crisis in his life. Should he himself also return? Obviously he could not find more Greeks and Macedonians at a moment's notice, and yet his entire expedition might end in disaster at this point. There was only one thing to do: to take a chance and, for the first time, to incorporate large numbers of Asiatics in his army.

Alexander's willingness to trust his own personal safety and the success of his expedition to barbarians must be placed at the top of the extraordinary ideas that now rapidly took form and unfolded to the world. And their motivation was the immediate need for survival.

The new Asiatic troops proved invaluable to Alexander during the two years in Bactria-Sogdiana. It was a time of guerrilla warfare, of constant marching, ambushes and treachery, of wounds and sickness. The opposition of the Macedonian nobility, moreover, remained; and one night at a banquet Alexander was taunted about his great debt to Philip and Philip's men. Finally, thoroughly drunk as he was this evening, he let his terrible temper get the better of him, and he murdered Clitus "the Black," as he was called, a friend since boyhood who had saved the King's life at the Granicus.

Somehow or other during these same two years, as we have said, Alexander found time to think. If the Asiatic troops were so loyal, could not some gesture be made to placate eastern Iran and bring the guerrilla warfare to an end? His solution was to marry Roxane, the captive daughter of a Bactrian prince, whom the soldiers pronounced the most beautiful of all the women they had seen in Asia, with the single exception of Darius's wife. Legend turned it into a love affair, but it was a political marriage, the beginning of a real effort to take Asia into full partnership with him. This, and the desire to legitimize his rule, led him in the year before his death also to marry Barsine, Darius' daughter. At that time, most of his friends took barbarian wives, and gifts were distributed to those soldiers, 10,000 in number, who in the course of all the marching had taken up more or less permanently with Asiatic girls.

Alexander's idea of a fusion of races did not mean that he planned a deliberate Hellenization of the East or a barbarization of the Greeks and Macedonians. Those who wished were free to pursue their own national life—and they represented the overwhelming majority—but at the same time there was to develop a new life based on an interchange and mixture of customs and blood. This new attitude toward the world was to be the driving and unifying force of his empire. As part of this program, he now ordered that 30,000 native youths should be taught the Greek language and trained in the use of Macedonian weapons. And to leave no doubt that these ideas were to be applied on an immense scale, he revealed his intention, once he had finished with the East, of marching against the West, to Italy and beyond. This was one of the first manifestations, surely, of a growing megalomania.

But what to do about an uncertain officer corps, as represented by the Macedonian opposition? Here was an immediate military problem, deserving treatment as drastic as that meted out to the mutiny of his cavalry. Alexander reached the decision to abandon the comradely relationship with his officers that had long characterized the Macedonian monarchy, and to put an end to wavering support and possible plots by becoming an autocrat. Or better, to put it in Greek terms, he decided, in this century which had already raised living men to divine status, to become a god.

The plan fell through for the moment, but when we look at Alexander's extraordinary ideas—on world conquest and his own relation to the state, on the use of barbarians in administration and army, the foundation of cities, a common culture, personal deification—we must conclude that there was no way to realize them except by autocratic action. Ideas, however, have a way of growing. In the year before his death, during a banquet of reconciliation with his men after another brief mutiny, Alexander prayed for partnership in the empire and for unity and concord in a joint commonwealth where all peoples were to be partners rather than subjects. It was this prayer, it has been said, that marks a revolution in human thought. It was picked up, first by Zeno, whose Stoicism preached the brotherhood of man, and then by Saint Paul in his stirring vision of a world in which there shall be "neither Greek nor Jew, barbarian nor Scythian, bond nor free."

When the time came to leave eastern Iran, Alexander recrossed the Hindu Kush by the Kaoshan Pass and continued down the Khyber Pass to India. This ancient land, with its ascetics and Brahmans, its marvels and curious customs, filled the Greeks with awe. But Alexander hurried on, for, being wholly ignorant of the size of India and even of the existence of China, he thought that Ocean—the great sea, so men believed, that ringed the inhabited land—lay not much farther east. A few years earlier, standing beside the Caspian Sea, he believed it to be a northern gulf of Ocean and organized an exploring expedition to find out. Now he thought he was near the eastern and natural limit of his empire, where great cities and harbors of his creation would produce a wonderful prosperity and serve to tie together in an economic whole the various sections of the state.

As Alexander traversed the Punjab, however, the great Indian rajah Porus opposed his crossing of the Hydaspes River, now known as the Jhelum. Alexander won a victory over him at great cost; but when, not much later, his men stood upon the high bank of the Hyphasis and gazed across the interminable plains extending to the horizon, their spirits sank. The rumor of more enemies, of men larger and braver than the other Indians, and of countless elephants, unsettled a morale that had already been weakened by the recent fighting. During the past eight and a half years Alexander's men had marched over 11,000 miles. Fatigued mentally and physically, they could not see the purpose of further marching and fighting in unknown lands. When Alexander learned that the army

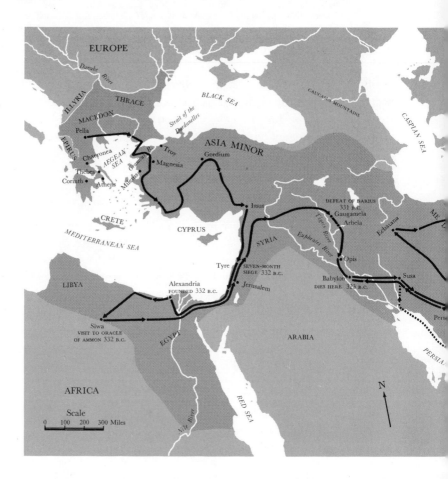

would go no farther and insisted upon returning home, he retired to his tent for three days—like Achilles—and hoped that the men would change their minds. But it was of no avail.

It has been a curious mutiny, for it had never occurred to the army to depose Alexander, the only man who could bring them safely home. To mark the farthest point of his advance Alexander erected twelve tremendous altars to the Olympian gods and offered sacrifice upon them, and celebrated gymnastic and cavalry contests. He also prepared armor that was larger than usual, and stalls for horses that were higher and bits that were heavier than those in common use, and left them scattered up and down to impress later generations with the manner of men who had come that way.

Alexander's men won their point, but it was he who chose the route home. In November, 326 B.C., the army, aboard ship and on foot, began the descent of the Indus river system. Indescribable

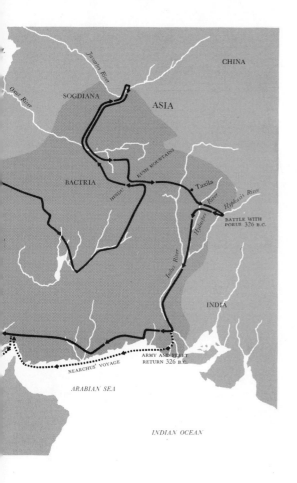

The cameo double-portrait above is thought to represent Alexander and his mother, Olympias. The odyssey of Alexander and his army is traced on the map; the shaded area represents the empire he sought to rule.

slaughter followed their progress, but in July of the following year the Indian Ocean was reached. Alexander's joy at seeing the southern limit of the inhabited world was great. All that now remained was to explore the route by land and sea between the Indus and Mesopotamia, and the empire would be a well-knit and self-sufficient whole.

Alexander knew something of the difficulties that lay ahead, for he had already sent westward, by a different route, many of his troops, most of his baggage, and his elephants. (He was too good a general to use the beasts in battle, for he recognized their unreliability, but he did employ them for transport and in hunting.) He had no real conception, however, of the torrid, arid wastes awaiting him, especially the 150 terrible desert miles in Baluchistan. His journey became one of the greatest marches in military history. His commissariat, for the only time in the expedition, failed him,   55 and he was unable to keep in touch with the fleet under Nearchus. Most of the camp followers died, but he got his army of 15,000 men back safely to Persepolis early in 324 B.C., almost exactly six years after his first triumphant entry.

Plans of further conquest, of the administration of his empire, of the exploration of Arabia, now filled Alexander's mind. But it was too much for him. His ceaseless mental and physical activity, the immense responsibilities of state, his long marches and dangerous wounds had so lowered his vitality that he was unable to throw off a fever. On June 13, 323 B.C., Alexander died at Babylon, not yet thirty-three years of age, after a reign of twelve years and eight months.

The world was never again to be the same. Gone forever, at least as a force in politics, was the small democratic city-state of the Greeks; gone, too, was the homogeneous civilization concentrated around the Aegean Sea. The high standards of taste, the freedom, responsibility, and intensity of Periclean life became things of the past. The world now belonged to the large monarchic state.

Nothing could be further from the truth than to imagine that, because Alexander's empire upon his death broke up into three or four large states, his conquests came to naught. The new kingdoms that resulted were ruled by Macedonians and Greeks for three centuries along Western lines, until the coming of Rome. The most striking fact about the Hellenistic age—as we term those extraordinary centuries after Alexander's death, when Hellenism was adopted by non-Greeks—is the unity of the large world that had been opened by his expedition.

Macedonians and Greeks who had been left behind in Bactria eventually mustered enough strength to march again across the Hindu Kush and conquer India as far as Calcutta. In the region of the Khyber Pass known as Gandhara, they created an art that was an extraordinary mixture of East and West. Hitherto Buddha had been merely an abstraction in art, but the only way Greek sculptors knew how to represent a god was in the form of a man. Thus when Chinese pilgrims to Buddha's birthplace passed through Gandhara, they brought back with them the new conception of Buddha. Except for this, however, the Farther East would be exactly the same today had Alexander and his men never existed.

It was distinctly otherwise westward. If some of Alexander's dreams took root slowly, such as that of co-operation between peoples, nevertheless his idea of the *oikoumenē*, the "inhabited world," found immediate acceptance. In the Hellenistic age man thought of himself more and more as a member of a world society, a society in which there might be (and were) sharp differences, but in which a common culture nevertheless acted as a natural bond. The new culture was different from that of Periclean days, for it was affected by the rapid rise of the ordinary man and by close contact with Orientalism. There could be no more vivid illustration of the unity of the world than the fact that the New Testament was written in Greek.

It was the culture of the Hellenistic age that civilized Rome and facilitated her creation of her own world state and then Christianity's conquest of that state. Only a mighty historical force would have brought that state into being. As such it is Alexander's monument; while his dreams have been, and still are, a challenge to humanity to substitute the idea of universalism, of solidarity of the world and co-operation between peoples, for narrowness of race and outlook.

It is one of the unedifying traits of human nature that man, given the opportunity, will not hesitate to exploit his fellow man. As Mr. Finley remarks, in the case of American slavery the racial difference between white and black could always be argued as a sure mark of inferiority on the part of the slave. But we tend to forget that almost all historical civilizations rested on exploitation, upon varying degrees of violation of the rights of others, upon the utilization of the victim's physical and cultural capabilities for one's own profit. In the United States slavery was localized and slaves were employed primarily in agriculture. But in the world of the Greeks and the Romans, with all its great achievements, it would have been utterly impossible to attain the wealth and leisure necessary for these achievements without the extensive use of slavery and the acceptance of slave-trading as an important industry. Mr. Finley here provides a masterful analysis of the many aspects of an all-important human institution as it affected the world of classical antiquity.

THE ANCIENT WORLD'S PECULIAR INSTITUTION

M. I. FINLEY

Aulos Kapreilios Timotheos does not appear in any history book. There is no reason why he should, but an accident of archaeology makes him a figure of some curiosity if not importance. He was a slave in the first century of our era who obtained his freedom and turned to slave dealing, an occupation in which he prospered enough to have an expensive, finely decorated marble tombstone seven feet high. The stone was found about twenty years ago at the site of the ancient Greek city of Amphipolis on the Strymon River, sixty-odd miles east of Salonika on the road to the Turkish border—and nothing like it exists on any other surviving Greek or Roman tombstone, though by now their number must be a hundred thousand or more. The stone has three sculptured panels: a typical funeral banquet scene at the top, a work scene in the middle, and a third showing eight slaves chained together at the neck, being led along in a file, accompanied by two women and two children who are not chained and preceded by a man who is obviously in charge, perhaps Timotheos himself for all we know. The

Roman military monuments often depicted prisoners, such as this enslaved Gaul on a first-century arch at Carpentras, France.

inscription in Greek reads simply: "Aulos Kapreilios Timotheos, freedman of Aulos, slave trader."

It is not his occupation that makes Timotheos a rare figure, but his publicly expressed pride in it. The ancient world was not altogether unlike the southern United States in this respect. After the Civil War a southern judge wrote: "In the South the calling of a slave trader was always hateful, odious, even among the slaveholders themselves. This is curious, but it is so." More than two thousand years earlier a character in Xenophon's *Symposium* said to Socrates: "It is poverty that compels some to steal, others to burgle, and others to become slavers." In neither case was the moral judgment quite so simple or so universally accepted as these statements might seem to suggest, nor was it carried to any practical conclusion, for the most respectable people depended on these same "hateful" men to provide them with the slaves without whom they could not imagine a civilized existence to be possible.

Yet contempt of the slaver was not uncommon, and this suggests that slavery itself was a little problematical, morally, even when it was taken most for granted. On this score ancient and modern slavery cannot be wholly equated. There were special circumstances in the southern states, pulling in contradictory directions. On one hand slavery was "*the* peculiar institution" and few southerners could have been unaware of the fact that most of the civilized world had abolished the practice and did not like it; whereas Greeks and Romans had no such external voice of conscience to contend with. On the other hand southern slaveowners found comfort in the color of their chattels and in its concomitant, the belief in the natural inferiority of black men—a defense mechanism of which the ancients could make relatively little use. The Negro in the old South could never lose the stigma of slavery, not even when, as an exception, he was freed or, as was often the case, when he had some white ancestry. But the descendants of an Aulos Kapreilios Timotheos could become ordinary free inhabitants of the Roman Empire, wholly indistinguishable from millions of others.

We have no clue to Timotheos's nationality. His first two names, Aulos Kapreilios, were those of his master (Aulus Caprilius in Latin), which he took upon receiving his freedom, according to the regular Roman practice. Timotheos was his name as a slave—a

The tombstone of the slave trader Aulos Kapreilios Timotheos,
discovered at the site of the Greek city of Amphipolis.

common Greek name that tells us nothing about him, since slaves rarely bore their "own" names but those given them by their masters. In more primitive times the Romans usually called their slaves Marcipor and Lucipor and the like—that is, "Marcus's boy" or "Lucius's boy"—but soon they became too numerous and required individual names so that Marcus's slaves could be distinguished from one another. When that happened there was no limit to the possibilities. The choice was a matter of fashion or of personal whim, though one rough rule of thumb was applied with some consistency. As Roman power spread to the east, the Empire was divided into a Greek-speaking half and a Latin-speaking half, and the naming of slaves tended to follow this division. It is more likely therefore that Timotheos came from the lower Danube, or the south Russian steppes, or perhaps the highlands of eastern Anatolia, than from Germany or North Africa.

To a buyer this question of nationality was important. It was generally believed that some nationalities made better slaves than others, temperamentally and vocationally. Prices varied accordingly, and Roman law (and probably Greek law, too) required the seller to state his chattel's origin specifically and accurately.

One example is worth looking at. In the year A.D. 151 a Greek from Alexandria purchased a girl in the market in Side, a city on the south coast of Anatolia (about two hundred miles west of Tarsus) that had a long tradition and notoriety as a center of slaving activity. He took the girl back to Egypt with him, and also the bill of sale—a bilingual document in Greek and Latin, written on papyrus, which was found in legible condition at the end of the nineteenth century. The girl is described in this way: "Sambatis, changed to Athenais, or by whatever other name she may be called, by nationality a Phrygian, about twelve years of age . . . in good health as required by ordinance, not subject to any legal charge, neither a wanderer nor a fugitive, free from the sacred disease [epilepsy]." The seller guaranteed all this under oath to the gods Hermes and Hephaestus, and under penalty of returning the price twice over should any of it be untrue. The phrase "or by whatever other name she may be called" is a typical lawyer's escape clause; in fact, the girl was born free and given a good Phrygian name, Sambatis, which was replaced by the Greek name Athenais when she was enslaved. How this happened cannot be determined, but it was well known in antiquity that Phrygians often sold their own children into captivity, a practice they continued even after Phrygia was incorporated into the Roman Empire. It is also not stated whether the buyer and seller were professional slave dealers, but Side was a long way to come from Egypt merely to purchase one little girl for oneself.

Bills of sale were usually written on perishable material, so that it is only by accident that a handful, written on papyrus or wax tablets, have survived. This is a pity, because there is no other evidence from which to build a statistical picture of the racial and national composition of the large slave populations of the ancient world. But the broad contours of the picture are clear enough, and they shifted with the times. The crucial point was that there were no specifically slave races or nationalities. Literally anyone and everyone might be enslaved, and which groups predominated at one time or another depended on politics and war. Greeks enslaved Greeks when they could, Romans enslaved Greeks, and they both enslaved anyone else they could lay their hands on by capture or trade.

The majority of slaves, however, were always "uncivilized" from the point of view of the Greeks and Romans. In principle the slave is an outsider, a "barbarian," and that sets him apart from all the other forms of involuntary labor known to history—from the Egyptian peasants who were conscripted to build the pyramids, from the clientes of early Rome, from debt-bondsmen, serfs, or peons. The slave is brought into a new society violently and traumatically, uprooted not only from his homeland but from everything which under normal circumstances provides human beings with social and psychological support. He is torn from his kin, from his fellows, from his religious institutions, and in their place he is given no new focus of relations other than his master and, in a very unreliable way, his fellow slaves. Nor can he expect support from other depressed groups within the new society to which he has been transported. He has lost control not only over his labor but also over his person (and his personality). Hence free sexual access to slaves is a fundamental condition of slavery, with complex exceptions in the rules regarding access of free females to slave males.

Inevitably the Greeks and Romans also made the attempt to justify slavery as an institution on the ground of the natural inferiority of the slaves. The attempt failed: it had to for several reasons. In the first place, there was too large a minority that could not be squeezed into the theory. For example, after the Romans defeated the Carthaginians under Hannibal, they turned east and conquered the Greek world, bringing back to Italy in the course of

the next two centuries hundreds of thousands of captives. Among the effects of this involuntary Greek invasion was a cultural revolution. "Captive Greece made captive her rude conqueror," said the Roman poet Horace, and it was manifestly impossible to maintain the doctrine of natural inferiority (which might do for Gauls or Germans) against a people who provided the bulk of the teachers and who introduced philosophy and the drama and the best sculpture and architecture into a society whose virtues had not previously lain in those directions.

In the second place, it was a common practice in antiquity to free one's slaves as a reward for faithful service, most often, perhaps, on one's deathbed. There were no rules about this, but some idea of the proportions that were sometimes reached can be gathered from one of the laws passed by the first of the Roman emperors, Augustus. He tried to put a brake on deathbed manumissions, probably to protect the interest of the heirs, and so he established maxima on a sliding scale, according to which no one man was allowed to free more than one hundred slaves in his will. After centuries of continuing manumission, who could distinguish the "naturally superior" from the "naturally inferior" among the inhabitants of Greek and Roman cities (especially in the absence of any distinction in skin color)?

Human nature being what it is, many individual slaveowners no doubt went right on wrapping themselves in their preordained superiority. But as an ideology the notion was abandoned, and in its place there developed one of the most remarkable contradictions in all history. "Slavery," wrote the Roman jurist Florentinus, "is an institution of the law of all nations whereby someone is subject to another *contrary to nature*." That definition became official: we find it enshrined in the great codification of the law by the Emperor Justinian, a Christian emperor, early in the sixth century. Yet no one, at least no one of consequence, drew the seemingly obvious conclusion that what was contrary to nature was wrong and ought to be abolished.

War was the key to the whole operation. The ancient world was one of unceasing warfare, and the accepted rule was that the victor had absolute rights over the persons and property of his captives, without distinction between soldiers and civilians. This right was not always exercised in full measure; sometimes tactical considera-

An act of manumission, from a Roman bas-relief. The master freed the kneeling bondsman by touching him. A freed slave is at left.

tions or pure magnanimity intervened, and sometimes more money could be raised by ransom than by sale into slavery. But the decision was the victor's alone, and a graph would show no more than occasional downward dips in the curve, never a long period (say fifty years) in which fairly large numbers of captives were not thrown onto the slave market. No total figures are available, but there can be no doubt that in the thousand years between 600 B.C. and A.D. 400, the Greeks and Romans between them disposed of several million men, women, and children in this way.

This is not to say that wars were normally undertaken simply as slave raids, though some surely were—as when Alexander the Great's father, King Philip II of Macedon, deliberately undertook an expedition into the Scythian regions north of the Black Sea in order to replenish his depleted treasury in 339 B.C. He is said to have brought back 20,000 women and children along with much other wealth. Granted that this was not a typical affair and that wars usually had other causes, it remains true that the prospect of booty, among which slaves bulked large, was never absent from the calculations—partly to help maintain the army in the field, always a difficult problem in antiquity, but chiefly to enrich both the state and the individual commanders and soldiers. Caesar went off to Gaul an impoverished nobleman; he died a multimillionaire, and Gallic captives played no small part in bringing about this change of fortune. When he took the town of the Aduatuci (probably Namur), he himself reported that 53,000 were sold off; and after the Battle of Alesia in 52 B.C. he gave one captive to each of his legionnaires as booty. Yet Caesar did not plunder to the limit; he often tried conciliatory tactics in the hope of dividing the Gallic tribes, as he did after Alesia when he restored 20,000 captives to the Aedui and Arverni. A century earlier 150,000 Epirotes from seventy towns in northwestern Greece had been sold off by the Roman state because they had supported the Macedonian king, Perseus, with whom the Romans were at war.

The figure 150,000 may be exaggerated, but human plunder even in quantities only half that size created problems for an army on the march. It could become completely bogged down, and sometimes in fact it was. In 218 B.C. King Philip V of Macedon invaded Elis in the northwestern Peloponnesus and soon found himself so overburdened with booty, which included more than 5,000 captives and masses of cattle, that his army, in the words of the historian Polybius, was rendered "useless for service." He therefore had to change his plans and march through difficult terrain to Heraea in

Arcadia, where he was able to auction off the booty.

This case is not typical. If it were, the military and therefore the political history of the ancient world would have been an altogether different one. Normally preparations were made beforehand for booty disposal, and they consisted above all in seeing to it that a crowd of peddlers and merchants came along, equipped with ready cash and means of transport. The booty was assembled at a designated spot and auctioned off (the Spartans, with their characteristic bluntness, gave the responsible officers the title of "booty-sellers"). What happened thereafter was the sole concern of the buyers, and the army was free to continue on its way, enriched by the proceeds.

Possibly the scene on the tombstone of Aulos Kapreilios Timotheos represents just such a situation, the removal on foot of slaves he had bought at an army sale. Certainly this would have been a very profitable business (providing the wherewithal for an expensive marble memorial), for slaves and other booty must have been extremely cheap to buy under such conditions. The only flaw was that war, for all its frequency, was nevertheless irregular and could not guarantee a steady flow of merchandise, and other sources had to be tapped as well. One of these was "piracy," an unfortunate label because it evokes the image of isolated Captain Kidds, whereas the reality was altogether different in scale and character: a continuous, organized activity, illegal yet (like rum-running) not unwelcome to many of its ultimate beneficiaries, the consumers. Among the Greeks even in classical times this was a traditional occupation in certain areas, especially in the western part of the Greek peninsula.

But that was small stuff compared with the later upsurge in the Roman Republic, beginning about 150 B.C. Then there arose in the eastern Mediterranean a complex business network of pirates, kidnappers, and slave dealers, with its headquarters apparently at Side and its main emporium on the island of Delos (whose docks were rebuilt and extended so that it was possible to turn over as many as 10,000 slaves in a day). The main impetus to this traffic was the rise in Italy and Sicily of the *latifundia*, large estates or ranches owned by absentee landlords and worked by slave gangs. The profit side of the trade left a mark on Delos that is still visible today in the excavated remains of the rich houses of the Italian traders.

Direct consequences of the trade were the two greatest slave revolts in antiquity, both in Sicily—the first beginning about

135 B.C., the second a generation later at the same time as the invasion of Gaul by the Cimbri and Tuetones. To meet that invasion, Marius was authorized to levy auxiliary troops wherever he could. When he appealed to Nicomedes of Bithynia (along the southwestern shore of the Black Sea), a "client-king" under Roman suzerainty, Nicomedes replied that he had no men to spare because most of his subjects had been carried off into slavery by Roman tax collectors. The Senate was alarmed (by the Germans, not by the complaint) and ordered provincial governors to release any "allied" subjects whom they found in slavery in their districts. Eight hundred were accordingly freed in Sicily, but this was an isolated action that hardly scratched the surface of the problem.

The needs of the *latifundia* owners were comparatively simple: quantity rather than quality of labor was what they were after. But important as they were, they were not the only consumers. In 54 B.C. Cicero wrote to his friend Atticus that Caesar's second expedition to Britain was causing concern in Rome. Among other things, it was now clear that there was no silver on the island and "no hope for booty other than slaves, among whom I believe you cannot expect any instructed in literature or music." The sneer need not be taken too seriously, but it does point to still another aspect of the slave procurement problem—the demand for specialist skills.

Slaves could be trained, of course, especially if they were bought young. All vocational training in antiquity was accomplished by the apprenticeship system, and slave boys or girls were often so taught alongside their free contemporaries. Gladiators were specially trained for their profession and obviously had to be, since no one was normally brought up from childhood with that aim in view. They were an exceptional group, requiring exceptional techniques that were developed in schools established for the purpose. Probably the earliest was in Capua, and it is no coincidence that Capua was the center from which the gladiator Spartacus organized the third great—and the most famous—slave revolt in antiquity (73–71 B.C.).

There were limits to the training of slaves, however, quite apart from strictly economic considerations. The right raw material was a necessary precondition: in the case of gladiators, Celts, Germans, and Thracians were sought, rather than Greeks or Syrians. Or in the case of the Athenian silver mines, the preference was for men with mining experience (Thracians and Paphlagonians), and the scale of the problem is shown by the fact that in the fourth century B.C. the concentration of slaves in these mines reached a peak of perhaps 30,000. What happened, then, if in any given decade war and piracy together slacked off or turned up mostly women and children?

In the year 477 B.C. or thereabouts the Athenians established a police force of 300 Scythian slaves, owned by the state and housed originally in tents in the public square—the Agora—and later on the Acropolis. The system lasted for a hundred years, and the number of men may eventually have been increased to a thousand. Now Scythians were famous as bowmen, an art little practiced among the Greeks, and they were sometimes employed in this capacity as mercenary troops. But the Athenians did not hire their Scythian policemen, they bought them. How on earth did they get this curious idea? And how could they count on regular replacements to keep the force up to par?

The answer is that there was already in existence by 500 B.C. a regular trade in "barbarians," who were bought from their own chieftains—captives in their own wars, children, human levies, and the like—exactly as most Negro slaves were obtained in more modern times. This trade had nothing to do with Greek or Roman military activity or with piracy. It was a purely private business carried on by traders who had their personal connections and methods in the various regions outside the Greco-Roman world proper. To return to Aulos Kapreilios Timotheos once more, it is likely that this was how he operated. Certainly the place where his tombstone was found was a main debouching point for traffic coming from the regions of the lower Danube into the Aegean Sea. Had he lived five hundred years earlier, the Athenian state could confidently have placed an order with him to supply fresh stock for its police force whenever needed.

As a commodity slaves created peculiar problems for the merchant. Apparently in the larger cities there were a few shops where slaves could be bought: in Rome in Nero's time they were concentrated near the temple of Castor in the Forum. But they were the exception. One could not keep on hand, like so much merchandise on the shelves, a supply of gladiators, pedagogues, musicians, skilled craftsmen, miners, young children, women for brothels or concubinage. The slave trade has always been conducted in a special way, and the ancient world was no exception. On the one hand there were the main slave markets where, probably on fixed dates, dealers and agents could count on large supplies being put up for sale. Some of the centers were the obvious larger towns, such as

Byzantium or Ephesus or Chios, but there were important lesser markets, too, like Tithorea in central Greece where there was a slave sale twice a year on the occasion of the semiannual festival in honor of the goddess Isis. On the other hand itinerant traders went with their slaves wherever there were potential customers, to garrison towns, country fairs, and what not.

The actual sale was normally by auction. The only surviving pictorial representations are on tombstones again, to be exact on two—one from Capua and the other from Arles—with substantially similar scenes. On the Arles stone the slave stands on a rotating platform while a man, presumably a possible buyer, lifts his single garment to reveal his very muscular legs and buttocks, and the auctioneer stands nearby in a characteristic pose with his arm outstretched. As the stoic philosopher Seneca observed, "When you buy a horse, you order its blanket to be removed; so, too, you pull the garments off a slave."

Seneca was one of the wealthiest men of his day, in an age (the first century A.D.) of enormous fortunes and luxurious living, and of course he possessed his quota of slaves. In one of his *Moral Epistles* he insists that a slave is a man with a soul like every free man; like you and me, he says. From this he concludes that one should live on familiar terms with one's slaves, dine with them, converse with them, inspire respect in them rather than fear—everything but free them.

Seneca was a Roman, but his attitude was more Greek than Roman. To the Greeks, as Nietzsche once remarked epigrammatically, both labor and slavery were "a necessary disgrace, of which one feels *ashamed*, as a disgrace and as a necessity at the same time." It would be more correct to say that the shame was generally subconscious; one sign was the almost complete silence of ancient writers about what was surely the ugliest side of the institution, the slave trade itself. The occasional exception usually has a special twist to it. Thus Herodotus tells a story about a dealer from Chios named Panionion, who specialized in handsome young boys whom he castrated and then sold, through the markets at Ephesus and Sardis, to the Persian court and other Eastern customers. One of his victims became the favorite eunuch of King Xerxes; when the opportunity fell his way, he took the appropriate revenge on Panionion and his four sons. Herodotus applauded, for in his view Panionion "gained his livelihood from the most impious of occupations," by which he meant not the slave trade as such but the traffic in eunuchs.

In this detail from the column of Marcus Aurelius in Rome, German prisoners of war are herded by soldiers toward a slave market.

This may seem a hairsplitting distinction, but distinctions have to be drawn. The ancient world was in many respects a brutal one by modern standards. The gladiatorial shows were surely among the most repellent of its habits—as the Greeks would have agreed until they, too, were finally corrupted by the Romans—yet there is abundant evidence that gladiators were proud of their successes and that not a few free men voluntarily joined their ranks. This, it can reasonably be argued, merely proves how deep the brutalization went. But what about the Paphlagonian named Atotas in the Athenian silver mines, who claimed descent from one of the Trojan heroes and whose tomb inscription included the boast, "No one could match me in skill"? The skill and artistry of slaves was to be seen everywhere, for they were not used only as crude labor in the fields but were employed in the potteries and textile mills, on temples and other public buildings, to perform the most delicate work. The psychology of the slave in the ancient world was obviously more complicated than mere sullen resentment, at least under "normal" conditions.

Even the slave trade had its shadings, so that it can serve as a barometer of the state of the society itself. It is no coincidence that the last century of the Roman Republic, a period in which moral and social values broke down badly, was the period of the most reckless slave hunting and of the great slave revolts. Then came the relatively quiet centuries of the early Roman Empire, followed by the long period in which ancient society itself finally dissolved. One incident is symptomatic: when the Goths achieved a massive breakthrough into Thrace in A.D. 376, the Roman armies were badly handicapped because many of their officers were more interested in the profits of slaving than in resisting the barbarians.

But by then slavery itself was a declining institution, not as the result of an abolitionist movement but in consequence of complex social and economic changes which replaced both the chattel slave and, to a large extent, the free peasant by a different kind of bondsman, the *colonus*, the *adscriptus glebi*, the serf. Neither moral values nor economic interests nor the social order were threatened by these subtle changes in the status of the underlying population. Nor did slavery disappear from Europe altogether. The legal problems created by the continued existence of slaves required more space in the sixth-century codification of the Emperor Justinian than any other topic. Philosophers, moralists, theologians, and jurists continued to propagate a variety of formulas which satisfied them and society at large that a man could be both a thing and a man at the same time. The Western world had to wait fifteen hundred years after Seneca for the radical final step, the proposal that slavery was so immoral that it ought to be abolished—and another three hundred years before abolition was brought about, by force and violence.

*The origins and development of Christianity present historians with
many and difficult problems, including the historicity of Jesus and the
gradual formulation of the new religion by Jesus' followers. Basically,
Christianity as we know it rests on the teachings not only of Jesus but
of Paul, who was not one of the original apostles, but a Hellenzied
Jew and a convert. S.G.F. Brandon here argues that while James and
the Jerusalem apostles saw in Jesus the Messiah of Israel and
constructed a religion based on this supposition, Paul assimilated
many of the religious ideas current in the Roman world of his time and
preached the role of Jesus as the savior of all mankind. In the
conflict which ensued the Jerusalem leaders appear to have imposed
their views, but the destruction of Jerusalem in* A.D. *70 and the
disappearance of the Jerusalem church left the field open to Paul's
broader, ecumenical religion, which was presently to decide the further
course of European history.*

*Mr. Brandon, Professor of Comparative Religion at Manchester
University, is the author of* Jesus and the Zealots *and* The Trial of
Jesus of Nazareth.

PAUL AND
HIS OPPONENTS

S. G. BRANDON

Whoever turns the pages of that collection of ancient Christian
writings called the New Testament must surely conclude
that Paul was the apostle par excellence of the early church. For no
less than thirteen separate items of that collection are entitled
"Epistles of Paul," whereas to no other apostle are more than two
letters assigned. And that is not all: not only do the writings of
Paul comprise a quarter of the whole content of the New Testament; the larger part of the Acts of the Apostles, which sets out to
record the early history of the Christian faith, is devoted to re-
counting his career.

But this impression of the primacy of Paul, both as a leader and
a teacher in the early church, is strangely belied by the internal
evidence of Paul's own writings. When we read many of these
documents, we at once sense an atmosphere of great tension. Paul
often appears profoundly concerned with what he regards as the
pernicious influence of certain opponents who operate among his
own converts; he sometimes uses the fiercest invective against
them, but in a curiously oblique way, never naming them.   73

Herein lies one of the fundamental problems that beset our understanding of the origins of Christianity. How is it that Paul's own letters are so full of bitter controversy, yet the space given to his letters in the New Testament, as well as the evidence of the Acts, so signally attest his pre-eminence as the great leader and exponent of the faith, a position that is also abundantly confirmed in later Christian tradition?

An attempt to answer this question takes us into the intricate study of one of the most crucial episodes in the history of mankind. It is a field, too, where in recent years many new evaluations of traditional views have been taking place. The attempt is worth making, for it will afford an insight into the dramatic clash of two powerful personalities with whom lay the future of one of the world's greatest religions.

It is necessary at the outset to appreciate the nature of our chief sources of information about Paul and his career. His own writings, of course, are of primary importance; but since they mostly comprise letters dealing with specific situations among the Christian communities that he had founded in various places in the Roman Empire, their interpretation is no easy task. Paul rarely outlines the situation with which he is dealing, because it was obviously well known to his readers; consequently we are obliged to reconstruct the issue from passing references and allusions. Moreover, it must be remembered that the Epistles are essentially ex parte accounts of the basic conflict; we have no documents giving us the case of Paul's opponents, and our chief information about it must be inferred from Paul's own statements.

The Acts of the Apostles constitutes our secondary source of information. When it was written, some four decades separated it from the events it records; in the interval the destruction of Jerusalem by the Romans in A.D. 70 had decisively altered the internal situation of the church. The Acts, moreover, is clearly motivated by an apologetic purpose; it is concerned with tracing the triumphant spread of Christianity from its beginnings in Jerusalem to its establishment in Rome, the metropolis of the world. Thus it gives an idealized picture of the past, passing lightly over the conflicts and representing the leading figures as amicably disposed to each other. However, the evidence of the Acts can be of great value when carefully interpreted, and it does supply us with two precious facts about Paul: that he was a Hellenized Jew, being a native of the Cilician city of Tarsus, and that he enjoyed the privilege of Roman citizenship.

Both our sources are clear on one point of basic significance: Paul had never been an original disciple of Jesus but had joined the church sometime after the Crucifixion. Another important point on which the sources agree is that Paul was not converted to the new faith by the original community of disciples living in Jerusalem. His independence of the Jerusalem Christians at this crucial stage in his career was a matter of supreme importance to Paul, and it provides the key to the role that he was destined to play in the development of the new faith. Paul gives us his own account of the events that led up to his conversion in a context of great significance. He is writing to his converts in Galatia, who are in danger of being won over by his opponents, and he seeks to prove to them the greater authority of his own teaching. The passage is from Epistle to the Galatians (1:11–20).

For I make known to you, brethren, as touching the gospel which was preached by me, that it is not after man. For neither did I receive it from man, nor was I taught it, but *it came to me* through revelation of Jesus Christ. For ye have heard of my manner of life in time past in the Jews' religion, how that beyond measure I persecuted the Church of God, and made havoc of it. And I advanced in the Jews' religion beyond many of mine own age among my countrymen, being more exceedingly zealous for the tradition of my fathers. But when it was the good pleasure of God, who separated me, *even* from my mother's womb, and called me through his grace, to reveal his Son in me, that I might preach him among the Gentiles; immediately I conferred not with flesh and blood. Neither went I up to Jerusalem to them which were apostles before me: but I went away into Arabia; and again I returned unto Damascus. Then after three years I went up to Jerusalem to visit Cephas, and tarried with him fifteen days. But other of the apostles saw I none, save James the Lord's brother. Now touching the things which I write unto you, behold, before God, I lie not.

The implications of this passage are immense. It informs us about three vital aspects of Paul's position. To defend his own teaching to his converts against that of his opponents Paul asserts that he had not derived it from any human source and, in particular, that he did not owe it to the original apostles at Jerusalem. This teaching, moreover, he claimed had been communicated to him directly by God for the express purpose of revealing "his Son in me, that I might preach him among the Gentiles." In other words, Paul maintains that his teaching was especially designed to be intelligible to those who were not Jews. He therefore admits by implication that his teaching differed from the tradition of the original apostles of Jerusalem, and he defends its novelty by claiming for it a direct divine origin.

HIC SAVLVS DNS CAECAT   HINC IVNDI EIHABLA   TERRAE TRAHIT CAECVS VT REQVEAT ·

Scenes from Paul's life, from a Carolingian Bible. At top, Paul falls blinded upon seeing the apparition of Christ. In the center panel, Ananias, at God's command, heals Paul, who begins his teaching (bottom).

We begin to perceive, then, the outlines of a truly amazing situation in the Christian church within some two decades of the Crucifixion. Paul is anxious to assert his independence of the Jerusalem apostles and to explain that his teaching has been divinely revealed for the Gentiles. Since he evidently had to defend this teaching against certain opponents, it becomes necessary to attempt to identify these opponents and the cause of their hostility to Paul.

In two separate writings Paul refers to these opponents and their rival teaching in very remarkable terms. In his Galatian letter (1:6–9) he writes in admonition to his converts:

I marvel that ye are so quickly removing from him that called you in the grace of Christ unto a different gospel; which is not another *gospel*: only there are some that trouble you, and would pervert the gospel of Christ. But though we, or an angel from heaven, should preach any gospel other than that we preached unto you, let him be anathema. As we have said before so say I now again: If any man preacheth unto you any gospel other than that which ye received, let him be anathema.

The extraordinary language used here is paralleled in another passage, which occurs in the Second Epistle to the Corinthians (11:3–6). A situation had apparently developed among his converts in the Greek city of Corinth similar to that with which Paul sought to deal in Galatia. He writes:

But I fear lest by any means, as the serpent beguiled Eve in his craftiness, your minds should be corrupted from the simplicity and the purity that is toward Christ. For if he that cometh preacheth another Jesus, whom we did not preach, or if ye received a different spirit, which ye did not receive, or a different gospel, which ye did not accept, ye do well to bear with *him*. For I reckon that I am not a whit behind the very chiefest apostles. But though *I* be rude in speech, yet *am I* not in knowledge; nay, in everything we have made *it* manifest among all men to you-ward.

Paul's language in both these passages is as amazing as it is significant. Paul does in fact attest to the presence in the Church of two rival interpretations of the faith. For the references to "another Jesus" and "a different gospel" must mean that Paul's opponents were teaching a different version of the meaning of the person and roles of Jesus from Paul's version.

But who *were* these opponents? Obviously they were not some obscure sect of heretics; otherwise Paul would surely have repudiated them with all that vehemence of utterance of which he was capable. Clearly they were men who could operate effectively enough within Paul's own mission-field to cause him profound concern. But, curiously, Paul never explicitly names them or questions their authority. He does, however, give a clue to their identity in the latter of the passages just quoted, when he significantly adds, after referring to this rival teaching, "I reckon that I am not a whit behind the very chiefest apostles."

In view of the facts just considered, and of Paul's concern to assert his independence of the Jerusalem apostles, there can indeed be little doubt that those opponents who taught "another Jesus" were either the leaders of the church in Jerusalem or their emissaries. In his Galatian epistle, describing a later visit to Jerusalem, Paul gives more details of these leaders. They formed a kind of triumvirate of what he calls *stuloi* (pillars); their names are James, Cephas, and John. The order in which these names are given is significant. James was certainly the leader; he precedes Cephas, *i.e.*, Peter, who had apparently been the leader of the apostles during the lifetime of Jesus. The fact that James was the brother of Jesus (Galatians 1:19) probably accounts, at least in part, for this pre-eminence. But a mystery seems to surround this James. According to the Gospels, he had not been an original disciple—indeed he had actually been unsympathetic to Jesus. The Acts is strangely silent about his antecedents; it represents him suddenly, without explanation, as the head of the church of Jerusalem. How he ousted Peter from the leadership of the new movement remains a veiled episode in the Christian documents. His blood relationship to Jesus obviously gave him great prestige, but it is evident that he was also a man of strong character and ability. In his Galatian letter Paul tells of a dispute at Antioch over whether Jewish Christians might eat with Gentile believers; Peter, who had agreed with Paul on the matter, had later withdrawn on the arrival of emissaries from James—surely a significant act of submission.

It was, then, the teaching of the Jerusalem church, presided over by James, from which Paul differed and again which he tacitly directs his innuendo by describing it as a "different gospel" that taught "another Jesus." But how did this Jerusalem gospel differ so radically from that of Paul? In brief, since it is certain that the Jerusalem Christians continued to worship in the Temple at Jerusalem and to practise the ritual customs of Judaism, it is evident that they did not regard their faith in Jesus as inconsistent with Jewish orthodoxy or as separating them from their national religion. To them Jesus was the promised Messiah of Israel. His death by crucifixion was a problem, since there was no expectation that the Messiah should die—rather he was to be the mighty champion who would free Israel from subjugation to a heathen conqueror.

But Jesus' death could be explained as a martyr's death for Israel at the hands of the Romans. And it was believed that God had raised him from this death, so that he might soon return with supernatural power to "restore the kingdom to Israel." Such, then, was the "gospel" of the Jerusalem Christians; it was conceived essentially in terms of Jewish thought, and it was calculated to emphasize and maintain that claim to a unique spiritual status and destiny that characterized Judaism. According to the evidence of the Acts, a considerable number of priests and Pharisees had, significantly, been won to the new movement.

If such was the "gospel of Jerusalem," what was Paul's version of the new faith? It would seem that before his conversion Paul was scandalized by the new movement because it taught "a crucified Messiah." On his conversion, whatever the true nature of that mysterious episode may be, Paul became convinced that the crucified Jesus was alive and of divine status. But he still had to explain to himself the apparent scandal of the Crucifixion. It was at this point, so it would seem, that Paul came to differ fundamentally from the Jerusalem Christians and to assert his original independence of them. To him the death of Jesus could not be just a martyr's death for Israel; it must have some more profound and universal meaning. It was in his attempt to interpret this meaning that Paul surely drew, though unconsciously, on his Hellenistic background.

This Hellenistic background teemed with religious cults and esoteric philosophies that promised salvation of various kinds. Consciously Paul would have vigorously rejected them as the service of false gods or "philosophy and vain deceit." But he could not have escaped their influence, since they reflected the aspirations and fears of contemporary Greco-Roman society and provided the current religious vocabulary. Two ideas of key importance that these cults and philosophies severally enshrined and propagated were those of the savior-god and of the fallen state of man. The classic pattern of the savior-god was afforded by the ancient Egyptian deity Osiris. The initiates of his mysteries believed that he had once died and risen again to life and that by ritual assimilation with him they too could win immortal life. The various esoteric philosophies that can be described as Gnostic taught that each human being was compounded of an immortal soul imprisoned in a physical body. This unhappy condition was due to an original fall of the soul from its abode of light and bliss and its involvement in matter. By thus becoming incarnated in this world the soul had also become subject to the demonic powers that inhabited the planets and controlled the world. From this state of perdition it could be rescued by acquiring a proper knowledge (gnosis) of its nature; emancipated from its involvement in matter, it would ascend through the celestial spheres to its original home.

Such ideas were foreign to orthodox Judaism. Hence it is significant that Paul, seeking to interpret the meaning of the Crucifixion, does so in terms that presuppose that mankind is enslaved by demonic powers, from whom they are redeemed through the death and resurrection of a divine savior. Thus he writes: "So we also, when we were children, were held in bondage under the *stoicheia* of the world. But when the fulness of the time came, God sent forth his Son, born of a woman, born under the law, that he might redeem them which were under the law, that we might receive the adoption of sons." The word *stoicheia*, which the Revised Standard Version translates as "elemental spirits," means in this context the demonic powers that were identified with the astral phenomena. Consequently Paul here envisages the human situation as one of subjection to these demonic powers until redemption is won by the incarnated Son of God. Paul clearly regards the crucifixion of Jesus as achieving this redemption, but of the way in which this was achieved he is not so clear. Sometimes he invokes the concepts of the Jewish sacrificial cultus, thereby implying that the death of Jesus was a sacrifice; but who demanded it and to whom it was made, he is not explicit. A more coherent conception, which links up with the thought of the Galatian passage just quoted, is found in his First Epistle to the Corinthians (2:7–8): "But we speak God's wisdom in a mystery, *even* the *wisdom* that hath been hidden, which God foreordained before the *aeons* unto our glory; which none of the *archontes* of this *aeon* knoweth; for had they known it, they would not have crucified the Lord of glory." In this passage Paul professes to explain the Crucifixion as an event, arranged for in a divine plan conceived before the *aeons*, whereby the *archontes* of this *aeon* were led, unwittingly, to crucify a supernatural being called "the Lord of glory." Since "*archontes* of this *aeon*" is in effect an alternative designation for the demonic powers described as the *stoicheia* in the Galatian letter, a further phase of Paul's interpretation of the death of Jesus can be discerned. In other words, the hold that the demonic powers had over mankind

Fra Bartolommeo painted Paul in 1514, showing him with a book of his epistles and the sword with which tradition says he was beheaded.

was broken when they were deceived into crucifying the "Lord of glory."

By employing ideas and terminology current in the Greco-Roman world, Paul thus fashioned an interpretation, intelligible to his Gentile converts, of a movement that was in origin and essence Jewish. But that was not all. Whereas the rite of circumcision was the form of initiation into the spiritual privileges of Judaism, baptism was adopted as the means of entry into the church of Christ. Paul's explanation of it is also indicative of the milieu of syncretistic faith and practice upon which he drew. He writes to the Christians in Rome:

Or are ye ignorant that all we who were baptized into Christ Jesus were baptized into his death? We were buried therefore with him through baptism into death: that like as Christ was raised from the dead through the glory of the Father, so we also might walk in newness of life. For if we have become united with *him* by the likeness of his death, we shall be also *by the likeness* of his resurrection.

In other words, according to Paul, in baptism the neophyte was ritually assimilated to Christ in his death in order to be one with him in his resurrection. When Paul wrote, for nearly three thousand years in Egypt resurrection from death had been sought by ritual assimilation with the dying-rising god Osiris.

Such, then, was the gospel with which Paul believed that he had been divinely entrusted for preaching to the Gentiles. In effect it replaced the presentation of Jesus as the Messiah of Israel by that of Jesus as the divine savior of mankind; and it presupposed that all men, whether Jew or Gentile, were equally in need of the same kind of salvation.

Such a gospel diverged fundamentally from the teaching of the Jerusalem Christians, and it was obnoxious to them. For not only did it equate the Jew with the Gentile, thereby robbing the former of his cherished sense of spiritual superiority; it made the Messiah of Israel into the savior of those heathen who had done him to death and who daily opposed his people.

When the Jerusalem leaders understood the nature and implications of Paul's teaching, they set about opposing it. They were in a strong position to do this: whereas they could repudiate Paul as a latecomer to the faith, he could not openly challenge their authority as the original disciples and eyewitnesses of Jesus. Accordingly they sent out their emissaries among Paul's converts, asserting that theirs was the original and authentic version of the faith.

As his letters eloquently attest, the activities of these Jerusalem emissaries seriously threatened Paul's position, undermining his authority with his converts and causing them to accept a "different gospel" and "another Jesus." The situation eventually became so serious that Paul resolved to go to Jerusalem in an attempt to negotiate some *modus vivendi* with the authorities there. He sought to strengthen his case by taking with him a delegation of his Gentile converts and a considerable sum of money, which he had collected from his churches for the support of the mother church of Jerusalem. Paul seems to have known that a visit to Jerusalem might be dangerous for him, and according to the narrative of the Acts, he received several divine warnings of impending danger. To have persisted in going against such advice surely attests that he felt the need to achieve an understanding with the Jerusalem leaders was urgent.

The outcome of the visit is recorded in Acts 21; its testimony must be evaluated in terms of that apologetic purpose that, as we have already noticed, inspires the work.

Paul was received by James in the presence of the elders of the Jerusalem church and is represented as reporting on the success of his work among the Gentiles. Paul's coming to Jerusalem must clearly have embarrassed the Christians there, and James comes quickly to the point about the matter:

Thou seest, brother, how many thousands there are among the Jews of them that have believed; and they are all zealous for the law; and they have been informed concerning thee, that thou teachest all the Jews which are among the Gentiles to forsake Moses, telling them not to circumcise their children, neither to walk after the customs. What is it therefore? They will certainly hear that thou art come.

The accusation was in fact a calumny, but it represented a plausible deduction from the logic of Paul's teaching. Reference to it by James was an astute move to solve the difficulty that Paul's visit had created. Accordingly he proposes a test of Paul's Jewish orthodoxy:

Do therefore this that we say to thee: We have four men which have a vow on them; these take, and purify thyself with them; and be at charges for them, that they may shave their heads: and all shall know that there is no truth in the things whereof they have been informed concerning thee; but that thou thyself also walkest orderly, keeping the law.

Paul was placed in a delimma. James had shrewdly detected the weakness of his position, in that while the logic of his teaching negated the peculiar spiritual claims of Judaism, he still endeavored

83

himself to remain an orthodox Jew. Now James challenged him to give a public demonstration of his orthodoxy, for the ceremony in which Paul should take part, *i.e.*, the discharge of the so-called Nazarite vow, was performed in the Temple. To refuse the test was tantamount to a declaration of apostasy from his native faith; but to accept it was to admit the validity of Judaism on the order of the Jerusalem church.

Paul felt obliged to submit, but the sequel was disastrous to his cause. While performing the rites in the Temple courts, he was set upon by a Jewish mob and only rescued from death by the intervention of the Roman guard from the nearby fortress of the Antonia. To escape subsequent trial and certain condemnation by the Jewish authorities, Paul invoked his right as a Roman citizen to be tried before the imperial tribunal. After recording his survival from shipwreck en route to Rome, the narrative of the Acts finally leaves Paul a prisoner there. What was his ultimate fate is unrecorded. According to ancient tradition he suffered martyrdom in Rome, and there is much reason for thinking that his appeal to Caesar did not prove successful.

The arrest of Paul probably took place in the year 55, and from that date he seems to have been removed from personal contact with his converts. What, then, was the fate of his work?

It would seem reasonable to conjecture, since Paul had previously felt his position to be gravely threatened by the Jerusalem Christians, that after his arrest the defeat of his cause was inevitable. His converts would have been left defenseless against the propaganda of the Jerusalem emissaries. That this did actually happen seems to be confirmed by the prophecy that is attributed to Paul when he took his farewell of the elders of the church of Ephesus; the prophecy is recorded by the author of Acts, who knew what had happened:

I know that after my departure grievous wolves shall enter in among you, not sparing the flock; and from among your own selves shall men arise, speaking perverse things to draw away the disciples after them.

It this situation had continued, without doubt Paul's interpretation of Christianity would have perished, and the faith evoked by Jesus would have remained but the belief of a small messianic sect within the fold of Judaism. But this was not to be. In the year 66 the Jewish nationalists raised the standard of revolt against Roman rule in Judaea. After four years of bitter warfare, the Jewish state was overthrown, Jerusalem ruined and its Temple destroyed. In

84

the course of that cataclysm the Christian church of Jerusalem disappeared.

In consequence of these tremendous events the future of Christianity was completely changed. The hold of the mother church of Jerusalem was broken, and the Gentile churches were left to work out their own destiny. This signal overthrow of Jewish Christianity led, understandably, to a rehabilitation of Paul's reputation as the great exponent of the faith. When the author of Acts wrote his story of the beginnings of the Church, magnifying the part played by Paul, others were searching for Paul's writings as the inspired teaching of a revered master and saint. Eventually the *Corpus Paulinum* was formed, becoming one of the earliest components of the New Testament, but bearing also within it evidence both of the eclipse and the rehabilitation of Paul in the mind of the Church. For the formation of Christian theology this rehabilitation was definitive. From Paul's teaching has stemmed the foundational doctrine of Christianity; namely, the incarnation of the Son of God, in the person of Jesus of Nazareth, to be the savior of mankind.

85

*A copper helmet plaque depicts King Agilulf,
the ruler of the Lombards from 592 to 615.*

Throughout history, from the earliest times of the hunting tribes, men have moved about in search of better living conditions. The early civilizations of Mesopotamia were repeatedly overwhelmed by less civilized peoples from Asia, as later Greece was overrun by Dorians and Egypt invaded by the Peoples of the Sea. In the Middle Ages the horsemen of Genghis Khan and Timur swept over much of central Europe. Indeed, as late as the nineteenth century some sixteen to twenty million people left Europe to settle on other continents.

The so-called "barbarian invasions," as Richard Winston points out, should be viewed less as violent attacks than as prolonged infiltration of the classical world. After all, there was at no time a population vacuum beyond the Roman frontiers. The Germanic peoples who lived there were influenced increasingly by Roman civilization. As the late Roman Empire became depopulated by epidemics, the "barbarians" were able to overcome the defenses against invasion of the inviting southern lands. Only occasionally, over the centuries, were the Germanic tribes driven on by invaders from Asia, much as, in the seventh century, the Byzantine Empire suffered the shock of the Arab tribes. Though little is known of the details, it has become increasingly clear that the "barbarian invasions" only gradually transformed the ancient world and inaugurated the Middle Ages.

Mr. Winston is well-known as the author of a biography of Charlemagne.

THE BARBARIANS

RICHARD WINSTON

Most of us have a vague general notion of the "barbarian invasions": wild hordes of almost naked blond-haired, blue-eyed Germanic warriors emerging from the swamps and forests of central Europe and charging with savage war whoops upon Roman armies corrupted and debilitated by an overrefined civilization. We see them smashing through the crumbling defenses of a doomed empire, ravaging and burning the flourishing cities of Gaul, Italy, and Spain, and ultimately bringing on the so-called Dark Ages in which the light of culture flickered and sputtered dimly in a few scattered monasteries. Slowly, then, the softening influence of Christianity supposedly converted these primitives to the milder habits of civilization, and out of the vigor they infused into a moribund society arose the states and culture that we call medieval.

It is a grand and rather satisfying panorama; it fits neatly into preconceptions about sin, punishment, fall, grace, and redemption.

But it is largely false. Modern historians, utilizing newly elaborated techniques in archaeology, epigraphy, toponymy, philology, source analysis, numismatics, historical geography, and so on, have thrown into question many of the elements in this picture. This is not to say that "modern" history knows all the answers, but historians today at least have a far better notion of how much they do not know.

Many tribes and peoples did move into the territory of the Roman Empire between the fourth and sixth centuries. Their numbers were relatively small—the Vandals, for example, counted no more than eighty thousand males before they crossed the Strait of Gibraltar to Africa, and probably less than half of these were fighting men. Nevertheless, many of these peoples succeeded in establishing political units within the Empire—until the Empire itself splintered.

The Huns came out of the vast central plains of Asia and advanced almost to Paris, as well as deep into Italy. Angles, Saxons, and Jutes crossed the North Sea from Denmark and northwestern Germany to take possession of England. The Franks made their way over the Rhine into northern Gaul and created the nation that still bears their name. The Burgundians seized the territory around Geneva and subsequently advanced as far as Lyon. Vandals and Suevians likewise breached the barrier of the Rhine and moved across present-day France into Spain. There the Suevians stayed, disappearing into the population, while the Vandals crossed to North Africa. Ostrogoths and Visigoths marched from Scandinavia to the extremities of Italy in the course of three centuries, and the Visigoths continued on into Spain. Alans traveled from the highlands of Persia to the Strait of Gibraltar. Lombards crossed Germany into what is now Hungary and then moved into the part of Italy that is known as Lombardy to this day.

With the exception of the Huns, the Alans, the Avars, the Bulgars, and the Magyars, the barbarians were Germans—that is, they spoke a Germanic language or dialect. They themselves seem to have been unconscious of their linguistic if not racial unity; they had no common word for themselves. The old German form of the word *deutsch* (meaning "of the people") did not come into general use until the eighth century, when it was introduced into Germany by Anglo-Saxon missionaries.

The word "German," according to the first-century Roman historian Tacitus, was in his own time comparatively new and had
been extended from the name of a tribe to the whole people.

Despite his many deficencies, Tacitus remains one of the principal sources for our notions about the Germans of the preinvasion period. In *Germania*, a brief, journalistic summary of the tribes of Germany. Tacitus draws a picture of a "distinct, unmixed race" of men with "fierce blue eyes, light hair, and huge frames fit only for sudden exertion." These men did in fact have a kind of war whoop, although there was an excellent rationale for it: the Germans, Tacitus says, roused their courage in war by singing heroic songs. As superstitious as the Romans, they regarded the note they struck in song as an augury of the outcome of battle. "For as their line shouts, they gain courage or feel alarm. . . . They aim chiefly at a harsh note and a confused roar, putting their shields to their mouths so that by reverberation it may swell to a fuller and deeper sound."

Tacitus pictures a people but recently entered into the Iron Age. Iron, he remarks, "is not plentiful among them, as we may infer from the character of their weapons." Few had swords or long lances. Their principal weapon was a spear with a short, narrow head, using little iron, which could either be thrown or used at close quarters. They wore no armor in battle, and only a few had metal or even leather helmets. Their brilliantly painted shields alone served them for defense. For the most part the Germans obtained their weapons from the Romans, by way of trade or booty; archaeological finds throughout Germany, Denmark, and the Baltic countries testify to the vast quantities of Roman arms imported by the barbarians.

Tacitus describes the dress of the barbarians as a cloak fastened by a clasp, or if none were available, by a thorn, and the "wealthiest are distinguished by a dress which is not flowing, like that of the Sarmatians and the Parthians, but is tight and exhibits each limb"—in other words, trousers. They also wore furs. The women "have the same dress as the men, except that they generally wrap themselves in linen garments embroidered with purple, but the upper part is not extended into sleeves. Thus the upper and lower arm is bare, and part of the breast is likewise revealed."

Their food was as simple as their dress: "wild fruit, fresh game and curdled milk." But they made beer—"their beverage consists of a liquor made out of barley or grain which has been fermented like wine"—and also bought Roman wine. "They satisfy their hunger without elaborate preparation and without delicacies. In quenching their thirst they are not equally moderate. If you indulge their love of drinking by supplying them with as much as they desire, you can overcome them by their own vices as easily as by weapons."

Although overfond of drink and warfare, these Germans were strict in their morals. They had formed a class society, with a nobility at the top, freemen in the middle, and slaves or semi-serfs at the bottom. They had an organized religion and a town-meeting form of democracy. Although confederations of tribes had kings, and smaller groupings chiefs, the final decisions rested with a popular assembly. There was, however, no fixed bureaucracy, nothing resembling a state—a *respublica* in the Roman sense—and no system of taxation. In such matters the Germans were far removed from the Roman concept of civilization. Throughout the German lands there were no real cities or towns, none of those concentrations of people that made Roman society so essentially urban.

Tacitus's picture of the early Germans resembles in some respects the eighteenth century's view of the Noble Savage. His nostalgia for the heroic days of the early Roman Republic may have prompted him to exaggerate such matters as the chastity of German women or the loyalty of the men toward their chiefs. Even his account of their appearance cannot be taken at face value. We do not know whether he ever visited the lands he describes. He may have based his description of the people on his observations of Roman slave markets and gladiatorial schools, without considering that slaves and gladiators would have been chosen for their stature and brawn. At any rate, Strabo remarks that the Germans scarcely differed in physique from the Gauls (whom Tacitus calls "effeminate") except perhaps for being some what more fair-haired. Skeletal finds suggest that the Germans were not notably taller than the Mediterraneans, and even in these early times they were by no means an "unmixed race." In the course of the subsequent migrations, moreover, a tremendous mingling of races took place.

The religion of these early Germans was a branch of that great pan-Eurasian polytheistic paganism that extended, with innumerable local variations, from India to the Hebrides, wherever peoples of Indo-European speech had settled: a religion with an elaborate mythology of gods and demigods, personifications of natural forces, and deified heroes. Like the Greeks, the Germans had sacred groves; like the Romans, they were fond of taking auguries; like the Hindus, they conceived of a cyclic universe—after the Twilight of the Gods a new round of birth and decay would begin.

Many of the characteristics of the early Germans merit comparison not with the Indians of North America but with the pioneers who conquered the continent. In fact, the Germans may once have enjoyed a higher state of civilization, but then adapted to the exigencies of a new land of swamps and forests. Such a retreat from civilization, rather than aboriginal primitiveness, is suggested by the unevenness of their cultural level. They were aware of writing, for example. Runes, peculiar Germanic alphabetic characters based on Greek, Latin, and possibly Etruscan antecedents, were in use at least as early as the second century. But instead of developing a literature, the Germans used their alphabet chiefly for magic and inscriptions. As metalworkers, they were capable of inlaying iron spearheads with silver ornamentation and producing beautiful gold filigree work. They were especially skilled in making body ornaments; but elegant ceramics, silver drinking vessels, and delicately incised combs were also within their powers.

Whatever the state of the German tribes in the first century A.D., it had greatly changed by the fourth century, when the "invasions" began. By then a stabilized Empire had long maintained fixed frontiers along the Rhine and the Danube, across which goods and slaves had constantly moved. The barbarians had acquired a liking for Roman luxuries and had learned the uses and abuses of money. The Romans had settled whole tribes within their borders or formed alliances with tribes just outside the borders. For centuries the Romans had been taking hostages from the tribes to guarantee that treaties would be honored. These hostages would later return home, bringing the fruits of Roman education and a taste for Roman life. Although Roman conquest had ceased after the reign of Trajan, cultural diffusion had continued. Throughout the German world a slow but steady Romanization had occurred.

The current had flowed the other way, too. There had been a "barbarization" of Roman society. Early in the third century the *Constitutio Antoniana* extended Roman citizenship to all free-born inhabitants of the Empire. This liberal measure made it increasingly difficult for the imperial government to recruit legionaries within the Empire, for military service had hitherto been one of the prime routes to Roman citizenship. The government therefore made efforts to enlist barbarians on the fringes of the Empire by offering high pay, citizenship, and land as rewards for assuming the burden that Roman citizens were unwilling to bear. Barbarians poured into the army and from there into Roman society. Barbarian gladiators, slaves, and freedmen had long since made the city of Rome a melting pot; now the barbarians were everywhere, often in positions of power and prestige.

Soon Romans began to ape the manners of the barbarians. The Western Emperor Honorius had to issue three successive edicts in the fourth and early fifth centuries banning the wearing of long hair and fur coats—barbarian costume—in the cities of the Empire. A more important sign of the times was the rise to high position in the Roman state of Stilicho the Vandal. This great Roman general virtually ruled the Empire for a time. He served as consul, married the emperor's adopted daughter, and married off his own daughter to the next emperor. He also served the Empire well in wars against his fellow barbarians.

For by the time of Stilicho and Honorius, in the late fourth century, what we generally consider to be the "invasions" had already begun. But when we examine them in detail, they look less like invasions than the consequences of Roman political maneuverings, which either staved off disaster or brought it on, according to the circumstances. Indeed, the barbarian "invasions" seem to prove, as so much history does, that statesmen can rarely predict the outcome of their policies.

The migrations began slowly. For centuries Germanic tribes of the north had been drifting southeastward into the steppes above the Black Sea—we do not really know why. By the third century A.D. the Goths and some other tribes had left their homes in the Scandinavian peninsula and along the shores of the Baltic Sea and moved into the region around the mouths of the Danube. There they lived amicably among smaller groups of Germanic peoples and a sizable population of Iranian nomads known as Alans.

These Alans, according to the description given by the fourth-century Roman historian Ammianus Marcellinus, "have no huts, nor do they use the plow. They feed themselves on meat and ample milk, live in their wagons which they provide with an arched roof of bark, and on these they move over the endless steppes. If they arrive at good pasturage, they drive their wagons into a circle. . . . On the wagon man and wife unite, offspring are born and raised. The wagon is their permanent dwelling, and no matter what the district they may wander in, their wagons are always home to the Alans."

From the Alans the Goths borrowed the use of horses and covered wagons. They also took over Alanic cavalry weapons and tactics, the use of body armor, long swords, and the lasso—the dreaded weapon of mounted tribes. Despite differences in language and culture, Alans and Goths intermarried and formed such close political alliances that the Romans soon came to regard them as one people. The Goths apparently acquired their distinctive dress from these nomads: baggy trousers with fringed cuffs extending sometimes to the ankles, sometimes to just below the knee.

For a time the Goths controlled a vast kingdom of indefinite boundaries extending from the Black Sea to the Baltic and including many tributary tribes. By the third century the Romans were paying them an annual subsidy to guard the frontier against the Sarmatians and other neighboring peoples. During most of that century the Goths made frequent armed raids into the Empire. Yet in intervals of peace they provided soldiers for Roman armies and collected their subsidies. In 332 a long period of peace with the Romans began, and during this time the Goths were converted to Christianity by Bishop Ulfilas, a Goth who had been educated in Constantinople and knew both Latin and Greek. He reduced the Gothic language to writing and translated much of the Bible into Gothic. Unfortunately for the future of the Goths, however, Ulfilas was an Arian, a follower of that Arius who had denied the identity of Jesus Christ with God the Father. The Arianism of the Goths subsequently poisoned their relationship with the Catholics of the Roman Empire who had accepted the Nicene Creed.

The peaceful coexistence of Goths and Romans and the slow Gothic penetration of the Roman world were rudely interrupted by the sudden descent of the Huns. Probably of Mongolian origin, the Huns in the course of their own migration from the east had gathered a great variety of nomadic tribes into their army. Their strange habits evoked terror in Europeans. They practiced cranial deformation, reputedly killed their old people, and burned their dead. They seemed to live in the saddle, allegedly ate their meat raw, rarely or never washed, and fought with unspeakable savagery. They are described as small in stature, with broad chests, disproportionately large heads, tiny eyes, and flattened noses. How much truth there is in this description we shall never know. In any case, the Huns apparently changed radically in the course of a century.

The sudden onslaught of the Huns in 374 and 375 shattered the Gothic and Alanic kingdom of the Ukraine. The Gothic king committed suicide; his successor was killed in battle. Part of one branch of the Gothic people, the Ostrogoths, submitted to the Huns, intermarried with them, and henceforth fought as their allies. The remaining Ostrogoths, together with another branch, the Visigoths, and a horde of Alans and other tribes, pleaded with the Eastern Emperor Valens for permission to cross the Danube.

Hesitantly Valens consented, and settled the Goths in Thrace. There the Romans took advantage of their desperate straits, charging such outrageous prices for bread and meat that the Visigoths revolted. At the great Battle of Adrianople on August 9, 378, they inflicted a crushing defeat upon the Romans, killing the emperor and almost annihilating the Roman army. With that battle the barbarian "invasions" may be said to have begun.

But "invasion" is scarcely the word. The Visigoths did not know how to consolidate their victory. After a brief plundering expedition and a futile attempt to capture Constantinople, they made peace with the new emperor of the East, Theodosius, who took them into his employ. Essentially they were mercenary soldiers of the Empire, settled like so many other Germans on Roman land in Thrace and Asia Minor, with their nobles often holding high offices in the imperial government and at the imperial court. As mercenaries, they rose in revolt when the successors of Theodosius attempted to reduce their pay. Under a young chief, Alaric, a disappointed office seeker, the Visigoths began a fifteen-year-long march through Greece, Illyria, and northern Italy, which eventually brought them to the walls of Rome. The only Roman general who could control the Visigoths, either by bribes or military force, was Stilicho the Vandal. After Stilicho's assassination in 408 on orders of the jealous Emperor Honorius, Rome was doomed. In August, 410, Alaric's Goths took Rome.

It is important for us to realize that the assault had been preceded by years of intricate negotiations, of requests by Alaric for a peace treaty, and of efforts by him to set up a puppet emperor of his own. But at last his patience ran out, and on August 24, 410, his men forced the Salerian Gate (or had it opened to them by partisans inside Rome). Alaric gave his soldiers permission to plunder Rome—he could hardly have withheld it—and the citizens were compelled by beatings and threats of death to give up their gold and valuables. But the Gothic forces respected the sanctuary of churches and largely obeyed Alaric's orders that no man was to be killed unless he was bearing arms and that no fires were to be set. The Goths were not a horde of wild men but a disciplined Roman army—so much so that Roman writers spoke with amazement of the good behavior of the conquerors.

Nevertheless, a shock ran through the Roman world as the news spread that Rome had fallen for the first time in eight hundred years. Saint Augustine began writing *The City of God* to answer the pagans' charge that Rome had been punished for abandoning her old gods. Saint Jerome felt obliged to quote Virgil's description of the sack of Troy as the appropriate epitaph for "the city which had captured the whole world." Yet Jerome's description of his friend Marcella's encounter with the Gothic soldiers shows them responding to her pleas and courteously escorting her and the young nun Principia to the safety of St. Paul's Church.

Alaric and his men next set out to invade North Africa—as the Vandals were later to do successfully—because North Africa was the granary of Rome. They reached the southern tip of Italy and attempted to cross the Strait of Messina, but their fleet was destroyed by a storm. Then, to compound the disaster, Alaric died suddenly, probably of disease. The Goths held a great funeral for their young king. They diverted the Busento River near the town of Cosenza and had their prisoners dig a grave for Alaric in the old riverbed. Vast quantities of booty—gold, silver, and weapons— were buried with the king, and then the river was turned back into its old channel. The prisoners were killed to preserve the secret of the burial place. That is the reason given by the historian Jordanes, himself a Goth; as we shall see, there was another motive for this massacre.

What had led to the fall of Rome was a failure not so much of Roman arms as of Roman diplomacy. Once Alaric was dead, his successor, Atawulf, proved willing to enter negotiations. The Visigoths took service with the Roman Emperor Honorius once more and were sent into Spain, which they helped defend against the Vandals, and into southern Gaul, where they fought against the Huns. From Gaul they were ultimately expelled by the Franks. The Visigoths in Spain, however, converted from Arianism to Catholicism in 587, and thereafter they merged with the people of Spain, whose language they had already adopted. Goths continued to reign until the Arab invasion destroyed their kingdom in 711. Even today the nobility of Spain boasts of Gothic descent.

The Goths had originally been sent to Spain to fight the Vandals, whose history had in some respects paralleled their own. The Vandals spoke a Germanic dialect akin to Gothic and seem to have originally been neighbors of the Goths in Scandinavia. In their move southward they established themselves somewhat to the west of the Goths, then moved farther westward toward the Roman *limes* on the Rhine. When Roman troops were withdrawn from the Rhine frontier to combat Alaric's invasion of Italy, the Vandals crossed into Gaul, accompanied by Burgundians, Suevians, and other Germans. Again it was not always a matter of invasion;

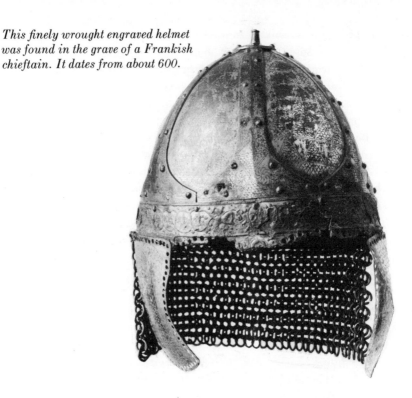

This finely wrought engraved helmet was found in the grave of a Frankish chieftain. It dates from about 600.

usually the tribes were invited to become Roman allies.

The Vandals next entered Spain. Driven from the Pyrenees by the Visigoths, they held their ground in southern Spain for a time, but the united power of Visigoths and Roman Spaniards was too much for them. They decided to go on to North Africa, and thus they carried out Alaric's dream. Although it was forbidden on pain of death, by Roman law, to teach barbarians how to build ships, the Vandals had not forgotten their Baltic heritage. They seized the vessels of fishermen, constructed ships of their own, and in 429 sailed across the Strait of Gibraltar to Tangier. The Romans, unable to defend North Africa, adopted their usual solution of offering an alliance to the barbarians. Gaiseric, the Vandal king, accepted, and within ten years he had built up an independent Vandal state under nominal Roman rule, with Carthage as its capital. Vikings before their time, the Vandals became a notable naval power that badly hampered Roman commerce.

In the middle of the fifth century, invited by a faction in Rome, the Vandals invaded Italy from the south. These newest assailants from Carthage were more successful than their Punic predecessors had been. In 455 they duplicated Alaric's feat of sacking Rome, but did little to justify the reputation for wanton destruction that has become associated with their name. As a matter of fact, the word "vandalism" seems to have been used first in the eighteenth century by the Bishop of Blois, who compared the destruction caused by the Jacobins in the French Revolution to the supposed crimes of the Vandals fourteen hundred years before.

The Vandals actually adapted with remarkable swiftness to Roman civilization. In North Africa they appointed Arian bishops for the major cities, abandoned their own language in favor of Latin, and took up the Roman customs of baths and circus spectacles. Within two generations they were displaying an interest in literature and even theology. But their kingdom did not survive long enough for any true cultural flowering. It collapsed like a house of cards in 533 when Belisarius, Justinian's great general, invaded North Africa. Belisarius captured Carthage within two weeks of his landing, and in a year's time he had destroyed the last vestiges of Vandal rule. Many Vandals took service in the Byzantine army, adding another element to the great ethnic melting pot that the Eastern Roman Empire had become. The Vandal nation vanished from history, leaving behind only a rather unjustified bad reputation.

The Huns, who initiated the great wave of migrations, likewise did not merit their reputation as savage and implacable enemies of civilization. After destroying the Gothic kingdom in the Ukraine, they settled down in the region north of the Danube and entered into reasonably good relations with the Roman Empire. They became a serious threat to western Europe only after Attila succeeded to the kingship in 434. With his motley army he terrorized the Balkans for the first fifteen years of his reign. But in the middle of the fifth century, at the same time that the Vandals were attacking Italy from the south, Attila invaded the west. Jordanes says he was bribed to do so by Gaiseric, the Vandal king. Attila had also been in touch with the rebellious peasants of Gaul, the Bagaudae. He had negotiated with one group of Franks and had received an offer of marriage from Honoria, the sister of Emperor Valentinian III. Honoria would scarcely have sent Attila her ring if she had thought him a savage, filthy, flat-nosed monster from the steppes.

Attila's raid across the Rhine into Gaul was checked by a "Roman" army consisting of Franks, Burgundians, Visigoths, Sarmatians, Saxons, Bretons, and Alans, under a general—Aëtius —who had been raised among the Huns and habitually hired Hunnish mercenaries. It seems hardly likely that the famous Battle of the Catalaunian Plains saved western Europe from domination by

Asiatic nomadism, as the traditional view has it. Attila headed a
confederation dominated by Germans, and the battle merely decided which of several different groups of Germans was to rule in
Gaul. Nor does the figure given by Jordanes, that 180,000 men fell
on both sides in the battle, seem at all likely. Attila's army was still
strong enough to withdraw in good order and invade Italy the following year. Aquileia, Milan, Pavia, and other cities were ravaged
or forced to pay tribute. But disease and hunger soon forced the
Huns to retreat.

The following year Attila died. His body was laid upon a bier in
a silken tent in the midst of an open field, and the Huns reverted to
their ancient traditions in celebrating the funeral rites of their
greatest king. After much riding and singing and an enormous
banquet, they buried the dead king in a triple coffin, the first layer
of gold, the second of silver, the third of iron. They filled the grave
with armor from slain enemies and with precious gems. To protect
it from grave robbers, they killed all the workmen—presumably
slaves—who had taken part in the burial. As we have seen, Jordanes reports a similar slaughter after the burial of Alaric; it is
probable that the killings also represented an ancient Scythian
ritual that the Huns as well as the Goths had brought with them
from their residence in Scythia. The Scythians strangled the victims so the king would have servants in the afterlife.

Attila left a great many sons, who promptly began quarreling
among themselves over the inheritance. The subject peoples seized
the opportunity to rise in revolt, and soon nothing was left of the
ephemeral Hunnish empire.

It was at this time, in the middle of the fifth century, after the
last of the Roman armies had been withdrawn, that Angles, Saxons,
and Jutes began pouring into England. Elsewhere the typical pattern of barbarian movement was that of the Franks, who infiltrated
rather than invaded the land that subsequently became France.
Only in Britain can we speak of a true invasion in which the invaders displaced the native population and destroyed its institutions. Everywhere else Roman civilization was elastic enough to
absorb the newcomers, although in the process many institutions
changed and the Empire itself became fragmented.

The great epic of the barbarian migrations, however, remains
the adventure of the Ostrogoths in Italy. The Ostrogoths, we re-
call, had been split into two parts by the onslaught of the Huns.
One group remained in Pannonia as satellites of the Huns and

fought loyally on the side of Attila on his expeditions into Gaul and Italy. After Attila's death they asserted their independence, and in a great battle under a king named Walamer they defeated the Huns. That same day in 455 a son was born to Walamer's brother. He was named Theoderic, meaning "ruler of the people," and he was destined to become just that.

After some difficulties with the Romans, Walamer and his Goths were hired, for three hundred pounds of gold a year, to guard the borders of the Empire. As assurance that they themselves would keep the peace, the king's nephew, Theoderic, then eight years old, was taken to Constantinople as a hostage. A handsome and intelligent boy, he became a favorite of the Emperor Leo. Theoderic enjoyed all the benefits of Roman education and observed the techniques of Roman government during his most impressionable years. At the age of eighteen he returned home to his father, Theudemer, who had succeeded Walamer on the throne.

Theudemer died in 473, and Theoderic became king of the Ostrogoths. By this time the Romans had assigned land in Macedonia to the restive Ostrogoths. When the Emperor Zeno was briefly expelled from Constantinople by a rebellion, Theoderic and his Goths supported him and assisted his return to office. Theoderic's rewards were the high-sounding title of patrician, the post of commanding general in the imperial army, and a lavish subsidy. Zeno, moreover, adopted him as his son—an act that implied he might some day succeed to the imperial throne. Zeno himself, after all, was by birth a barbarian from Isauria in Asia Minor.

In spite of this honor and subsequent distinctions—a consulship, a triumph, an equestrian statue in Constantinople—Theoderic's relationship with Zeno underwent many fluctuations. The emperor could not help but regard him as a dangerous rival who was too successfully gathering around himself the scattered Gothic troops of the Eastern Empire. In 488, after a dangerous clash in which Theoderic's troops blockaded Constantinople for a time, Zeno got rid of him by sending him to Italy to drive out the German usurper Odovacar, who twelve years before had deposed Romulus Augustulus, the last Roman Emperor of the West.

Ostrogoths were probably a minority in the multinational army that Theoderic assembled at Novae, in what is now Bulgaria, and he commanded it in his capacity of Roman general rather than Ostrogothic king. There were a strong contingent of Rugians and the usual motley array of barbarians from many different tribes. But Theoderic had the qualities of leadership necessary to hold the disparate elements together during a year-long march to Italy.

The conquest of Italy proceeded rapidly, although Odovacar held out in virtually impregnable Ravenna after Theoderic had seized the rest of the peninsula. Imperial naval forces blockaded Ravenna from the sea while Theoderic's army kept it surrounded on land. Nevertheless, the siege lasted four years, and even then, Odovacar was strong enough to extract from Theoderic an agreement to divide the sovereignty over Italy. Theoderic honored the agreement for exactly ten days. On the ides of March, 493, he invited his co-regent to a palace banquet and assassinated him.

After this unsavory beginning, Theoderic ruled Italy as a remarkably benevolent despot for thirty-three years, providing the longest period of peace and prosperity the country had known for centuries. His early training at the court of Constantinople had imbued him with a respect for Roman law and administration. He sought out competent men for high offices, fostered literature and learning, and devoted himself to restoring the buildings, roads, mines, fisheries, agriculture, and commerce of Italy. In religion he displayed a rare tolerance toward his Catholic subjects, as well as toward pagans and Jews. And he indulged himself in the passion of kings: building. Palaces, baths, churches, and theatres rose in Rome, Ravenna, Verona, and many smaller cities.

Throughout his long reign Theoderic maintained a dutiful courtesy toward the Roman emperor in Constantinople, whose sovereignty he recognized. Although he styled himself "king," he was not called "King of the Goths"—or Germans, or Romans—but simply *Flavius Theodericus rex*. The combination of the Roman "Flavius" with the barbarian "Theoderic" expresses the dual nature of his reign. He used the titles Augustus and triumphator, but not Caesar or imperator. His influence extended far beyond the boundaries of Italy; at times he was the recognized leader of the West. But he accepted his legal inferiority to the legitimate emperor and was content with the official position, as far as Constantinople was concerned, of Master of the Soldiers for Italy. Thus did the most formidable of the barbarian kings strive to preserve the Roman Empire.

Such are the uncertainties of history that the efforts of the last Latin-speaking emperor of the East, the great Justinian, undermined Theoderic's work and finally doomed the Western Empire. After Theoderic's death Justinian tried to recapture the lands the Empire had lost in western Europe. His general, Belisarius, had easily accomplished this task in North Africa and then turned his attention to Italy. But it took twenty years of desperate fighting before the imperial forces under Belisarius and Narses finally defeated the last of the Gothic armies. Italy was so ravaged by this war that she never recovered. She easily fell prey to a new group of barbarians who had come as allies of the Byzantines. These Lombards, it is said, were not so civilized as the Goths. At any rate, they still fashioned drinking cups from the skulls of their enemies. Lacking the organizational talents of the Goths, moreover, they splintered Italy into numerous petty duchies.

But even this last major wave of barbarians to enter Italy came by invitation and merely outstayed their welcome. If any generalization is justifiable, it is that this was the usual course of events in the so-called barbarian invasions.

The movement of the Lombards into Italy was not the last of the great migrations. The Lombards were followed by Avars, the Avars by Magyars and Turks and various Slavic tribes. From the north came a wave of truly barbarian invaders: the Vikings. The Celts expelled from England by the Saxons invaded what is now Brittany.

By the end of the sixth century the Roman Empire of the West had ceased to exist as an effective government. Britain had become a network of Anglo-Saxon kingdoms from which the Latin language and Roman influence had almost entirely vanished. Spain continued to be dominated by Visigothic kings. The Eastern Empire had retained only bridgeheads in a fragmented Italy in which the Lombards were steadily gaining ground. Almost by default the pope acquired administrative powers in Rome and its surrounding territories, and something like the Papal States came into being *de facto* long before they were created *de jure* by Charlemagne's father, Pepin.

Central Gaul and part of what is now Switzerland were held by the Burgundians. In northern Gaul the bloodthirsty Clovis had established what was to become one of the most successful of the barbarian kingdoms. The Franks had not migrated far, and once they established a power base in Roman territory, they pushed their conquests into Germany as well as Gaul, civilizing the barbarians to the east even as they themselves absorbed Roman ways. They were able to maintain the Roman system of taxation until they had devised a substitute. By the time the Roman system collapsed for want of a civil service to maintain it, the barbarian rulers were deriving their revenues from vast personal estates. They had also organized a makeshift military government of counts and dukes to replace the elaborate Roman bureaucracy. But the era of a strong central government had disappeared from Gaul and would not be restored until the advent of the Carolingians.

Perhaps the most dramatic social changes, aside from the intrusion of a new, barbarian upper class, were the slow but steady desiccation of the Roman school system and the abandonment of Roman law. In Aquitaine, Italy, and North Africa schools for the laity continued to exist for some time, but the quality of education declined. In other parts of Europe the church gradually assumed the task of teaching. Ultimately medieval education became something very different from Roman education. Nevertheless, it would be unwise to overstress the differences. Education was still education in the Latin classics—as, indeed, it remained until very recently.

The emergence of medieval civilization from that of the Romans is far too complex a subject to be dealt with briefly. Ultimately, of course, the entire quality of life changed. But in the period of the last barbarian invasions and immediately afterward such medieval phenomena as chivalry, Scholasticism, and Gothic cathedrals still lay far in the future. Despite the political upheavals, many aspects of life remained unchanged, especially in the southern part of western Europe.

Christians were inclined to interpret the chaos of the times as a sign that the last days were coming. Thus Saint Ambrose could write, "we are indeed in the twilight of this world." Nevertheless, the emperor in Constantinople was still *the* emperor. The popes acknowledged their subservience to him even though they were becoming virtually independent. The chanceries of barbarian kings continued to date documents by the reigns of the emperors in Constantinople. Throughout western Europe the literate continued to write in Latin, and the common people—including the barbarians —spoke dialects of Latin for the most part. Only in England was there a violent rupture with tradition, and only there did a barbarian vernacular take the place of Latin.

One of the few great breaks with the past did come about as a consequence of the barbarian migrations. Many aqueducts were destroyed during the sieges of the cities, and after the reign of Theoderic no new aqueducts were built, nor any of the old ones repaired. The most dramatic destruction took place at Rome itself, where in the middle of the sixth century the Goths besieging Belisarius cut the great aqueducts. After the war the patricians had to abandon their palaces on the hills of Rome and come down to the
banks of the Tiber, where the poor lived, drawing their water from

the river or from wells. Without piped water the hills were uninhabitable. Moreover, all the great Roman baths now became useless, and the popes who thereafter ruled Rome may have been glad that these relics of pagan life could no longer corrupt Christian morals. Torrents of water from the broken aqueducts poured out over the flat plain of the Campagna, transforming what had been fruitful wheat fields into malarial swamps, the source of the dreaded Roman fever.

The cities of the empire were already shrinking because of the decline of commerce, the displacements of political power, and the ravages of disease. The frightful bubonic plague of 542–543 reduced the population of Europe at least as severely as the Black Death of the fourteenth century did. The disruption of the water supplies completed the ruin of the great urban centers. And as the moribund cities died of thirst, medieval rustication began.

Rustication is the key word in defining the essential difference between Roman and early medieval civilization. With the end of the Empire came a return to agrarianism that was in some part the result of barbarian influence—for many of the barbarians feared the walled towns of the Romans. "A walled enclosure seemed to them a net in which men were caught, and the city itself a town to bury them alive," Ammianus Marcellinus commented. But the resurgence of agrarian life resulted mainly from complex economic and political forces that had their origins in the Empire itself— the general insecurity of life, the slowing of trade, the destruction of the middle class, the breakdown of central government, the shift from a money economy to a natural economy, and so on. Europe returned to the soil, and centuries were to pass before a new cycle of urbanization could begin. When towns once again sprang up, the "barbarians"—who could no longer by any stretch of the imagination be called that—built the novel institutions that link medieval urban society with the modern world.

A seventh-century bronze disc features a warrior.

*The huge empire constructed by Charlemagne in the course of his
religious wars against Saxons, Lombards, Avars, and Saracens was
too extensive to be efficiently administered by anyone of lesser stature.
Its disintegration was hardly less spectacular than its formation. But
during his long reign the great emperor held it together by force of
personality and by the assistance of the enlightened, progressive men
whom he enlisted in his service. Despite the breakdown of the empire,
it did re-establish the tradition of a united Christian (Roman) Empire
and a common European culture. Add to this the fact that
Charlemagne was a man of insatiable curiosity who actually
attempted to renew the classical culture, and it becomes
understandable that his person and career soon became legendary.
In his achievements and aspirations he did indeed set the standards
for the Western-Christian civilization that was to follow.*

   *Miss Pernoud is the author of numerous studies of medieval
history, including a biography of Eleanor of Aquitaine.*

THE AGE
OF CHARLEMAGNE

RÉGINE PERNOUD

In the history of the Western world three great heroes have at
separate times held sway over most of the European continent
—Caesar, Charlemagne, and Napoleon. Of the three, it may be
argued, Charlemagne has had the most profound and lasting influence on the course of human events. Lord Bryce, writing about a
century ago, had no doubt about it. The coronation of Charlemagne
as the first Holy Roman Emperor on Christmas Day A.D. 800 was,
to quote from Bryce's own rich, rounded periods, "one of those
very few events of which, taking them singly, it may be said that
if they had not happened, the history of the world would have been
different." It was from that moment, when Charlemagne was acclaimed emperor, wrote Bryce, that modern history began.

   Be that as it may, those large statements serve to remind us that
the historical importance of Charlemagne's reign was far greater
than its material achievements. Within a few generations after his
death, in 814, the great empire he had so laboriously pieced to-

*In a ninth-century sculpture in a Swiss church, Charlemagne wears
a French tunic and carries the orb and scepter of imperial Rome.*

gether was already a shambles. In his later years the aging emperor is said to have wept at the thought of the menacing advances of the Vikings along the northern and western fringes of his realm. Now, ever more boldly, the dreaded longboats with their high dragon prows were slipping up the Seine, the Loire, and other waterways, spreading terror and destroying every vestige of imperial authority wherever their raids reached. Paris itself was sacked in 845. A year later, Saracens raiding from the south attacked Rome and violated St. Peter's and the tombs of the Apostles. Then nomadic hordes of Magyars pressed in to ravage the eastern borders of the empire. And, in the meantime, Charlemagne's heirs and descendants were incapable of maintaining any semblance of political unity within the crumbling empire. Once again Europe divided into a dismal miscellany of contending and often hostile forces.

Yet the great emperor had left an indelible impress on the minds of men. It was in the generations of dissolution following his death that legends of fabulous grandeur started to cluster around his memory. He was remembered as "the Emperor with the Flowery Beard," gigantic in size and two hundred years old, who was held in awe from Britain to Baghdad; and as the invincible Christian conqueror, inspired by angels, whose sword *Joyeuse* had contained the point of the lance used in the Passion. He was credited with miraculous prowess and implausible virtue. According to some chronicles he would arise from the dead to vanquish the enemies of his realm; according to others he did in fact so rise to take part in the Crusades. He soon became the center of an epic cycle of romance, best remembered in the *Chanson de Roland*, that spread enchantment throughout the Middle Ages and down the centuries to our own day. In 1165 he was even transformed into a saint by the antipope Paschal III; and, to reduce his legend to the most elementary, everyday reality, the day of Saint Charlemagne, the "inventory of schools," was a cherished holiday for the school children of France until recent times.

However extravagant their growth, the legends about Charlemagne were rooted in historical realities, and these, even in the most factual chronicles, often enough have an epic quality that challenges the imagination. In 772, the first year of his reign as sole king of the Franks, the young warrior led his troops through the dark forests of Germany on the first of his many campaigns against the fierce Saxons of the North. On their Holy Heath in Westphalia, their most revered sanctuary, Charlemagne cut down the Irminsul, the wooden column that stood as an ancient pagan symbol of the very bearer of the universe—a gesture as expressive, if not as decisive, as that of Alexander the Great when he cut the Gordian knot in Phrygia more than a millennium earlier. At the end of his career, it is told, Charlemagne was accompanied on all his royal progresses by an elephant, Abul Abbas by name—the most prized among the lavish gifts from the Caliph Harun al-Rashid, who was to be immortalized in *The Arabian Nights* as Charlemagne was in the *Chanson de Roland.* To the Middle Ages the elephant was a beast of fabulous propensities, and when Abul Abbas died on one of Charlemagne's last campaigns against the Danes, it was taken as an omen of darkest import. The campaign was in fact indecisive, and the emperor did in fact die three years later.

These episodes, selected from the start and the finish of his reign, are more or less typical of Charlemagne's life story as it has come down to us. In the historical record as in the legend, he almost appears as a figure somewhat larger than life. Actually, judging from observations made when his skeleton was examined about a century ago, he must have been around six feet four inches tall (in spite of legend, he was apparently beardless). A man of immense energy and strength, he was a superb horseman and an accomplished swimmer. His wives, mistresses, and concubines were numerous, but his amorous indulgences at no time interfered with his conduct of state affairs or his almost incessant military exploits. He was a man of insatiable intellectual curiosity, many-sided in his interests and demanding of those from whom he could learn. Although no verifiable portrait of him has survived, he obviously had a commanding presence. Few men in history, indeed, have displayed such an impressive personality; and it was largely by the force of his personal influence that he gave shape to the trends of his age and direction to things that were to come.

The greatest achievement of that Carolingian age was in effect nothing less than the founding of Europe; that is to say, the welding of the fresh vigor and energy of the Teutonic north to the civilized traditions of the Roman south in the name of the Christian faith. Geographically speaking Europe is not a natural unity; it is rather a physically disparate extension of Asia. But out of the fusion of the Carolingian period there evolved a common European consciousness which, in spite of constant tensions and intermittent bloody ordeals over the centuries since, continues to assert itself. It was in this new Europe, as Henri Pirenne has remarked, that was elaborated the Western civilization which was one day to become that of the whole world. And nothing reveals the greatness of Charlemagne more clearly than the zeal with which this almost unlettered warrior attended, supervised, and encouraged the birth of the new and viable culture. Viewed in historical perspective his coronation marked the consolidation of this achievement. The ceremony changed nothing in fact; but it did give formal recognition to Charlemagne as the Christian emperor in the West and a rival of the Byzantine emperor in the East.

It is also true that much that Charlemagne accomplished had been initiated by others before his accession to power. Indeed the foundations upon which he built so splendidly had been laid long before his birth. History is constantly breaking out of the compartments assigned to it for the sake of convenience by historians, revealing new continuities with both past and future. So, if we settle on a birth date for the Carolingian age, it involves a fairly arbitrary selection. Nevertheless, the year 732 marks a sharp turning point in the destinies of the Frankish state, a point to which the ascendancy of Charlemagne can be directly traced. It was in this year that Charles Martel, grandfather of the emperor-to-be and then the presiding administrator for the helpless Merovingian king, checked the advancing Saracens at a great battle near Poitiers. By chance this crucial encounter took place precisely one century after the death of Mohammed. In the course of that hundred years the fanatically militant followers of the Prophet had overrun Asia and Africa, from the Indian Ocean to the Atlantic, gaining recruits as they progressed; they had crossed over into Spain and conquered the kingdom of the Visigoths; and, aided by large hordes of converted Berbers from North Africa, they had then swarmed over the Pyrenees.

The fear provoked by their deep penetration into what is now France was real and desperate; the shock of relief that followed their repulse reverberated down the years to come—echoes can be found in the much later legends of Charlemagne, who was therein confused with his grandfather as the Christian victor at Poitiers. In any event, it was in the wake of this repulse that the line of Charles Martel in the person of his son Pepin, father of Charlemagne, was established to rule the Franks.

More than two centuries before, the Franks forged the first true European state to take shape from the general wreckage that followed the invasion of barbarian tribes and the fall of Rome. With the conversion of their great ruler, Clovis, about 496, and the attendant mass conversion of his followers, the Franks became the stalwart champions of Roman Catholicism north of the Alps, in a continent otherwise given to paganism and, more subtly divisive of Christian authority, Arianism—that widespread form of heresy that denied the true Divinity of Jesus Christ. To this large, central area newly opened to the faith streamed emissaries from papal Rome and, even more important, monks and missionaries from England and Ireland. The latter included the most learned and devout men of the time, and at a point when Continental civilization had all but vanished, their work among the Franks and among the heathen beyond the frontiers helped to lay the foundations of a new age.

It is claimed that the greatest of all these Anglo-Saxon pilgrims, Saint Boniface of Crediton, had a deeper influence on the history of Europe than any other Englishman who has ever lived. In any case, it was he, the so-called "Apostle of Germany," who founded the German Church and who sowed the seeds of a new cultural life throughout those dark lands wherever his voice was heard. And when the Merovingian line of Clovis had degenerated beyond any hope of resuscitation, it was he who anointed Pepin with sacral oil, and in the name of Saint Peter, as king of the Franks.

A few years later, Pope Stephen II, with great travail, crossed the Alps and journeyed north to the abbey church of St. Denis where he personally anointed Pepin afresh—and, for good measure, Pepin's two sons, Charles (the future Charlemagne, then twelve years old) and Carloman. He not only anointed them kings of the Franks but proclaimed them "Patricians of the Romans," a title which in effect made them protectors of Rome. Alienated from his titular lord (the Roman emperor at Constantinople) by serious differences in religious policy, threatened by the territorial encroachments of the Lombards in Italy, and harassed by powerful family groups within Rome itself, the Holy Father needed the help which Pepin quickly supplied. In several campaigns Pepin established papal authority over territory that had been usurped by the Lombards—thus laying the foundation of the Papal States, which endured for more than a millennium, and at the same time marking the beginning of the imperial mission of the Carolingians as leaders and organizers of Western Christendom.

Before his death in 768, Pepin had by and large succeeded in consolidating his Frankish kingdom. Although the Lombards were still to cause trouble, their territorial aggression in Italy had been thwarted, and Pepin had placed the northern part of the peninsula under his own protection. The Saracens had finally been driven out of France altogether, and Pepin had added to his realm their earlier holdings in the southwest as well as the duchy of Aquitaine. To the east, Bavaria acknowledged his authority, and the Saxons had been contained along the northern frontier. When, upon the death of his brother and co-heir in 771, Charlemagne—at twenty-nine—became sole king of the Franks, he was already indisputably the strongest ruler in western Europe.

For the next thirty-odd years, by almost incessant warfare, Charlemagne strengthened and amplified his position until his dominions stretched from the Mediterranean and northern Spain to the North Sea, and from the Atlantic to the Elbe and the lower Danube, uniting most of the lands that are now France, West Germany, Austria, Switzerland, Liechtenstein, the Netherlands, Belgium, Luxembourg, and a good half of Italy. He quickly and finally destroyed the power of the Lombards and assumed for his own purposes the iron crown of that kingdom and all its considerable wealth. In successive bloody campaigns he virtually obliterated the Avars, the savage mounted nomads from the Eurasian steppes who had been the scourge of eastern Europe and who had laid siege to Constantinople itself.

The most celebrated of all Charlemagne's campaigns and the most famous of all medieval wars was his ill-fated expedition in 778 against the infidel Saracens of Spain. Although he had recruited a formidable "international" army, including warriors from all parts of his realm, and had been promised the support of Spanish collaborationists, Charlemagne was unable to win a decisive victory; and he soon retreated across the Pyrenees. Here it was, in the defile of Roncesvalles, that the Frankish rear guard was cut to pieces by a guerrilla band of Christian Basques, a misadventure which was not immediately reported with any great emphasis but which grew in story and legend until, as described in the *Chanson de Roland*, it became one of the most popular epic tragedies of all history. Henry Adams wrote that in the later Middle Ages it was a story "chanted by every minstrel—known by heart, from beginning to end, by every man, woman and child, lay or clerical—translated into every tongue—more intensely felt, if possible, in Italy and Spain than in Normandy and England. . . ."

Both before and after that debacle, it required eighteen separate campaigns to subdue the Saxons and to force them to baptism in the Christian faith. In the course of one of these, forty-five hundred men were beheaded in a single day, and a third of the rebellious population was resettled in distant places. "After he had thus taken vengeance," the annals calmly recite, "the king went into winter camp at Thionville and there celebrated Christmas and Easter as usual." Although his spiritual advisers reminded him that such butchery and deprivation were not the most persuasive methods of conversion, to Charles these were wars of religion; as the anointed leader of Roman Catholic Christians he fought with the sword for the cross. To this exalted leadership the Holy Father himself must pay due regard. "It is my duty," Charlemagne reminded Pope Leo III—he who was later to crown the emperor—"with the help of divine piety, to defend the Holy Church of Christ with arms on the outside against the raids of pagans and the ravages of the unfaithful, and within to protect it by diffusion of the Catholic faith. It is your duty, very holy Father, lifting your hands towards God with Moses, to help the success of our arms with your prayers." In another letter the king indirectly but emphatically admonished the pope "to live honestly and to give special attention to observing the holy canons," and in all ways to run an incorruptible, exem-

A silver-gilt panel from Charlemagne's shrine in Aachen depicts the emperor weeping over the slaughter of his knights at Roncesvalles in the Pyrenees, an event immortalized in the Chanson de Roland.

plary office. Charlemagne presided over his kingdom of God on earth with all the theocratic powers of the ancient Hebrew kings; indeed, among his intimates he chose to be addressed as David.

To those looking for more recent parallels, he seemed the re-embodiment of Roman imperial authority. More than eight centuries had passed since Julius Caesar had conquered Gaul, and more than three centuries had passed since the last Caesar of the West had given over to the remote Eastern emperor at Constantinople the dominion of the European Roman world. But the conviction that the Roman Empire of Caesar and Augustus had never ceased to exist faded very slowly. That empire, as one historian has observed, seemed to be "a necessary mode of being of the world, above the accidents of historical facts." For all its despotism, it had established peace and order, to which men's minds turned with stubborn nostalgia throughout the long, convulsive period of the barbarian invasions. And, in spite of the violence and cruelty with which Charlemagne imposed his sway over Europe, men were beginning to sense again the blessings of the Pax Romana.

In 799 violence broke out in Rome, and Pope Leo was assaulted on the city's streets. The pope had already sent Charlemagne the keys to the grave of Saint Peter and the standard of the Eternal City, and had pledged his loyalty and obedience to his Frankish protector. Now he fled north to beseech the king for his aid. Charlemagne crossed the Alps again, restored order in Rome, and re-established the papal authority and dignity. It was during this interval, in 800, while Christmas Day Mass was being celebrated, that the grateful pope crowned Charlemagne with the diadem of the Caesars. He had become, as the crowds acclaimed him, "Charles Augustus, crowned by God, the great and peace-giving Emperor of the Romans." Whether this ceremony was planned in advance, and with Charlemagne's approval, may never be known. In the light of the future that did not matter. The crown fit securely and becomingly where it was placed, and in time, even the emperors of the East acknowledged as much.

Charlemagne did not revive the Roman Empire, except in name. At his coronation as emperor he wore the Roman long tunic and cloak, but it is significant that he never thus dressed again—and that he never returned to Rome after this epochal visit. In spite of his consuming interest in the revival, preservation, and dissemination of classical culture, which gave his reign the character of an early medieval renaissance. Charlemagne remained always a Frank. He chose as a new and permanent capital the old watering town of

Pope Leo III crowns Charlemagne emperor in Rome on Christmas Day, 800.
Jean Fouquet painted this manuscript illumination in the fifteenth century.

Aachen, between the Rhine and the Meuse, an area with which his Carolingian forebears had long been associated. And here he built a splendid palace with a church that seemed to his contemporaries a structure "half human, half divine"; and at Aachen he gathered about him wise and capable men to instruct him and to guide him in his role as a Christian monarch.

For untold centuries past the Mediterranean had been the maternal, nourishing element of all intellectual vigor and of all creative spirit. Urban life at Athens, Alexandria, Rome, and Constantinople had fed the growth of all civilizing tendencies and developments from time out of mind. Now the center of cultural ferment, in Europe at least, had shifted to the heartland of the rural dominions of the Franks—to a land that a few centuries earlier had been identified with long northern nights, dark forests, and crude barbarism.

The administration of Charlemagne's huge and miscellaneous empire was a highly personal operation. Through his inheritance and by his conquests, peoples of many varied tribal traditions— Lombards, Burgundians, Franks, Saxons, and Bavarians, among others, not to mention Romans—had been brought within the imperial jurisdiction. He did not attempt to abolish their customary laws; but he apparently had these committed to writing, and then proceeded to refine them and add to them a voluminous flow of capitularies, or ordinances, of his own, which were final, absolute, and beyond appeal. To be sure that these promulgations were known, respected, and observed throughout the land, Charlemagne dispatched pairs of royal emissaries called *missi dominici*—usually consisting of one secular representative, a count, and one cleric, a bishop or an abbot, who were responsible directly to the emperor. They checked periodically in the most intimate detail on the behavior of his subjects, from the efficiency of high public officials to the sex habits of the lowliest monks. Although, as one of his capitularies stated, "the emperor cannot exercise the needful care and discipline upon each individual," through his *missi* Charlemagne did try to be everywhere at once in his realm. The welfare of his subjects rested almost completely in his own two hands. He was in effect, a contemporary phrase stated, "Lord and Father, King and Priest, the Leader and Guide of all Christians." And it may be fairly said that no one with such great power has abused it less.

Nothing better illustrates Charlemagne's vision of his "universal" state and of his own responsibility, under God, for its welfare than his determination to raise the educational standards of his people and to restore for their benefit the neglected knowledge of the past. The seed of such a revival had already been planted in an abysmally illiterate society by Boniface and his fellow missionaries a generation or two earlier. Now, forced by the enthusiasm of the king, it came to flower during his lifetime. There was no more eager student in the realm than Charlemagne himself. His interest in his own self-improvement appeared at times almost pathetic. For the age, Charlemagne had a well-informed if not brilliant mind; but he never mastered the art of writing, although we are told he "used to carry with him and keep under the pillow of his couch tablets and writing sheets that he might in his spare moments accustom himself to the formation of letters." To satisfy and exercise his own intellectual curiosity as well as to further his reforms, he gathered about him the brightest and most competent minds of the time. The old palace school of earlier kings was transformed into an academy of distinguished theologians and scholars who were enlisted from all parts of the realm and beyond. Alcuin, the most prominent of them all, was an Anglo-Saxon; Paul the Deacon, Paulinus of Aquileia, and Peter of Pisa came from Italy; Clement and Dungal were Irish; Theodulf and Agobard were Visigoths from Spain; and Einhard and Angilbert were Germans—that is, Franks.

The intellectual excitement that Charlemagne instigated by this recruitment of learned men, which was centered in the palace school, was to spread throughout his empire, largely by way of the monastic and episcopal centers of the land. Indeed, in an agrarian world the great Carolingian abbeys as Tours, St. Gall, Reichenau, Fulda, Lorsch, Corbie, and others became the creative sources of civilization, as cities had been and were to be in both earlier and later societies. They were the basic social and economic centers of the age, and within their precincts were developed those traditions of art and letters, of architecture and liturgy, of music and calligraphy, which were to remain the essential cultural endowment of the centuries to come. They long survived the emperor's death and the political chaos that followed. Indeed, in later years King Alfred sent to the Franks for scholars who could help in the re-education of England. It can be claimed that in providing for the needs of his rude Christian society, Charlemagne laid the foundation of all modern education.

As one single token of this lasting influence, the page you are reading is printed in letters derived from the calligraphy developed in Carolingian manuscripts, called the Carolingian minuscule, a style of writing that became standard in most of western Europe.

More than 90 per cent of the oldest surviving classical Latin texts have come down to us in the form of copies made in the Carolingian period, or in copies of them. For a long time these were mistakenly considered to be Roman manuscripts, and the characters themselves still are called "roman" letters.

In arts and architecture as in letters Charlemagne hoped to enrich and invigorate his northern world by a return to the forms and traditions of the earlier Roman Empire. Thus the design of his palace chapel at Aachen, which provided a model for many other Carolingian churches, was based on the church of San Vitale at Ravenna. To complete this structure he purloined classical columns, bronze gratings, and other ancient elements from Italy. This "marvel of workmanship," as Einhard described it, was the crowning ornament of the emperor's capital. In the end it was no imitation of any older model, but a vigorous northern interpretation that served to stimulate the development of new architectural styles and concepts; and in this creative fusion it is typical of Carolingian art.

The murals, mosaics, and sculptured reliefs that adorned such Carolingian structures have, along with the buildings themselves, almost entirely disappeared. It is in the so-called minor arts—ivories, metalwork, and particularly, brilliantly illuminated manuscripts—that the spirit of the age is most expressively revealed to us. The most characteristic—and the most significant—feature of Carolingian illumination is its tendency to return to the classical tradition, particularly in its renewed interest in the representation of the human figure. Some such illustrations in eighth- and ninth-century manuscripts are startlingly reminiscent of classical likenesses painted on the walls of Pompeii and elsewhere eight centuries earlier—illustrations no doubt based on long-lost late Roman and Byzantine models. Yet neither the Roman occupation of earlier centuries nor the classical revival of Charlemagne's time destroyed the rich cultural traditions of the Celtic, Germanic, and other "barbarian" people who had migrated to the western European continent. For barbarism is not savagery but rather a degree or stage of social organization; it is a tribal culture rather than one of a settled, authoritarian state. These people brought with them a heritage in their arts as in their folkways that was deeply rooted in a distant past, and in part inherited from the Scythians, Sarmatians, and other eastern tribes with whom they had come in contact during their earlier migrations. In a number of Carolingian manuscripts magnificent ornamental initials reflect that love of intri-

cately patterned flat decoration typical of the art of the migration
period—an old art that had been remembered by Irish and Anglo-
Saxon illuminators and returned in refined forms to the Continent
by missionaries from the British Isles. In others the pictures are
almost set in motion by a dynamic expression of energy, a vibrant
rhythmic quality that recalls the linear tensions of Celtic ornamentation (and also heralds the expressionism of much later German
Gothic art).

Charlemagne recalled from threatened obscurity the ancient
traditions of art, as he had salvaged from possible destruction
classical manuscripts of enduring importance. The "renaissance"
he had fostered gained momentum, attaining an even more complete development in the generation following his death in 814.
Some of the finest of such manuscript illuminations as we have
mentioned were created during the reign of his grandson, Charles
the Bald. But in his efforts to revive the ideals of classical antiquity,
as is so often the case in such "revivals," Charlemagne merely performed the last rites over the past; and, as is also often the case, he
signaled the advent of something new and different.

In the arts as in the rest of the cultural pattern that evolved in
Carolingian times, the many conflicts between the traditions of the
northern tribesmen and the inheritance of classical civilization
were slowly resolved. The antique conception of the human figure,
presented as an illusion of corporeal reality, and the barbarian
preference for vigorous, flat patterns, ultimately merged into a
fresh idiom. The human figures and other subjects are not realis-
tically defined but are transformed into symbols used to animate
the walls of a building or the pages of a book. By the end of the
ninth century these new principles had been decisively formulated,
and from them stemmed inevitably the glories of the Romanesque
art that followed.

By an old, established, and highly misleading convention, the
term Middle Ages has been applied to that long period between the
fall of Rome and the beginning of the Renaissance, as though the
medieval world was simply a way station between antiquity and
modern times. By an even more unfortunate convention this millennium has been broadly labeled the Dark Ages—implying a time
of intellectual and cultural stagnation. Actually it was a period of
assimilation, of ferment, and of consolidation. There were indeed
years of relative "darkness"; but there were also interludes of
radiant accomplishment. None of these had greater import for the
future of Western civilization than the age of Charlemagne.

*Although scholars have long since rejected the harsh judgments on
Byzantine history of the "enlightened" historians such as Gibbon, it
still requires something of an effort of the imagination to think of the
Eastern Empire as an integral part of European history. Yet the story
of the West would have been very different had not the Byzantine
Empire held back the pressure of the infidels over hundreds of years.
Basic differences were bound to continue between the Germanic-Roman
culture of the West and the essentially Greek culture of the East. The
Greek culture had persisted through centuries of Roman domination
and reasserted itself as the West fell prey to the "barbarians." As we
now realize, however, the Greek culture of the East continued to
influence the West long before the Renaissance and played a crucial
role in preserving and transmitting the classical heritage. In
Byzantine history there were periods of weakness, corruption, and
general disreputability, but the story of its thousand-year existence is
on the whole as impressive as it is important.*

*Mr. Sherrard, formerly deputy director of the British School of
Archaeology in Athens, has published a study of* The Greek East and
the Latin West.

BYZANTIUM: THE OTHER HALF OF THE WORLD

PHILIP SHERRARD

I t is only recently that the word "Byzantium" has been freed
from the contumely attached to it by several generations of un-
comprehending, humanist-minded historians. Pre-eminent among
them was Edward Gibbon, for whom Byzantine history was "a
tedious and uniform tale of weakness and misery" in which "not a
single discovery was made to exalt the dignity or promote the hap-
piness of mankind." Christian Byzantium—or rather the triumph
of Christianity itself—marked for Gibbon the end of the "classical"
civilization he so much admired, marked indeed the decline and fall
of the Roman Empire. At the end of his vast work he notes mod-
estly: "I have described the triumph of barbarism and religion."

Some hundred years later another historian, William Lecky, was
still echoing Gibbon's contempt: "Of that Byzantine Empire, the
universal verdict of history is that it constitutes, without a single

*Constantine the Great holds a model of Constantinople, his imperial
capital; detail of a tenth-century mosaic in Hagia Sophia.*

119

exception, the most thoroughly base and despicable form that civilization has yet assumed. . . . [It] is a monotonous story of the intrigues of priests, eunuchs, and women, of poisonings, of conspiracies, of uniform ingratitude, of perpetual fratricides."

Judgments like this, which could be multiplied, are not likely to be made today, or to carry much weight if they are. Byzantine history and civilization have become legitimate objects of academic attention. There are now institutes, such as that at Dumbarton Oaks in Washington, where notable scholars devote themselves entirely to the gathering, sifting, and assessing of Byzantine material. As a result, Byzantine society is no longer regarded as the stagnant playground of decadent voluptuaries, immersed in sensuality and bestirring themselves only when provoked by some outburst of public spleen in the Hippodrome, or by some hair-splitting theological subtlety thrown into their midst by fanatic monks. In art, literature, statesmanship, diplomacy, and war, Byzantium's achievements are now recognized, even admired. The philosopher Alfred North Whitehead went so far as to assert that its culture was superior to that of classical Rome, and some distinguished historians have claimed that it afforded greater opportunities for living a civilized life than the Pax Augusta. It might in fact seem that the wheel has come full circle, and that Gibbon's thesis is being reversed: it is no longer a question of Rome's decline and fall, but of Byzantium's ascent and triumph.

For in fact the Byzantine Empire was not simply the Roman Empire extended in a semiparalytic state through another thousand-odd years of slow ossification and decay. This was a new creation, growing out of the Roman past but essentially different from it. Indeed, it was precisely a failure of ideology in the Empire of the Caesars that made a new form of society imperative if Western civilization was to survive. Already in the second century A.D. the Roman Empire was threatened with disruption. There were civil wars within and frontier wars without; legions mutinied, Goths and Parthians bestirred themselves. The highly centralized administrative machinery creaked under the strain. Disaster was averted for the time being by Diocletian, who came to power in A.D. 284. He introduced a series of measures to decentralize and stabilize the Empire, now split for this purpose into four great compartments. But these reforms only postponed matters, for after his death, as after the death of Alexander the Great, struggles broke out between the rulers of the various parts of the Empire as they contended for the imperial throne. And it was only in A.D. 323

that the triumphant survivor was able to take the steps that ultimately created the empire of the Byzantines.

This survivor was Constantine, known to history because of the
magnitude of his achievements as Constantine the Great. He was
born in Moesia, the province of the modern Serbs and Bulgars, and
as a youth was sent to the court of Nicomedia in Asia Minor, which
Diocletian had already chosen for his headquarters in preference to
Rome. After serving in Persia and Egypt, he was acclaimed Caesar
at York, in England, where his father had died while on a punitive
expedition against the Scots. The next six years Constantine spent
in Gaul and Italy as co-emperor with Maxentius, and in A.D. 312
he captured Rome from his colleague. This made him sole emperor in the West, with Licinius, sole emperor in the East, as his
only rival. His final triumph did not come until A.D. 323 with the
defeat and capture of Licinius, after a struggle into which both
parties had thrown all their strength.

Faced now with the task of arresting the disintegration of the
Empire and of welding its heterogeneous elements, both territorial
and cultural, into a new coherence, Constantine made it his first
concern to choose and construct a new imperial capital. Where
should this be? Rome was the scene of conspiracy and intrigue,
while to the north and west were lands of unreclaimed barbarity.
The East seemed the obvious choice: there was the main focus of
trade; it was there that some bulwark had to be found to resist the
Parthians and to check the westerly migrations from the steppes;
and it was there that Christianity was rapidly gaining an ascendancy sufficient to displace the dead or dying ideologies of the ancient world. And if the East was obvious, what better site could
there be than the small town of Byzantium? Set on a triangular
peninsula commanding the mouth of the Bosporus, which links the
Sea of Marmara with the Black Sea and divides Europe from Asia,
Byzantium seemed to meet all the requirements. The climate was
cool and healthy. Along one side of the triangular peninsula was an
inlet that formed a perfect natural harbor: the Golden Horn. To
the south lay the Aegean and the rich gardens of Asia Minor,
source of all the earth's fruits, and beyond, the flax fields of Egypt.
To the east, as far as India and China, stretched the trade routes
along which passed those treasured spices and medicaments—pepper and musk, cloves and nutmeg, cinnamon and camphor, sugar
and ginger, aloes and balsam—that were to lend such refinement
to the Byzantine cuisine; and thence, too, came the ivory and
amber, pearls and precious stones, porcelain and glass, muslin, taf-

feta, and damask that were to be the raw materials of Byzantine reliquaries and embroideries. To the north lay Russia and those ports of the Black Sea through which flowed wheat and furs, honey and gold, wax and slaves. Byzantium's natural defenses were, as Constantine had discovered during the war with Licinius, as good as could be desired; and he must have sensed prodigious possibilities as he chose this site and marked out with his own hands the confines of the new city to which he gave his name, and which for more than a thousand years was to be the focus of Western civilization.

Materials for its building were at hand in the marbles of Proconnesus, a nearby island, and in the wood from forests bordering the Black Sea. Edifice after imperial edifice began to rise on the spacious platform, once the ancient acropolis, of the peninsula that divided the Sea of Marmara from the still waters of the Golden Horn. To the east of this platform was the Senate House; to the south was the Great Palace, a dense group of buildings stretching through gardens down to the shore, where for many centuries stood the porphyry pavilion of the empresses; to the west lay the Forum and the vast theatre of the Hippodrome, capable of seating forty thousand people and containing works of art Constantine had rifled from the entire classical world: four great bronze horses (eventually removed to the façade of St. Mark's in Venice, where they remain to this day); the bronze eagle and Calydonian boar; the bronze triple pillar from Delphi, bearing the names of the thirty-one Greek states that had triumphed over the armies of the Persian Xerxes at Plataea in 479 B.C.; and much more. Northeast of the Hippodrome, on the headland most visible to ships approaching from the south, Constantine placed the Church of the Holy Wisdom, Hagia Sophia. Enlarged by his son Constantius and rebuilt in the sixth century by the emperor Justinian, it was eventually to be recognized as the crowning glory of the Empire.

Constantine also set up a huge column—ten drums of porphyry, bound in metal—rising from a white marble plinth and supporting a Greek Apollo whose head was replaced by that of the Emperor encircled with the golden rays of the sun. Within the plinth were enshrined such purported relics of special veneration as a casket holding crumbs from the bread with which Christ fed the five thousand, the adze with which Noah built the ark, the alabaster box of ointment with which Mary anointed Jesus, and the crosses of the two thieves crucified with Jesus of Nazareth which the Emperor's mother, Saint Helena of York, had recently brought from Jerusalem. The inscription on the plinth of Constantine's column read: "O Christ, Ruler and Master of the World, to Thee have I now consecrated this obedient City. . . ." On May 11, A.D. 330, the city was solemnly dedicated and the Byzantine Empire inaugurated.

For this empire Constantine the Great laid both the temporal and spiritual foundations, and in it he fused together the great political legacy of Rome, the equally great cultural legacy of the Hellenic world, and the explosive dynamism of the Christian faith. It was to last for 1,123 years, and to be governed by no less than eighty-eight effective rulers in succession.

For convenience this long period can be divided into phases. The first—from the foundation of Constantinople in 330 to the death of the emperor Anastasius in 518—was one of growth and trial. Thanks partly to its geographical position, the new city escaped the barbarian devastations that visited the West. Only in one battle, at Adrianople in 378, were the armies of the Eastern Empire defeated by the Goths; and it may in part have been the recollection of this defeat that prompted Cyrus, prefect of the emperor Theodosius II, to build a huge triple line of walls to the landward side of the seagirt promontory on which Constantinople stands. The impressive ruins of these walls may still be seen.

The second phase, from 518 to 610, or from Justin I to Phocas, is marked above all by the reign of the emperor Justinian and his wife Theodora. Fired by an ambition to bring within the orbit of Byzantium all those alienated lands of the old Roman Empire, and to establish his imperial government over the whole of the Mediterranean and Western world, Justinian embarked on a policy of territorial aggrandizement which strained the resources of the Empire to their limits. In twenty years (533–554), he brought northern Africa, Italy, southern Spain, and the islands of Sicily, Corsica, Sardinia, and the Balearics under Byzantine rule. At the same time he initiated a series of internal reforms. In spite of the wealth and splendor of the imperial capital, the whole administrative machinery was in urgent need of overhaul, and so great was popular discontent over the various abuses that in 532 a revolt, known as the Nika riot, broke out at Constantinople and all but cost Justinian his throne. That it did not was due to the courage of Theodora and, it must be added, to the loyalty and brutality of the imperial guards who, after half the original city of Constantinople had been burned to the ground, put down the revolt by slaughtering some thirty thousand of the insurgents in the Hippodrome.

Justinian, in order to remove the causes of the riot, set about at 123 once to centralize the administration, abolishing the sale of offices and tightening up provincial government. But his greatest work, already begun in the opening years of his reign, was the recodification of Roman law. In a series of volumes, collectively known as the *Codex Justinianus*, the primary rules of social existence as defined by Roman law were reformulated in accordance with the Christian ethic. It became the civil code not only of Byzantium but of much of the Western world in subsequent centuries. Finally, Justinian set about repairing the damage caused to the capital by the fires of the Nika riot. Various new civic buildings were erected, and a bronze equestrian statue of the Emperor himself, wearing what was referred to as the armor of Achilles, was set up on a huge column in the main public square, the Augustaeum. Above all, the great church of Constantinople, Hagia Sophia, had to be reconstructed. In five years and ten months the two major architects, Isidore the Milesian and Anthemius of Tralles, raised a building that was to be forever after the pride and pivot of the Byzantine world, a visible expression of the vital consciousness—compounded of Roman, Greek, and Christian elements—of the Byzantine people.

For behind the pageant of the eleven-hundred-odd years of their history lies a deliberate and unchanging pattern, a particular vision of human life and its purposes that gives an underlying unity to the shifting scenes of the historical drama. Byzantium was above all a Christian empire; before we can understand its unique nature, we must try to discern what meaning and relevance this fact had for the Byzantines themselves. Here we may have recourse to the image of the dome. Set over all, seeming to contain and embrace in its simple unity all the diversity and multitude that lies below it, the dome is the Byzantine architectural form par excellence. And the dome of all Byzantine domes was that of Hagia Sophia—a dome so light, as the contemporary historian Procopius wrote, that it "does not appear to rest upon a solid foundation, but to cover the place beneath as though it were suspended from heaven by the fabled golden chain."

It was the desire to make visible a certain complex of ideas, and not any structural or utilitarian interest in a means of covering space, that impelled the Emperor Justinian and the subsequent builders of Byzantine architecture to give such prominence to the dome and to the building of domed churches and palaces. It was wholly natural that the visitor who approached the holy city of

Constantinople from across the dolphin-torn silvery blue of the

Sea of Marmara, and rounded the promontory to enter the Golden Horn, saw rising on the spacious platform of the headland—over the masts of the merchantmen and the roofs of the warehouses, over the Hippodrome and the Senate House and the Great Imperial Palace, over the public square of the Augustaeum with its armor-clad statue of the Emperor on his enormous column—the huge domed mass of Hagia Sophia.

For this church expressed that consciousness of a transcendent reality, of a supernatural presence, which lay at the heart of Byzantine life. It was a replica of heaven upon earth, of Paradise, of the house of God. And the crowning glory of the church was the dome, invested with a symbolism both divine and royal. Situated at the central point of the earthly and heavenly kingdom, scene of the manifestation of the Christian Saviour, the dome was thus a symbol of transcendent power and authority as well as of the Resurrection and the coming of the Kingdom of God in which human life and society would be fulfilled. In it were thus embodied the multiple ideals and purposes which gave Byzantium its *raison d'être* and which the Empire, in theory at least, was consciously intended to realize.

But if Christ was the spiritual ruler of Byzantium, his temporal instrument for achieving the corporate salvation of his chosen nation was the Christian emperor. Although formally elected by the Senate and proclaimed by the people and the army, the emperor was in fact regarded as chosen by divine decree and therefore as occupying a position superior to that of other mortals. "Glory to God who has designated you as basileus, who has glorified you, who has manifested His grace to you" ran the acclamation which followed the imperial coronation. Temporal representative of Christ, the emperor was equal to the Apostles, *isapostolos;* and the mystical procession of his days as well as the elaborations of court ceremonial were patterned on the example of his celestial paradigm. His costume was like an icon. At Easter he donned the garb of resurrection, and appeared surrounded by twelve apostles, his body swathed in white bands. Twelve guests sat at his table at meals. His receptions were not so much audiences as epiphanies, divine appearances. In the Sacred Palace they took place in an octagonal room crowned with an immense cupola and furnished with glittering chandeliers, golden lions, golden griffins, golden birds perched on golden branches, the birds breaking into song when some mysterious device was set in motion. At the heart of all this, on the imperial throne, was the sovereign himself, clothed

in gold, bathed in sanctity. Sacred, too, was all he touched—his garments, his letters, the golden imperial seal. To insult him was to blaspheme. To revolt against his authority was to invite excommunication. Rebellion was apostasy. And this sanctity of the sovereign flowed over into that of his ministers, and indeed into the whole imperial administration. Entrance into public office was a kind of ordination; to leave it was to lay down a sacred trust. The veneration due to the emperor in this way conferred on the whole imperial service a truly hieratic character.

Indeed this civil service—massive and proficient, inherited directly from Rome—was the backbone of the state. Down to Justinian's day it used Latin as its official language and preserved Latin titles for its senior officials (Praetorian Prefect, Magister Militum, Quaestor Sacri Palatii, and so on). But from the seventh century onward the service gradually assumed a new form. Greek became the official language. Greek designations replaced the Latin titles of ministers and high officials. Of these the most numerous were the logothetes, ministers of internal and foreign affairs, of public revenues and imperial estates, and of the military chest. Generally, though not necessarily, these great functionaries were recruited, after passing a stiff examination, from distinguished families with a tradition of public service. They were nominated, promoted, and dismissed by the emperor; it was he who conferred upon them the emblems of office, and it was with him that the actuality of power lay. No parliament or senate encumbered the emperor in his dealings with his officials or stultified the everyday working of the state machine. The same was true where provincial administration was concerned: each province was ruled by a general, or strategos, directly appointed by the emperor and directly responsible to him. At the same time, as a check against the abuse of power on the part of the military governor and the growth of local despotisms, a representative of the civil interest was appointed alongside him, though in a subordinate position; and he, too, was in direct communication with the emperor. This combination of highly trained officials and military aristocrats all personally known to, chosen by, and directly responsible to the emperor, made the Byzantine administration one of the most centralized and at the same time one of the most efficient of which we have a record.

The grime of centuries and the hanging medallions of Arabic script have only slightly dimmed the immense majesty of Hagia Sophia.

If the regulation and administration of the material and temporal side of life lay with the emperor and his service, the spiritual and eternal side of life was most fully represented not by the bishops and clergy, as might be imagined, but by the monasteries and hermitages. It is impossible to overestimate the significance of the role played by monasticism in Byzantium. It was not simply that monasteries were places in which deposed emperor and downtrodden peasant alike could find refuge—a kind of safety valve through which rejected or disruptive elements might be discharged without the system exploding. It was that the monasteries, and more particularly the craggy fastness or desert cave of the hermits, were the forging-houses of what the Byzantines regarded as the highest types of humanity, the types in which the Christian ideal was realized to the fullest possible extent on earth. The emperor might be God's elect. The saint or the holy man was more: he was a living holocaust of divine energies, the incarnation of the Holy Spirit, witness of God, and in a certain sense God himself. For the Byzantines saw the highest type of humanity fulfilled not in those who lived a terrestrial life of moral rectitude or judicious piety, but in those who through earnest battle had broken the barrier between man and God, and had fused the two once more into a vital conjunction. It was this union that the saint or the holy man had accomplished.

The saint or the holy man was a mediator between earth and heaven. He was a present source of mercy, miracle, and guidance, the father of the people among whom he dwelt, their healer and deliverer. Mortal life was a constant warfare between myriad unseen forces, divine and demoniac, ever-present, overwhelming, unappeasable. Where else could a man turn but to those who through divine power could subject even the demons to their bidding? Let disease or other affliction come, the holy man was at hand with his healing grace. Let taxgatherer extort or landowner oppress, the ascetic saint was there to defend against the rapine and injustice of the powerful. Let the emperor himself, out of considerations of state, seek to impose some dogma contrary to the faith and, weather-wracked and gaunt, the man of God would descend from pillar or mountain retreat to head the opposition that brought the erring sovereign to heel. For what had the ascetic to fear at the hands of the powerful, even if they were the hands of the emperor himself? He had already renounced the world and all its ways. All that could be taken from him now was his mortal life, and if he were to lose that through violence laid upon him, it might well be but to gain a martyr's crown and so to become an even stronger focal point of popular worship and superhuman aid than he already was. Fanatic to us though they may often appear, the fact remains that throughout the Byzantine period it was from their ranks—the ranks of the monks and the nuns—that came those heroic men and women who guarded the Empire's conscience, its spiritual lifeblood. Through them the springs of its inspiration flowed and, barren though it may seem to say it in an age of disbelief, to them was Byzantium chiefly indebted for all that was most vital in her achievement.

Between the material and the temporal, represented in Byzantium by the emperor and the imperial body politic, and the spiritual and the eternal, represented by the saints, there is the image-forming world of the soul, the world of the imagination. It is the world of Byzantine art, which not only gave expression to the divine and supernatural aspirations of man, but also to those transcendental realities which are the objects of his spiritual quest. Its sources and intent therefore coincided with those of Christianity itself, and like other forms of Christian worship its chief function was to serve the religion to which it owed its existence. The forms and figures of Byzantine art reflect that necessity. The symbolism is intelligible, clear, subtle, allowing for the intrusion of no pleasing sentiment or vacant naturalism. All is simplified, all reduced to essentials, all subordinate to the spiritual truth which is being conveyed. To this sparse geometry of symbolic content, color gave the flesh, color employed not merely as an adjunct to the modeling but fired with an independent life. But one must also remark the subtlety of contour, the impeccable sense of proportion, the superb grasp of the whole that brought all the elaborate detail into harmony with the overriding symbolic pattern; and finally the unbridled richness of material employed—stones, metals, fabrics, marbles, and mosaic. Having absorbed all this, one may understand something of the magnificence of this art, and of its sophisticated splendor.

The first flowering of Byzantine art begins with the foundation of Constantinople in A.D. 330 and reaches its golden age under Justinian in the sixth century. This period coincided with the final decadence of Hellenistic art, which had spread across the Mediterranean and Anatolian world from Rome to Bactria—unrooted, cosmopolitan, dominated by the natural world and with the natural human form as its final measure and norm. Already in the Near East the revival of Persia and the foundation of the Sasanian em-

129

pire in A.D. 226 had brought a reaction and a return to a more hieratic convention. Byzantine art may be seen as the result of the imposition of Oriental forms on a Hellenistic ground. In it an almost preternatural insight into the significance of intelligible forms is fused with a lyrical sensuality that prevents stylization from becoming academic and lifeless, the mere repetition of formulas. This fusion seems to have been achieved in Justinian's reign, if one is to judge from the astonishing mosaics recently restored to their full brilliance in the apse of the Church of Saint Catherine on Mount Sinai. At the same time there came about the architectural fusion of the early Christian basilica (square atrium or narthex, rounded apse, and long naves flanked by twin or quadruple rows of pillars) with the domed octagon or rotunda—a fusion crystallized in Justinian's new church of Hagia Sophia. "Solomon, I have surpassed thee," Justinian is reported to have said when first he viewed the immense majesty of the completed edifice; and he celebrated its dedication with a banquet at which six thousand sheep, a thousand each of oxen, pigs, and poultry, and half a thousand deer were roasted for the delectation of court and populace alike.

This church remains, even as the secularized museum it is today, Justinian's most enduring monument. His attempt to reconstitute the Roman Empire proved politically a great burden; and the ensuing phase of Byzantine history, opening with the reign of Heraclius in 610 and ending with that of Theodosius III in 717, was one in which the existence of the whole Empire was imperiled. First came the onslaughts of the Persian armies under Khosrau II in the East, followed by the attacks of the Avars and the Lombards in the West. Then, in 634, within three years after the death of Mohammed, his Arab followers from Medina attacked the Byzantine garrisons of Palestine. By 640, Palestine was lost and Egypt invaded; by 641, the year Heraclius died, Alexandria was evacuated and Persia and Armenia were overrun. Cyprus fell, and in 655 the Byzantine fleet, under the Emperor Constans II, was defeated off the coast of Lycia. But largely as a result of the discovery and effective use of a new weapon, Greek fire, the Moslems were finally brought to a halt on both land and sea, and in 678 peace was concluded. Much reduced in size, the Byzantine Empire was from then on centered on Constantinople and the Greek seaboard, while connections with the West grew correspondingly weaker; it was at this time, for instance, that the last vestiges of Latin were dropped from official imperial usage.

130   The fourth phase, from 717 to 867, began with a restoration of

the prestige of Byzantine arms under the Isaurian emperors Leo and Constantine V Copronymus. The Moslems attacked again and laid siege to Constantinople itself, but the Byzantines, with the considerable aid of frost and famine, inflicted a loss of some one hundred fifty thousand men on the besiegers. That defeat stemmed for a time the tide of Arab expansion: the capital of the Abbasid caliphs was now transferred to the distant city of Baghdad.

But the great event of this phase of Byzantine history lay not in the field of military triumph or of internal reform, but in that of religion. The worship of sacred images, or icons, had by this time become an integral part of Orthodox Christianity. And thus when the Emperor Leo, supported by his puritanical followers from the hinterland of Asia Minor, launched an attack on image worship in an edict of 726, reaction was immediate and intense. Riots in the capital were soon followed by insurrection in Greece, Byzantine authority in Italy was fatally undermined, and the whole Empire was split asunder. Even the restoration of the worship of images by the empress Irene in 787 did not bring an end to the troubles. In 815, with the advent of a new emperor from Armenia, icons were once again proscribed; and it was only because most orthodox Christians, and particularly the monks, remained so intransigent in their attachment to sacred pictures that the iconoclasts, or "image-breakers," were finally defeated.

The restoration of images after these struggles ushers in a new period of Byzantine art, which continues through the eleventh and twelfth centuries. It is a period marked by the huge patronage of such emperors as Basil I the Macedonian, whose reconquest of imperial territories at the end of the ninth century launched the Empire's most prosperous times; Constantine VII Porphyrogenitus, who as a patron of the arts has been compared to Hadrian and Lorenzo the Magnificent; and Alexius I Comnenus, whose life and character were recorded so graphically by his daughter Anna. This was the period of Byzantine culture's widest diffusion. Of the profane art of the time, such as that which decorated the Great Palace at Constantinople, little or nothing remains, and our notion of it must be derived chiefly from contemporary chronicles. But of ecclesiastical art, refined and spiritualized after the attacks of the iconoclasts, memorials exist as far apart geographically as the mosaics in Santa Sophia at Kiev and the enthroned Christ at Monreale in Sicily; lying between them, in Greece, are such masterpieces as the monastery churches of Daphne, near Athens, Saint Luke in Phocis, and Nea Moni on the island of Chios.

An ivory carving dating from the tenth century portrays Christ crowning Constantine VII as the emperor of Byzantium.

A single dynasty, that of the Macedonians, fills the two hundred years between 867 and 1057. It was a period of territorial expansion and internal prosperity, in which the forces of Islam were thrust back to the deserts of Arabia and the hills of Kurdistan, while many of the lost provinces and cities of the East were reclaimed. In 961 the capture of Crete restored control of the Aegean to the Byzantine navy, and by 1014 the emperor Basil II Bulgaroctonos (the Bulgar-slayer) had reduced the whole Balkan peninsula to imperial rule. External success was marked by a corresponding prodigality at home. All the world's wealth seemed to pour through the trade routes of the Levant, overland from India and beyond, or down the great Russian rivers and the Black Sea into the queen of cities, there to furnish fresh magnificence in art and architecture. The only signs of trouble to come were the increasing independence of the great feudal overlords; the growing alienation of the West, soon to lead to official schism with Rome; and the deepening shadow of the Seljuk Turks converging on the northeast frontiers.

Between 1053 and the sack of Constantinople by the Fourth Crusaders in 1204 these threats materialized. With the death of the last ruler of the Macedonian house in 1053 a thirty-year struggle for the possession of the throne broke out among the great feudal families, only resolved by the accession, in 1081, of Alexius I Comnenus, succeeded in turn by his son and grandson. Meanwhile the Seljuk Turks were continuing to expand, and in 1071 they routed the Byzantine armies at Manzikert, near Lake Van in eastern Anatolia, taking the emperor Romanus IV Diogenes prisoner. This defeat was the prelude to the loss of the greater part of Byzantine territory in Asia Minor. Six years after Manzikert the Turks occupied Jerusalem, and their possession of the holy places there both incited the chivalry and tempted the land hunger of the West. The First Crusade was launched by the Council of Clermont in 1095. Already relationships between the Orthodox Christian churches and the church at Rome had been strained beyond the breaking point, and a state of open schism had been proclaimed and ratified by Patriarch and Pope alike. Hence, to the crusaders the Greeks of Byzantium were neither Christians nor brothers, and were in fact scarcely less legitimate objects for their ill-disciplined and rapacious armies than the Moslems themselves. The Second Crusade in 1147, led by the Emperor Conrad Hohenstaufen and King Louis VII of France, looted and raped its way through Byzantine lands till its final defeat by the Turks. In the Third Crusade of 1189 a Norman-Sicilian fleet sacked Salonika with particular brutality. But it was with the Fourth Crusade that the full depredation of the Western host broke over the Byzantines: in 1204 the Latins assaulted and took Constantinople, the virgin city was handed over to wholesale plunder, and the accumulated treasures of nearly nine centuries, including those works of classical art which Constantine the Great had brought to his capital, were committed to destruction. It is one of the ironies of history that it was the soldiers of the Cross who were responsible for the rape of the queen of Christian cities and that it was they who prepared the way for the overthrow of the Christian empire.

During the Latin occupation of Constantinople the Byzantine capital was transferred to Nicaea in Asia Minor, and the next-to-last phase of Byzantine history covers the fifty-seven years of exile. In the European territories of the Empire a series of petty semi-feudal dependencies, of which the most important were the kingdom of Thessalonica under Boniface of Montferrat, the barony of Athens, and the principality of Achaia, were set up in vassalage to Baldwin of Flanders, Latin emperor-elect in Constantinople. But this attempt of Western chivalry to take over the Empire proved as abortive as it was misconceived. Within a year Baldwin and Boniface were at war with each other, and both were killed before three years were out. Henry of Flanders, Baldwin's brother, survived only till 1216, to be succeeded by the children of his sister, Yelande. Of these the youngest, Baldwin II, came to the throne at the age of eleven in 1228, and reigned until Michael VIII Palaeologus—concluding a treaty with the Genoese which granted them, in return for naval assistance, the privileges held by the Venetians in Greek lands—crossed from Nicaea to Europe and in 1261 recaptured Constantinople. Baldwin II, the Latin Patriarch, and the Venetians fled.

And so the Byzantine Empire, diminished but still vigorous, entered upon the final phase of its history, under the dynasty of the Palaeologi. The period was one of gallant rear-guard actions against overwhelming odds. The Empire itself was confined to Nicaea and the northwest corner of Asia Minor, Constantinople and Thrace, Salonika and part of Macedonia, and a few islands. The capital had been devastated and deserted; the working of the administrative machinery had been disrupted; Italians monopolized the trade; Bulgars, Serbs, and above all the Turks menaced every frontier; and still another crusade against the Greeks threatened from the West. After the death of Michael VIII in 1282, civil war over the succession further weakened the state. Meanwhile, the

Turks were gradually advancing. By 1345 they had crossed from Asia Minor to Europe. Soon they had overrun the whole Balkan peninsula, and it was only their defeat by the Tartar army of Tamerlane in 1402 that prevented them from taking Constantinople itself. Even so, the respite was short. Some twenty years later the Turks had entered Albania and the Peloponnesus. Salonika was captured in 1430. In a last desperate attempt to secure help from the West, the Emperor John VIII Palaeologus tried to persuade his bishops to cede to the demands of the Roman Church. Union between the Orthodox and Latin churches was actually celebrated at Florence in 1439. But it proved an empty formality: at Constantinople neither monks, clergy, nor people accepted the decision, and in any case the Western forces sent to assist the Byzantines were defeated at Varna on the Black Sea in 1444. Still the Byzantines behind the walls of Constantinople held out. But in 1451 Mohammed II became the leader of the Ottoman Turks: the last years had come.

The sense of impending doom was vivid throughout this final period under the Palaeologi emperors, and yet it saw a renaissance of the arts of which the paintings at Mistra in the Peloponnesus and the decorations of many churches in Constantinople itself, allow us to gauge the mastery. Even if weakened by the naturalism that later reduced art in Italy to the level of sensation, the hieratic form of these works still reflects the vigor and audacity of the Byzantine spiritual intellect, sharpened as this had been by recent controversies with theologians of the Latin West. If one needed to demonstrate the fact that the Byzantines, far from being moribund, effete, the hidebound victims of a religio-political system of their own making, retained their creative vitality even after a thousand years and more of historical existence, then the art and intellectual activity of this final period are there to supply the needed evidence.

The persistence of the classical tradition through the whole Byzantine period has already been indicated; and it may be added that if the Byzantines were not humanists, in that they did not regard man and his reason as the measure of reality, yet the study of the humanities was, except for a short period during the iconoclast struggles, an indispensable part of their intellectual training. Of music it is impossible to estimate the full richness: ecclesiastical music has survived in numerous manuscripts, but interpretation is difficult and uncertain. It seems safe to say, however, that the chants were akin to the Gregorian, which may in fact have derived from them. Literature, like the music and painting, was largely in the service of the Church, and reflected the same spiritual qualities. In the major theological works are enshrined the meditations of some of the most profound doctrinal masters of the Christian tradition, while the vast body of liturgical writings—hymns, prayers, and offices—combines theological penetration with rich lyrical imagery in a manner that is both dignified and immensely moving. Of secular poetry little is left, apart from a handful of epigrams such as those by Paul the Silentiary and Agathias which adorn several pages of the Greek Anthology; though there is that unique product of medieval Greek literature, the epic of Digenes Akritas, in which chivalresque adventure, Persian romance, and mythological imagery are expressed in a language reflecting the rhythms and strength of popular speech. The products of craftsmanship, in reliquaries of jewelers and goldsmiths' work, in glass, enamels, ivories, and fabrics, and in such other minor arts as the illumination of manuscripts—these emphasize on a smaller scale what architecture, painting, and literature demonstrate on a larger one, that the Byzantines were among the world's most perfect artificers.

One thing yet should be mentioned, and that is the role of Byzantium in the growth of Western civilization. For not only were the borders of Byzantium for the greater part of her historical existence more or less coterminous with those of Western civilization itself; but by the time of her overthrow in 1453 she had already planted seeds from which were to grow some of the major developments of modern Europe. Perhaps the two most important concern Italy and Russia; in any case they will suffice to indicate the magnitude of the Byzantine legacy. Where Italy is concerned, the old theory that the fall of Constantinople loosed a flood of scholars and classical manuscripts upon the Italian world, and thus kindled the Renaissance, has long been discarded. Nonetheless, through those long centuries which separate the ancient Greco-Roman world from the Renaissance, the classical tradition—the literature and art of ancient Greece—was part of the living heritage of the Byzantine world, and it was through Byzantium that it was transmitted to Renaissance Italy and hence to the whole of the modern Western world.

Where Russia is concerned, the direct influence of Byzantium is less through culture than through religion and imperial tradition. The conversion of Russia to Christianity was largely linked with the activities of Olga, daughter-in-law of Rurik, the founder of the Russian state, and of her grandson Vladimir. Olga visited Constantinople in order to "learn about God," and there she was baptized, with the Emperor Constantine VII Porphyrogenitus as her godfather. Vladimir, after assisting the Emperor Basil II Bulgaroctonos to put down a revolt, was given Basil's sister in marriage; thenceforth, from 989, Christianity became the official religion of the Russian state. The final seal of Byzantine influence on Russia was set when, in 1472, after the fall of Constantinople, Sophia Palaeologina, survivor of the Palaeologue dynasty, married Ivan III of Muscovy. It was she who introduced Byzantine court ceremonial into the Russian court; the Kremlin was built at Moscow in imitation of the Great Palace at Constantinople; and the Byzantine bureaucratic system, its titles and usages, and even the double-headed eagle and the designation "Autocrat," borne by the Byzantine emperors for eleven hundred years, were adopted by the Russian state. Not for nothing was Moscow to be known as the third and final Rome.

Its predecessor lasted for a little more than a millennium, and then the city of Constantine was invested by the Turks. Mohammed II brought his giant artillery into action; the final preparations for assault were made. Within the city the last Byzantine emperor, Constantine XI Dragases Palaeologus, remained with his people despite frequent appeals to escape. On the afternoon of May 28, 1453, a day of ill omen, the last Christian service was held in the great church of Hagia Sophia. Relics and icons were brought out. After the service, Emperor and Patriarch bade public farewell. Then all took their posts to await the attack. Before the dawn of May 29 it came. A breach was forced in the great walls and the Sultan's soldiery poured through. The Emperor, discarding the insignia of his office, plunged into the fighting and was killed on the ramparts. Constantinople fell, and with its fall the Byzantine Empire was at an end.

The celebrated Bayeux Tapestry is, technically, an embroidered
hanging rather than a tapestry. It is thought to have been
commissioned a few years after the Battle of Hastings by William of
Normandy's half-brother, Odo, Bishop of Bayeux and Earl of Kent.
The embroidery was probably done by a team of women, who worked
on panels of bleached linen following an artist's sketches; the final
result, stitched together, is 230 feet long and 20 inches wide. In this
scene, Harold of England, looking unhappy, swears on two reliquaries
an oath of fealty to William (left). Harold's breaking of the oath
gave William the excuse he needed to invade England. Other scenes
from the tapestry illustrate Mr. Bishop's essay.

*Every schoolchild knows that 1066 is one of the decisive dates of
European history, marking one of the great Norman conquests and
ending, once and for all, the Anglo-Saxon period of English history.
How the invasion of England by William the Conqueror, Duke of
Normandy, and the Battle of Hastings came about is as dramatic as it
is a well-authenticated story. To this must be added the existence of
that wonderful and unique Bayeux Tapestry, which recounts the entire
episode in vivid and spirited fashion. Beautifully displayed, as it now
is, the tapestry must leave an indelible impression on the viewer. It has
certainly aided the author immeasurably in constructing his
fascinating narrative.*
Mr. Bishop, a frequent contributor to Horizon *and* The New
Yorker, *is Professor of Romance Literature, Emeritus, at Cornell
University and the author of numerous biographical studies.*

1066

MORRIS BISHOP

On a jocund day in 1027, or possibly 1028, the tanner's beautiful
daughter Arlette, or possibly Herleve, was dancing in the road
below the castle of Falaise, in Normandy. So says one chronicler;
another asserts that she was washing the family linen in the brook,
with her skirts tucked high. A third maintains that she was washing her beautiful feet. Perhaps all three authorities can be accorded; perhaps she did the laundry, danced in the road, and then
washed her beautiful feet. At any rate, all agree that young Duke
Robert "the Magnificent" (or "the Devil") of Normandy observed
Arlette (or Herleve) and swept her into the castle, and that in 1028
(or possibly 1027) was born William the Bastard, who determined
the direction of European history for these nine hundred years.

The stain of bastardy discolored his character and his life. When
he attacked Alençon in 1051, the garrison of an outlying guard-
house hung some hides on their walls and shouted: "Hides for the
tanner!" ("Hides" had the undermeaning of "whores.") William
took the mockery ill. He burned the thirty-two guardsmen out of
their stronghold, cut off their hands and feet, and catapulted the
one hundred and twenty-eight extremities into the city, which
surrendered.

He was a brooding, angry boy. When he was about seven, his
father named him successor to the dukedom and went pilgrim to

Jerusalem, dying on the journey. But woe to the land whose prince
is a child, and double woe if he is a bastard! His mother married a
viscount and left William in the care of guardians. The nobles immediately disregarded their oaths of fidelity, built forbidden castles, and entered upon a course of mutual extermination. They
killed William's guardian and his tutor. A party sought William in
the castle of his seneschal and stabbed the seneschal in his bed,
unaware that the boy was clutching him under the tossed bed-
clothes. He emerged later covered with blood. While his maternal
uncle hid him in the homes of peasants and woodcutters of the
Norman forest, a vassal of the seneschal tracked down the assassins
and stabbed them in *their* beds, according to the precedent they
had set.

The savage nobles, and even the king of France, took advantage
of the little duke's weakness. But fortunately they were too jealous
of one another to unite effectively against him. The leader of the
rebels was Roger de Tosny, who had fought the infidel in Spain,
and whose wont it was to serve the boiled head of a Saracen at his
mess, no doubt as a kind of centerpiece. He and many other mal-
contents were killed in a gigantic tourney to the death (the widows
of the dead married the unwed victors). William thus was able to
assume command of his faithful when barely adolescent. He was
familiar with plots, bloodshed, torture, death. He had no boyhood,
and evidently no education, except in war. He learned that he
must rule or be ruled, kill or be killed. He must fight and win; he
must seize and hold. He was taking the character and learning the
trade of the Conqueror.

He was tall for his times; his extant femur indicates a height of
five feet ten inches. He was muscular and enduring, but in middle
age he got fat. He had a harsh, guttural voice. In the famous
Bayeux Tapestry he looks more French than Viking, perhaps with
good reason, for his mother may have been French and his paternal
grandmother, Judith of Brittany, was apparently Celtic. Probably
he was only a quarter Scandinavian. (The tapestry likenesses are
unreliable, however; William's hair appears now black, now red,
now yellow or blue.) He was devout, temperate in eating and
drinking—he hated drunkenness and drinkers—and chaste. He
seems never to have had a mistress or concubine. He courted, first
for advantage and then for love, Matilda, daughter of the count of
Flanders. She was a great match, a descendant of Charlemagne
and Alfred the Great of England. She was very small; her skeleton
stands only four feet two inches high. But she burst with vigor and

spirit. The story runs that when the marriage was proposed, she cried: "I would rather be a veiled nun than be given to a bastard!" But William was not a Conqueror for nothing. He invaded her quarters, dragged her round the room by the hair, and kicked her until she gave her consent. The union was very happy. Tiny Matilda bore him nine children (possibly ten), gave him constant good advice, and served as regent on occasion.

We look now across the Channel to England. Its ruler was Edward ("the Confessor"). His mother was William's great-aunt. He spent most of his life in Normandy, until he was summoned to rule England in 1042. Edward was very good, very weak, and childless —more monk than king, everyone said, and impotent besides. He packed his government and his church with Normans. William paid him a visit in Westminster and reported afterward that Edward had formally offered him the succession to the English throne. Probably he did; but there were no witnesses, and the crown was not Edward's to offer.

The most powerful man in England was Harold, son of Earl Godwin of Wessex and brother of Edward's queen. He was very tall, mighty, blond, Nordic; he was also honorable, hearty, and gay, a sportsman, an English country gentleman, much beloved in his time and still beloved. The England that he controlled, under the king, had a population of about a million and a quarter. It was a civilized land with effective government and administration, laws, currency, communications; it had its own thriving literature, its own distinctive art; it was far more peaceful than Normandy. If we could visit it, we should recognize much that is familiar—the rolling, furrowed fields, the huddling thatch-roofed villages, the graceful dispositions of English landscape. But we should see no castles and great houses and only rare, humble churches; for roads we should have only the weedy, pitted Roman ways and farmers' tracks. Chiefly we should be struck by the great forests of oak, ash, and beech, where wolves still dwelt, as did woodcutters and charcoal burners and swineherds.

In 1064 Edward the Confessor was sixty-two years old and was worried about his own future and England's. Out of concern for the first he was building Westminster Abbey, but his provisions for the second are obscure and disputed. (Here and elsewhere we shall not argue the case, but shall choose the likeliest presumption and go on.) King Edward, then, sent Harold to the Continent, very likely to confirm his choice of William as his successor, or to make some sort of deal with him.

Harold undertook the unwelcome task. His ship missed its mark and came ashore near Saint-Valéry at the mouth of the Somme, on the territory of Count Guy de Ponthieu. Count Guy treated him as a shipwrecked sailor; that is, he clapped him in a dungeon and held him for a thumping ransom. But Duke William demanded Harold's release and sent a deputation to conduct him in all honor to Rouen.

William and Harold immediately liked and respected each other. They hunted, hawked, and feasted together, and certainly talked politics. (Harold must have had adequate French.) William took Harold to a little war against Brittany and rewarded his prowess by dubbing him knight. This honor was a trap; according to feudal practice the knight was bound by fealty to the dubber. William could not bear to let his dear friend depart for England. Finally he made a bargain: he would give Harold his daughter's hand in marriage and free return to England, but he would require Harold's oath that he would support William's succession to the English throne. Harold agreed, being well aware that an ordinary oath made under duress is not binding.

The ceremony of oath taking was held in Bayeux. William had his clergy assemble the holiest relics of the dukedom, and concealed them in a chest. Harold swore to be William's man. And then, as described in the doggerel verse of the Norman chronicler Wace:

> *Then kneeling, and still with his hand on the Chest*
> *In reverent guise he his lips to it press'd.*
> *As he rose to his feet, the Duke took his hand,*
> *And fast by the Chest bade him still keep his stand;*
> *The Pall he uprais'd, and made Harold aware*
> *How solemn an Oath on such Relics he sware.*
> *And he, when he saw what was hid by the Veil,*
> *And what he had sworn upon, felt his heart quail.*

Well may his heart have quailed. He could not deny having sworn; there were too many witnesses. He could not dismiss the sanctity of the oath; the guarantors were the holy saints themselves. William had got the feudal world, the Church, and heaven itself to support his claim to the English crown.

Harold returned to England to make his ominous report to the king. He dodged marrying William's daughter, in ungentlemanly style, and ruled England as a sort of prime minister while everyone waited for King Edward to die. In 1065 Harold was forced to depose his troublesome younger brother, Tostig, from his earldom of Northumbria. Tostig went to Flanders and devoted himself to plotting against the English regime.

In April 1066, Halley's comet (in the upper border of the tapestry, looking like a space capsule) flamed through the sky. Harold, newly crowned as king of England, gets the news of this fearful omen.

On January 5, 1066, Edward the Confessor died. On his death-bed he named Harold heir to the kingdom. But according to English custom this was a mere nomination; the nobles chose their king from the men of royal blood. Already the great were gathered expectantly in London. They met as soon as their king had ceased to breathe and elected Harold as his successor. On the very day of Edward's burial in the new Westminster Abbey, Harold was crowned by the Archbishop of York.

Thus the terrible year of 1066 began. In April appeared a portent in the heavens—a long-tailed comet, as large as a full moon; it was visible for two weeks. This was Halley's comet, which returns every seventy-six years, always bringing trouble.

William was now determined to be king of England. He made his preparations with the utmost astuteness. He appealed to public opinion—noble public opinion, of course—by demanding that Harold renounce his usurped crown. He asked the pope's blessing on a punitive expedition into England, a country recalcitrant toward papal authority, lax in enforcing clerical celibacy, and dilatory in remitting Peter's pence to Rome. The pope replied by authorizing William to invade England and to see to the collection of Peter's pence; he also sent a bull excommunicating Harold and his partisans, a consecrated battle banner, and a diamond ring containing a hair and a tooth of Saint Peter. Thus the Western conscience was rallied to the support of the invader. A dynastic quarrel, a plundering raid, took on the character of a crusade.

William dealt with his nobles in general councils and in innumerable private interviews. His country was momentarily at peace, and his gentlemen were bored. He made alluring promises of land, loot, rank, and feudal rights in a rich land that had lost the way of war. He went beyond Normandy to tempt adventurers; important contingents from Brittany and Flanders responded. He organized a fifth column of Normans and pro-Normans in England. He entertained Harold's disgruntled brother, Tostig, and encouraged him to make a probing attack on the southern English coast and to form an offensive alliance with the Norwegian freebooter king, Harold Hardrada.

William assembled his men, perhaps eight thousand combatants, plus sailors, grooms, armorers, cooks, and so on. They were quartered along the Norman coast, with headquarters at the mouth of the Dives River, which was then a capacious port. (You may still sleep there in the Hostellerie de Guillaume le Conquérant, roundly alleged to be William's own billet.) The knights supplied their own horses, armor, and weapons, but these had to be inspected and supplemented. The chief need was transport; says Wace of the building of the ships:

> *The Ports of all Normandy teem'd with new life,*
> *Wherever you turn'd preparation was rife.*
> *Materials and Timber were haul'd to the shore,*
> *Bolts fashion'd, Planks jointed, or brought out of store:*
> *Boats fitted, Ships rigging, Masts rais'd, Sails outspread,*
> *With foresight and outlay in readiness made.*

Military men estimate that the transports numbered about seven hundred. If, as seems likely, they were built to a common plan, this is a very early example of mass production. The craft resembled the Viking long ships, long and narrow with shallow draft. Each had a single sail and mast. There were no oars except for a steering oar near the stern on the starboard side; rowers would take too much precious space. The boats could probably not work at all to windward. They must have been very cranky, and restless horses must have been a serious menace in the slightest sea. William was taking a terrific chance on having a fair following wind and not too much of it. And if his expedition should come to grief, his chances of re-embarkation and return were poor.

It was a brilliant supply operation, which included even a prefabricated fort ready for immediate erection. We long to know more; for instance, were tents or other shelter carried? If you let your men sleep out under England's whipping autumnal rains, half of them will be down with terrible colds or pneumonia, weapons and coats of mail will rust, bowstrings will lose their resilience, and there will be no hot food.

The fleet was reported ready in mid-August. Meanwhile Harold had assembled the English militia, the fyrd, to guard against Tostig's raids on the south coast and against the Norman threat. Tostig then went north to plan, with Harold Hardrada, an invasion of England's east coast before winter.

William had now only to wait for a suitable wind to carry him to England. But the breeze blew steadily from the north. During a lull, in mid-September, William moved his fleet northeast along the Norman coast to Saint-Valéry-sur-Somme, forty miles nearer England than Dives. Again he sat down to wait in vain for the wind, which had to be exactly right. Or was his delay deliberate? Had his intelligence sources predicted what actually occurred? In early September Harold was forced to disband his coast-guarding militia, which was raging to get in the neglected harvest. And there is a good likelihood that William was in touch with Tostig and Harold Hardrada, and was glad to time his invasion with that in the north.

Harold Hardrada, with about three hundred Viking dragon ships, entered the Humber and, by September 18, had pushed upstream to Riccall. His army disembarked and marched on York, nine miles away. The earls of Mercia and Northumberland met him at Gate Fulford. In a long and bloody battle the earls were utterly worsted.

When King Harold, in London, got news of the northern invasion, he immediately assembled his housecarls, or permanent picked troops, and what militiamen he could find. His specialty in war was speed and surprise. His army, mounted, went north on Ermine Street, the old Roman road, making the two hundred miles to York at the rate of forty miles a day, a remarkable feat for both horses and men. He met the Norsemen at Stamford Bridge, beyond York, on September 25. In a great battle his saddle-sore troops destroyed the enemy and killed Harold Hardrada and Tostig. The invaders, who had come in three hundred ships, went home in twenty-four.

Three days after Stamford Bridge, Duke William landed in the south.

On September 27, the persistent west wind at Saint-Valéry had shifted to the south. William gave the crucial order. The ships were

*September 27, 1066: William the Conqueror's great adventure begins.
On a prancing charger, William leads his men to their Viking-style
ships at the embarkation port of Saint-Valéry in Normandy.*

pulled into the water and loaded with men, horses, and gear. By
sunset the fleet was assembled in the Channel. William took his
place in his flagship with its elaborately carved figureheads, fore
and aft. He hoisted a masthead beacon, flaming in an iron basket,
as a guide. But at dawn he found that he had lost his convoy.
Whatever he felt, he betrayed no qualms. He ordered a very special
breakfast, with spiced wine, and displayed "a memorable gayety."
And then the flotilla began to appear. It reached the coast at
Pevensey at 8:30 A.M.

The crossing was a remarkable feat of navigation, though the
distance is only sixty miles. The fleet had to find a sandy or shingly
beach on which to disembark, and much of the English south
coast was cliff or marsh or forbidding shore. Apparently William
aimed for Pevensey and hit it square. The pilots navigated by the
stars and intuition, for they had no compasses, and the crescent
moon set at 9:15 P.M. Yet only two vessels were lost. One of them
carried the expedition's soothsayer. "No great loss," said William;
"he couldn't predict his own fate."

Pevensey was a spit of land at the entrance to a shallow tidal
harbor, now filled in and transformed into a sheep pasture. A
Roman fort stood, and still stands, on the spit. The position is well
defensible; a small force of archers could have raised havoc with
146 the Normans wading in from the sea. But the English fyrd had

gone home, and the landing was unopposed.

The masts were unstepped and the boats were hauled in as far as possible. The archers were the first ashore. They fanned out in search of hostile troops, and found none. Then the mailed knights and the horses. (How were the horses disembarked over the high sides of the transports? Perhaps ramps were carried, and the horses led into the sea when the boats grounded.) Finally the service troops, the carpenters, farriers, cooks, unloading the supplies and equipment. The efficient amphibious operation is a tribute to the planners. And, like other such operations, it was blessed by the general's good luck.

Disembarking, William stumbled and fell. This was an evil omen. But William cried: "By the splendor of God, I here have taken the land in both my hands!" It is a well-beloved story, but kill-joy scholars point out that Julius Caesar, landing in Africa, likewise fell, seized the earth, and exclaimed: "*Teneo te, Africa!*"

William's plan was clear: to seize a strong, defensible beachhead from which he could ravage the countryside, supply his troops, and eventually provoke battle with the enemy under favorable circumstances. For he must fight and conquer, and that soon: time was against him. But Pevensey was too narrow and restricted a base. He therefore moved about ten miles east to Hastings, which in those days formed a kind of peninsula protected on three sides by water. (Possibly he had been aiming for Hastings in the first place.) There he made an entrenched camp and within a day put up his prefabricated fort.

Meanwhile a faithful Sussex thane galloped north, two hundred and fifty miles, to inform Harold of the invasion. The news could not have reached him before October 1 or 2. Harold did not waste a moment. He assembled his housecarls, still battle-sore, and those few archers and militiamen who could be mounted, and rode at top speed to London. It was the second long forced march in a fortnight. On the way he picked up recruits, ordered to follow him on foot. Others joined him in London.

Harold was in a rage. He was provoked by news that William was systematically ravaging and burning the south coast. Not waiting for the fyrd to assemble from all England, he marched out of London on October 11. He took the highway to Rochester, then turned south on the old Roman way through the dense forest of the Weald to Hastings. His army, mostly dismounted, covered nineteen miles a day. This is amazing speed, when one considers the weight of equipment, the ruggedness of the road, the many swamps, thickets, and sharp little hills, and the difficulties of supply in the barely inhabited forest country.

Harold's army, of perhaps nine thousand men, was composed of the housecarls and a contingent of the fyrd. According to the authoritative study of Lieutenant Colonel Charles H. Lemmon (*The Norman Conquest*, 1966), "the housecarls, a royal bodyguard instituted by Cnut, were professional men-at-arms who were dressed in short, close-fitting leather jerkins, on which iron rings were sewn, trousers bound with thongs, and sandals. They wore their hair long, and their heads were covered by steel caps with nasal pieces and long leather flaps which fell over their shoulders. They carried pointed shields made of lime wood, which measured about 36 inches by 15 inches. Their principal weapon was the long Danish battle-axe, with which a horse and rider could be cut down at a blow; but the axemen had to be supported by swordsmen and javelin throwers, and they may have fought in combat groups like the one shown on the Bayeux Tapestry, as they were noted for their perfect drill in action. After supplying a bodyguard for the king, their chief function in battle was to stiffen the ranks of the fyrd."

The fyrd, the national levy, was composed of peasants, ill trained if trained at all. They wore leather jerkins and caps and were armed with farm tools, such as scythes and pitchforks, and miscellaneous spears, short axes, and slings. Very few were archers. But at least they had Saxon courage and the Englishman's hatred of the invader.

On the evening of October 13 Harold emerged from the forest and encamped on the edge of open farm land, recently harvested. His position was on Caldbec Hill, in the present village of Battle, seven miles from Hastings shore and perhaps three or four from William's camp. His men were dog-tired and probably hungry.

William's scouts promptly informed him of Harold's arrival. He had an immediate choice to make. He could await Harold's move against his entrenched camp or he could attack. If he waited Harold might also wait, until overwhelming reinforcements should arrive. He chose to attack while the English were still disorganized. He moved north at dawn on the fourteenth. He found the English deploying in a very strong position just below the summit of a small hill, with their flanks protected by marshy streams and with open fields before them.

The visitor to Battle Abbey today stands among the Saxon ghosts on a southward-looking terrace, while the scholarly guide explains the action. The ground drops away, not sharply but a little more than gently, enough to wind an attacker wearing a thirty-

pound suit of chain mail and carrying weapons. The English formed
a "shield-wall," with the housecarls in the front line, the fyrd
behind.

Halfway down the slope William deployed his army, with the
archers foremost, the cavalry next, the infantry in the rear. The
banner blessed by the pope waved overhead. William, wearing a
bag of relics at his throat, rode to and fro giving final orders.

The minstrel Taillefer, the eternal exhibitionist, gained William's permission to strike the first blow. He rode in front of the
Normans chanting a song about Roland, the legendary hero, tossed
his sword high in the air, and caught it by the hilt. He then galloped straight at the enemy, and with spear under arm impaled an
Englishman; he was chopped down by battle axes.

Now the Norman archers moved forward to their effective range
—about a hundred yards—and let loose a volley. But they were
shooting uphill against men crouching behind their shields. The
chief product of the attack was a chorus of gibes and taunts. The
archers' arrows were soon exhausted. They depended for replenish-
ment on picking up the opponents' spent shafts, and of these there
were few.

The next stage is not clear. It may have been a Norman cavalry
charge. Not many people today, outside of the movies, have taken
part in a cavalry charge. But the present writer, a trooper on the
Mexican border in 1916, can testify that there is no greater thrill in
life than to gallop knee to knee against even a simulated foe, and
that there is nothing more terrifying than to stand firm while a
wall of maddened horses charges one down. But the maddest horses
will refuse before a row of planted pikes; and a proper cavalry
charge demands long training of men and particularly of horses.
This training William's army did not have. It seems more likely
that his knights skirmished along the line, throwing javelins and
looking for weaknesses. A horseman might spear a trembling Saxon,
but before he could withdraw he and his mount were cut down by
the mighty two-handed axes.

The decisive clash was clearly of infantry against infantry. The
attackers had the advantage of armor, being mostly clad in linked
chain mail, and probably they were more agile than the English in
thrusting with their long swords. But they were fighting uphill;
and the English had the advantage of reach with their five-foot
axes, which could sever a horse's neck or cleave a helmet or a
mailed shoulder, driving the chain-mail links into the wound.

The battle resolved itself, then, into a series of hand-to-hand

149

Early in the fighting at Hastings, the Norman cavalry is brought up short by the formidable English infantry. Behind the shelter of their shield-wall, the Englishmen hurl lances, spears, and a mace.

When the English broke ranks to pursue their "retreating" foe, the Norman cavalry got in amongst the foot-soldiers, as seen here. Both sides are shown wearing identical chain mail and helmets.

engagements. At length the Breton contingent on William's left
wavered and fell back. The English broke ranks and started in pursuit. The rumor ran among the Normans that William was killed.
He doffed his helmet and rode to and fro reassuring his men, and
sent his mounted knights to ride down and pick off the scattered
English one by one.

A long lull followed, while both armies re-formed. William
launched his cavalry in full force against the English position.
They were met by a storm of stones, javelins, and Saxon throwing
axes. The melee was long, fierce, and bloody. Harold's two brothers
were killed, but the English line held.

According to the Norman chroniclers, William now practiced
one of the oldest tricks in the military bag, the "Feigned Retreat."
But this trick is also one of the most difficult; it requires perfect
battlefield control and timing and well-trained troops, or else the
feigned retreat is very likely to turn into a real one. Modern military men are inclined to think that the Norman cavalry in the center gave way, and that the English broke ranks to pursue them.
The temptation was great; the field was covered with dead Norman knights, while the wounded were crawling or limping away.
Each wore an expensive suit of chain mail, the most precious of
loot. The Bayeux Tapestry shows many scenes of survivors pulling
coats of mail over the heads of dead men, in some cases apparently
first removing the head.

William seized his opportunity. He ordered his cavalry on left
and right to close in on the pursuers. In the open the horsemen
were easily able to run down and destroy the foot soldiers. (One
notes that there is no mention anywhere of prisoners. Nor, for that
matter, of surgeons, medical corpsmen, stretcher-bearers. The
wounded were left to die or—to die.)

William now ordered a direct attack in full strength on the English position. He bade his archers, who were now re-equipped, to
shoot high in order to catch the enemy with descending shafts. It is
commonly said that Harold was thus wounded by an arrow in the
eye, but this may be a misinterpretation of a scene in the tapestry.
The Normans, massed and fierce for victory, broke through the
English defense. The chronicler says that the dead stood so close
that they had hardly room to fall. Panicking Englishmen began to
run for the shelter of the forest. Harold was struck down by Norman knights. On the exact spot where he fell William decreed that
the altar of a great commemorative church, Battle Abbey, should
stand.

At the bloody climax of the battle, one of William's knights charges up
a rise against members of Harold's fyrd, or militia. Two of the
militiamen tumble head over heels down the hill, and two others flee.

In the final section of the Bayeux Tapestry, Harold's housecarls make
a last desperate stand. The fallen knight at left center, under attack
by a Norman horseman, is thought to be Harold himself.

The Normans had won the battle and, as it turned out, the war. Harold and all his brothers were dead; there was no other serious claimant, besides William, for the English crown. From now on it was all mopping up. William moved cautiously, consolidating his hold on the southeast, striking terror by his spoliation, and also enduring a long attack of dysentery. He circled about London, entered the city, and on Christmas Day, 1066, was crowned king of the English in Westminster Abbey.

The day of Hastings, October 14, 1066, was one of the decisive days of all history. The battle itself was nip and tuck; the shift of a few elements, a gift of luck, could have given the victory to the Anglo-Saxons.

If Harold had won at Hastings—and had survived—William would have had no choice but to renounce his adventure. He could not have prevailed against the aroused masses of the island, led by their determined king. He could not possibly have raised reinforcements in France. There is little likelihood that anyone would have attempted an invasion of England during the next millennium— at least by water. England would have strengthened its bonds with Scandinavia while remaining distrustful of the western Continent —even more distrustful than is the present case. The native Anglo-Saxon culture, art, and literature would have developed in unimaginable ways. I should be writing these words, and you would be reading them, not in English but in Anglo-Saxon, and William the Conqueror would be dimly known in history only as William the Bastard.

*Of all the Holy Roman Emperors of the Middle Ages, those of the
Hohenstaufen family were the most attractive. Frederick Barbarossa,
the crusader, and Frederick II, stupor mundi, "the wonder of the
world," made a profound impression on their own time and have
proved historically memorable. Both were foiled in their political
aspirations, for they failed to break the power and influence of the
papacy and tried in vain to subjugate the Italian communes. Yet they
made their mark by the strength of their personalities and by their
daring. Of the two, Barbarossa was very much a medieval figure, but
his grandson, Frederick II, astounded his contemporaries not only by
the brilliance of his Sicilian court but by the modernity of his mind
and the breadth and depth of his interests and knowledge. In the
emancipation of his intellect he was indeed a forerunner of
Renaissance man, as in his political realism he foreshadowed the
despots of the late Middle Ages.*

*Mr. Stillman has taught at the Johns Hopkins University and
is currently director of the Hudson Institute's European division
in Paris.*

FREDERICK II: WONDER OF THE WORLD

EDMUND STILLMAN

I taly south of Naples is the Mezzogiorno—the land of the noonday sun. In the Mezzogiorno ignorance and poverty seem endemic. Not many travelers even in our day penetrate there. The
land is craggy, barren, and disease-ridden; and the north—the
Italy of avant-garde films, *la dolce vita*, and aggressive modern
capitalism—seems far away. In the south the traditions of organized banditry and vendetta still endure; the peasants are sunk in a
kind of sullen apathy that even the communists cannot shake.

There has been little of love and compassion in the history of the
Mezzogiorno. But it was not always a wasteland. Nine hundred
years ago in this forgotten region of Europe the Moslem East, Byzantium, and the barbarian North all fused together in a civilization of wealth, glitter, and intellectual brilliance under the Norman
kings of Sicily. And here in the thirteenth century a grand ide-
ological drama was played out: the dream of a united, powerful,

*A portrait of Frederick is the frontispiece of his pioneering work on
ornithology. Other scenes from the book illustrate this essay.*

and ultimately secular Europe (a dream of our own time) clashed with an older dream of God's universal order on earth. In the events of this drama we can discern the collision of the skeptical spirit of the yet-distant Renaissance with the static, believing spirit of the Middle Ages.

Yet it is not quite so. The roles and characters of the actors are oddly mixed, so that the worldliness of popes is matched by the brutal despotism of the champions of a secular empire. In the end neither side won. The dream of secular society went down in a welter of futility and blood. The religious vision was painfully corrupted by the desperate struggle for survival, dooming itself in the aftermath of ostensible victory to the contempt of believing and thinking men.

It is a drama rich in personalities—great medieval popes and kings. But the single greatest figure of the drama, indeed perhaps the single greatest figure of the thirteenth century, was Frederick II of Hohenstaufen, Holy Roman Emperor, king of Sicily, king of Jerusalem, lecher, scientist, political prophet, mathematician, lawmaker, poet, linguist, sinner thrice excommunicated and consigned by Dante to hell to roast forever in an incandescent tomb; a man known to his contemporaries, without the slightest flattery, as *stupor mundi*, "the wonder of the world."

If, seven hundred years later, there is any touching feature to this terrible drama, it is an aging woman's love for the defenseless child born late in her life, and the love of the man that child became for the Mezzogiorno. For Frederick, Italy, especially the south, was the soul of the world and ultimately the cause of his ruination. To him Apulia, Lucania, Calabria, and Sicily were *il Regno, the* kingdom, "a haven," as he put it, "amidst the floods and a pleasure garden amidst a waste of thorns." At the height of his career, straddling Europe and the Levant, he marveled that God had flattered Palestine so when He might have loved Italy instead.

Every biography must begin with the banal fact of birth. Frederick Roger of Hohenstaufen was born in the Italian hill town of Iesi on the day after Christmas, A.D. 1194. But there was nothing banal in the circumstances of his birth nor in his inheritance. On his paternal side he was a Hohenstaufen—a family that the popes at Rome, with a unanimity born of experience, called the devil's brood. His grandfather was Frederick I, called Barbarossa, generally conceded by historians to have been the greatest of the German Holy Roman Emperors, a man who had fought to stale-

mate the pretensions of the papacy and who so seized the imagina-
not died on crusade but instead slept with his warriors in the bow-
els of the Kyffhäuser mountain, whence he would emerge on his
great war horse when the German people called.

Frederick's father was Henry VI, a man devoid of Barbarossa's
largeness of style but one just as ambitious, a cold-blooded intri-
guer and killer hated by wife and family, whose short reign was
spent in an incessant struggle for the hegemony of Europe and
whose early death less than three years after Frederick's birth was
greeted by the papacy with profoundest relief.

More attractive perhaps, but no softer, was his mother's legacy.
On his mother's side Frederick was Norman, but not of the house of
the Norman kings of England. Constance was a princess of a different line, the last legitimate representative of a clan of Norman
freebooters who had descended on Italy like wolves in the eleventh
century, serving as faithless mercenaries to Byzantine and Lombard overlords, fattening on the incessant warfare they helped to
foment in the southern marches of Christendom. Finally, in the
glittering figures of Robert Guiscard and his brother Roger they
had seized Sicily and southern Italy, a domain that dwarfed the
roughly contemporary conquest of England in the cold North Atlantic: the commerce of the port of Palermo yielded more revenue
to Count Roger of Sicily than the Normans could extract from all
of twelfth-century England. And Palermo was only a part of the
much greater whole—a kingdom built on the threefold heritage of
the Byzantine emperors at Constantinople who had held the island
and southern Italy for centuries, the Saracen emirs of Sicily, and
the restless North.

Frederick's mother was at the time of her marriage to Henry
Hohenstaufen a spinster of thirty-one, long since reconciled to a
life of barren piety; some said she had become a nun. But when it
appeared she would fall heir, in her plain person, to the gorgeous
Norman patrimony, she was judged a fit wife even for a future
Holy Roman Emperor, eleven years her junior, who aspired to
govern the world. Miraculously, after nine childless years of marriage Constance gave birth to Frederick at Iesi—in a pavilion
erected in the market place in plain sight of hundreds of towns-
men, so we are told, lest there be any question thereafter of the
legitimate birth of her son. Other chroniclers record only that fifteen cardinals and bishops stood crowded in the tent and were
judged sufficient witness to the point.   157

Like many a latecomer to motherhood, Constance proved a doting parent. Frederick, so the chroniclers record, was everything to her, and though Dante has placed her in paradise as the very type of the devout and dutiful woman, there is an ugly suspicion that she did not stick at intriguing for the murder of her hated husband in order to advance her son to the throne. The plot, real or imagined, was betrayed to Henry, and young Frederick may have been exposed to the sight of the tortures inflicted on the suspects. There was to be no shortage of torture in Frederick's life.

The Norman kings of Sicily had been vassals of the popes. They had gained a dubious legitimacy by swearing to be the popes' men, and whatever the extent of their ambitions and their later perfidies, they had mainly directed their avarice and longing, not against the secular domain of the popes in central Italy, but against the Moslems and Byzantines of the East. As the popes' men—and formidable warriors they were—they had fought the German emperors, who wanted to recreate the long-dead Roman Empire in the implausible guise of a union of Germany and Italy. For the popes, who aspired to a countersupremacy over the worldly power of kings and yet exercised only an insecure territorial sovereignty of their own in central Italy—the *patrimonium Petri*—it was a condition of survival to keep the Holy Roman emperors at bay. Now the popes' Norman shield was gone, for by marrying Constance and gaining her Sicilian inheritance, a German emperor had achieved at last what it had always been papal policy to prevent. He had turned the popes' southern flank; his rival, the spiritual power of Rome, was thus caught between hammer and anvil.

The papacy was saved by Henry's sudden death, from dysentery, in 1197. This was for the papacy an almost miraculous deliverance. But for the three-year-old Frederick his father's death was a personal catastrophe: his mother, worn out by years and anxiety, was herself in poor health and, sensing her approaching death, could think of nothing better to do than, in desperation, commit the child to the care of Pope Innocent III. In her last act of policy Frederick was crowned king at Palermo in May, 1198, and six months later his mother was dead.

The guardianship of the pope was casual. A rival unfriendly to Frederick succeeded to the throne of the Holy Roman Empire. The kingdom of Sicily, which was Frederick's sole inheritance, fell into anarchy, and the boy himself was left to run wild in the streets of Palermo. Frederick may not actually have gone hungy—the poor townsfolk are said to have fed him from their meager stores—but he learned about neglect and want. Yet some of his most attractive qualities surely stem from his years as a barefooted *ragazzo* of Palermo. These were his quickness of wit, his self-reliance, and the determination to prevail; he acquired as well a polyglot command of French, Arabic, Greek, and Italian and a permanent addiction to the lands of the sun.

Frederick might have died of neglect or as the victim of obscure political murder if the new Holy Roman Emperor, Otto of the Welf house of Brunswick, had proved faithful to his pledges. A member of a family who were sworn enemies to the Hohenstaufens, Otto had taken power as a friend to the popes, promising to submit to the spiritual authority of the church. But once again the office made the man: a pliant tool before his coronation as emperor, after he held power Otto undertook the conquest of Sicily. Pope Innocent III, faced with the need to undercut his imperial rival, remembered the dirty, half-starving *ragazzo* of Palermo, by now almost grown. He excommunicated Otto and had Frederick elected emperor. Three years later, in 1214, Otto was defeated by the French king, who was acting on the pope's behalf. Frederick's fortunes were made.

Innocent III has been hailed as one of the three greatest of the medieval popes. He was the man who presided over the rise of the Franciscan and Dominican orders; he hammered at the Waldensian heretics and engineered the great crusade against the Albigensian heretics of southern France; he saw the Greek schismatics of Byzantium humbled by the fourth crusade. Fortunately for his peace of mind he did not live to see his former ward become the deadliest enemy the medieval papacy ever faced; for he died just two years after Otto's defeat. No more than any other ambitious medieval king would Frederick, holding the reality of power, remain a faithful vassal of the popes.

The conflict between the spiritual and the temporal is the leitmotif of medieval history, but it is a curiously ambiguous controversy. The ostensible spiritual contender, the papacy, seeks a temporal authority; and the papacy's temporal enemies, the medieval kings, aspire to a spiritual dominion as well.

To us, seven hundred years later, the terms of the struggle are strange, though they may be made a little more comprehensible by the observation that behind this battle between two abstract conceptions of government lay a conflict involving cold cash as well. The medieval church was vast in its holdings, and each increment to its revenues and prerogatives was a diminution of those of the secular lords. Yet the prize was more than real estate or hard cash. In the medieval mind there was an almost magical conception of man's place in nature and of the honor that fell to the one who disposed over the rule of mankind.

By the late Middle Ages the papacy had acquired such administrative expertise and power that the popes claimed supreme authority. What was the pope? "The royal High Priest of the Christian church, the *verus imperator* of the Christian Empire, the first judge of Christendom, these three are one and of one origin: they are the Pope," writes the modern German historian Ernst Kantorowicz. "The pope . . . was not . . . the representative of any man, but the representative of Christ himself, and through him the representative of God." According to one medieval propagandist, Manegold of Lautenbach, the Holy Roman Emperor was, by contrast, no more than a swineherd.

Yet the kings of this world, not surprisingly, were unwilling to see themselves as mere swineherds, agents of papal authority and direction. Indeed, for Frederick especially, the emperor was himself the earthy incarnation of divine justice and power. Condemning to unspeakable torture those who had plotted his death, Frederick, then at the height of his career, proclaimed that the criminals had not merely struck at his own person: by striking at the emperor the traitors had "imperilled the fabric of the world." In this view, as Kantorowicz puts it, "If God is present on earth . . . [and] has condescended to reveal himself as Justice in unconsecrated precincts, the State can no longer be conceived as 'sinful,' a relative good amid the total evil of the world; but becomes forthwith an absolute good in its own right." It is for this reason that such progenitors of modern German autocracy as Nietzsche and the historian Treitschke hailed Frederick for his politics and that in our time the Nazis cited him as an early incarnation of the *Führerprinzip*.

This much at least of the bitter controversy is easily comprehensible to us today. And to the degree that emperor and pope quarreled not about the mere division of earthly revenues but about the nature of conscience, the role of the state, and indeed about the nature of man as a social animal—inherently reasonable or inherently bestial and standing in need of constant brutal correction—their quarrel is relevant even to our own time.

But for Frederick it was no mere abstract controversy. Any biographer of Frederick must reckon with the fact that this stupendous talent and imagination were marred by megalomania. At

Frederick's treatise demonstrates the use of leather thongs, or jesses, to handle falcons, even at birdbath sessions (right).

his best, Frederick was an intellect two or three centuries in advance of his time—as skeptical a scientific theorist as Francis Bacon, as daring a political schemer as Cesare Borgia. If he was not a compassionate man, he was nevertheless capable of tolerance for men of all faiths. But at his worst, Frederick was a man who could chop off the thumb of a scribe for misspelling the imperial name and condemn his oldest friend, suspected of treason, to hideous torture. Frederick was less concerned with the abstract issue of spiritual power versus secular than with *his* majesty, *his* prerogatives, *his* near divinity. Frederick foreshadowed not only the intellectual achievements but the manic pride of the High Renaissance. In the pious medieval environment he came perilously close to blasphemy when he saw in himself a kind of second Christ, incarnate in the person of the Holy Roman Emperor, ruler of the world; so that the little town of Iesi where Frederick was born became, in his words, "our Bethlehem," and he proclaimed that portents had attended his birth.

The court that Frederick maintained in the south was one of the most brilliant in history. Nothing like it had been seen in the Christian West before, not even in the great days of Charlemagne. The rude court of that Frankish emperor could not boast steam baths and plumbing to rival those of ancient Rome, a menagerie of wild beasts from distant Africa and India, a wholly secular university that challenged the intellectual monopoly of the medieval church, and a secular bureaucracy that was the product of this education and that regulated the foreign commerce into the port of Palermo down to the finest detail. It was a court where for the first time poets, as Dante noted approvingly a century later, sang a   161

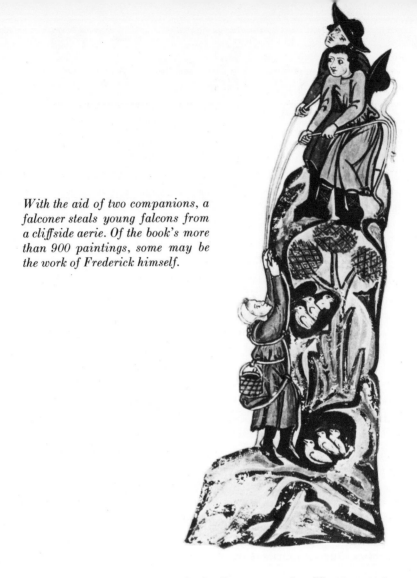

With the aid of two companions, a falconer steals young falcons from a cliffside aerie. Of the book's more than 900 paintings, some may be the work of Frederick himself.

sophisticated early verse in the Italian vernacular. There eunuchs guarded harems of Moorish women, and the pious were daily offended by the brazen comings and goings of infidel Moslem and Jewish alchemists, philosophers, astrologers, and mathematicians.

In intellectual terms the court of Frederick deserves nothing but praise. In an age hopelessly wed to the supernatural, the brilliant Frederican courts at Palermo, Foggia, and Castel del Monte truly justified the epithet the age applied to Frederick—*stupor mundi et immutator mirabilis*, "wonder of the world and marvelous innovator."

Some of the greatest names of medieval humanism and science

revolved in Frederick's orbit. Among them were the jurist and polemicist Pietro della Vigna, the mathematician Leonardo Fibonacci, who is said to have introduced to Europe Arabic numerals and the concept of the zero, and the astrologer and philosopher Michael Scot. These men, together with a learned slave reportedly sent to Frederick by the sultan of Egypt, examined the mysteries of the natural world. Why, asked Frederick, puzzling over the phenomenon of the refraction of light, does a lance in water appear bent? Why does the sun appear red as it nears the horizon?

Frederick's curiosity was limitless and wholly unconstrained by such few notions of mercy as lighted a savage age. One monkish chronicler relates that Frederick, "Wanting to find out what kind of speech children would have when they grew up, if they spoke to no one before hand . . . bade foster mothers and nurses to suckle the children, to bathe and wash them, but in no way to prattle with them, for he wanted to learn whether they would speak the Hebrew language, which was the oldest, or Greek, or Latin, or Arabic, or perhaps the language of their parents, of whom they had been born. But he labored in vain, because the children all died. For they could not live without the petting and the joyful faces and loving words of their foster mothers."

His excursions into ornithology were less self-defeating. He was enough a man of his time to share a passion for the hunt, or at least for the art of falconry, but he was apart from his time in his intelligent and detached curiosity about birds and all their ways. For his illegitimate son Manfred he compiled a great compendium of knowledge on birds, not merely falcons: his work deals with skeletal structure, plumage, and the presumed mechanics of flight, as well as with the training of falcons and their diseases. "Our intention is to set forth the things which are, as they are," he writes, establishing the empiricist's credo. "We have often experimented." Aristotle and the authority of the ancients did not overawe him. "We have followed Aristotle where necessary," he writes, "but we have learned from experience that he appears frequently to deviate from the truth. . . ."

But for all his proto-modernity Frederick emerges more as the type of an Oriental potentate than as the common variety of medieval king or Renaissance despot. Indeed, it was in the Levant, where, bowing to intense papal pressure, he undertook a serio-comic crusade to liberate the Holy Land, that Frederick seems to have found his spiritual home. The histrionics of medieval crusading clearly bored him, and it is an ironic comment on the brave but bumbling military operations of the times that this cynical atheist, who contemptuously dismissed the holiness of the Sepulcher, should have accomplished more by skillful negotiation (in Arabic, to the entranced delight of his enemies) than all his earnest but inept contemporaries could accomplish by their battles. What did Frederick care for the cause itself? The answer must be nothing. "There have been three great impostors in history," he once wearily observed. "Moses, Jesus, and Mohammed." Or so his papal enemies swear he blasphemed. Others, knowing Frederick's respect for the Moslems, were less certain he took the Lord Mohammed's name in vain.

If military operations in the Holy Land were to Frederick an ineffable bore, military operations closer to home were not. From the day he secured himself in the *Regno*, returning from a Germany that he chose thenceforth virtually to ignore, he was engaged in incessant war. But this was a war for the glory of the Hohenstaufens, waged against the insolent communes of central and northern Italy allied to Frederick's enemies. Delivery of the Holy Sepulcher was no part of Frederick's true interest; indeed, so long did he delay in the discharge of this obligation that he was excommunicated for the sin—and then denounced for undertaking the obligation without first making his act of contrition. But the fight to deliver royal power from the challenge of papal pretension and the encroachments of upstart city bourgeoisie and proletarians became his burning political cause.

Frederick in effect was driven to fight in this Italian arena because his larger German ambitions had all been rebuked. The Holy Roman Empire was too huge a conception for political health. The emperors could not, like the French, English, and Spanish kings, secure a territorial base from which in time they could control their unruly barons. Frederick's clan has been criticized for its Italian ambitions; but it was the unsatisfied longing for a compact imperial base, to be used as a springboard for power, that led the Hohenstaufen emperors again and again over the Alps and into Italy. Their hope was always that with a secure Italian base behind them they could strike north once again to assert their rule.

But for them power over Italy was always a will-o'-the-wisp. Their Italian ambitions led them into inevitable collision not only with the popes but also with the cities of Tuscany and the north Lombard plain. Behind their walls, in the thirteenth century, a new world was struggling toward birth. It was a postfeudal world, a society of pushing urban middle classes and proletarians, of new mercantile interests and incipient nationalism—all incompatible with the despotic ambitions of Frederick and his imperial kind.

In the field the citizen armies of the Italian communes were seldom more than a helpless rabble. If caught in the open they inevitably fell victim to the professional arms of Frederick's German and Saracen knights. But such was the primitive state of military art in the thirteenth century that the citizens, behind their walls, were nearly always safe from Frederick's wrath. Time and again he moved against them, and time and again, despite ephemeral successes, the combination of papal denunciation and Lombard doggedness in defense ensured Frederick's failure.

And fail he did. *Stupor mundi*, wonder of the world, outstanding political intelligence of his time though he might be, in collision with these nascent forces he proved helpless. He could not in the end transcend the materials and the inherent limitations of his age.

All the cruelty, all the implacable discharge of hate, the butchery of captured rabble, could not break the spirit of the towns, bolstered as they were by the blessing of the popes and by their own will to resist. Frederick might love his Italy, but to the Italians he was a German king. He died in 1250, a defeated and bitterly disappointed man. He had built the first secular European state, codified laws, regulated commerce, fostered progress in the governmental interest, challenged medieval obscurantism and ecclesiastical pretension; but his work did not live long beyond him.

His two surviving legitimate sons had proved either weak or traitorous. Neither was competent to succeed Frederick. Into the vacuum in Italy moved the best of his sons—that Manfred for whom he had written the falconry book, Frederick's bastard by his beloved Bianca Lancia. Manfred intrigued bloodily for his father's legacy. For twelve years he maintained the semblance of Frederick's glories in southern Italy, only to be defeated and killed in 1266 by a great French punitive expedition that invaded Italy at papal request. The Hohenstaufen line—the devil's brood—was virtually at an end.

What Frederick built did not endure. Viewed in retrospect, his dream of a powerful secular empire could never have succeeded, though Frederick would have done anything in the wild pursuit of his vision. For him no brutality, no breach of faith, was too much. But his vision was out of its time. It is almost as if history had made a bizarre experiment and then had dropped it for another. The future lay with the middle-class, urban, capitalistic society that was then struggling into being in Italy.

165

The Venetian patriciate was one of the most successful oligarchies of
European history. Merciless in its treatment of opponents or potential
opponents, it maintained an efficient administration over huge areas
and for centuries. It likewise managed to formulate comprehensive
policies of trade and expansion and to see that they were energetically
implemented. The shameless attack and sack of Constantinople by the
Fourth Crusade in 1204 marked the beginning of three centuries of
Venetian power in the Levant, a period during which many Venetian
notables became feudal potentates in the Aegean Islands and in Greece
proper. During the rise of the Ottoman Turks in the fourteenth
century the Venetians bargained with them for trade privileges and
indirectly abetted their expansion.

Only at the end of the fifteenth century, after the fall of
Constantinople to the Turks, did the Venetians begin to suffer reverses.
The great explorations and the involvement of Venice in Italian
politics contributed to the city's decline, but it remained a power to be
reckoned with through most of the sixteenth century. And that century
was, incidentally, the apogee of the Venetian cultural achievement.
Unique in its location, in its institutions, in its policies, the city
of the lagoons was easily one of the really great cities of the Middle
Ages. Its story is brilliantly reviewed here by James Morris, author of
The World of Venice.

VENICE:
THE TRIUMPHANT CITY

JAMES MORRIS

On a spring morning in 1797 lookouts on the fort of Sant'
Andrea, at the sea gate of Venice, reported the approach of a
French warship, *Libérateur de l'Italie*. Revolutionary France was
rampant then; Napoleon himself commanded the French armies in
Italy. But for five centuries no foreign ship of war had entered
Venetian waters without permission. When the frigate failed to
answer signals, the fortress commander gave the order to open fire;
and so on an April day at the end of the eighteenth century the
commander wrote finis to the story of the Venetian Republic.

The ship was halted and boarded. Its commander was killed in
the melee, and Napoleon was given, as he wished, a *casus belli*. The
Venetians, he stormed, were "dripping with French blood," and

A Venetian doge, figurehead that he may have been, was impressive
indeed. This is Doge Andrea Gritti, painted by Titian c. 1540.   167

anyway, time had expired for their preposterous state and all its antique ceremonial trappings. "I have 80,000 men and twenty gunboats," he said in ultimatum (he was twenty-eight years old and brash). "I will be an Attila for the State of Venice." He refused to treat for peace, and on May 16 three thousand hardened French soldiers disembarked upon the Piazza San Marco, the symbolic showplace of Venetian splendor. "*J'ai occupé ce matin la ville de Venise*," a French commander of troops laconically reported.

Napoleon was the first general ever to accomplish the capture of Venice, for a thousand years one of the marvels of Europe—a water prodigy, an empire, a legend; the loveliest city man had ever built, its natural element the sea, its vocation the pursuit of magnificence. As the French moved into the sumptuous Palace of the Doges, for so long one of the prime movers of European history, the Venetian style and spirit died at last. A tree of liberty was erected in the Piazza, the lion-flags of Venice fluttered down, and an era limply ended.

At the northwestern corner of the Adriatic, where the rivers Brenta, Sile, and Piave enter the sea, there lies a marshy crescent lagoon, part lake, part sea, part estuary, speckled with islets and protected by a long outer line of sandbanks. In the comfortable days of the Roman Empire it was inhabited only by fishermen and occasional sportsmen, for it was malarial and melancholy. As the old order crumbled, though, and successive waves of barbarians swept into Italy from the north, the peoples of the neighboring mainland cities—Padua, Concordia, Altinum, Aquileia—came to look upon the marshes as a place of refuge in times of particular tumult. At first, it seems, they had no intention of moving permanently into the lagoon; but as successive waves of Goths, Huns, Avars, and Herulians swept over northeastern Italy, and as it became apparent to successive generations that the good old days would never return, groups of refugees took to the marshes as a new homeland where civilization might start again.

Omens and prophecies encouraged them in this hope, and holy men sometimes led their migrations, carrying sacred objects with them, quoting pertinent Scriptures, and reporting apposite miracles. And so during the fifth and sixth centuries, while a fitful and intermittent exodus continued, a water community was established in the lagoon. There some of the Roman assurance survived in a stable social order and a Christian certainty: "they would receive no man of servile condition," we are told, "or a murderer, or [a man] of wicked life." One by one the little islands were colonized, each with its own church, from Torcello, the first and northern-most settlement, to Chioggia, at the southern end of the lagoon. By the end of the sixth century there were twelve loosely associated townships, forming a more or less independent political entity.

It was a strange commonwealth from the start; a country whose "roads" were canals dredged from the natural rivulets and chan-nels of the lagoon and whose early buildings of wattles and thatch stood on piles among the reeds. Boats were the only transport, fish was the only natural food, rain the only drinking water. This rude environment was exploited by a cultivated sort of pioneer, for these were settlers brought up to the high, if faded, standards of im-perial Rome. They soon acquired the skills of boatmen and fisher-men, and gradually hammered out common institutions. By 697 the separate settlements had elected a doge, or duke, to be the sovereign of them all and to represent them in dealings with the rest of the world. At first a democracy, the republic of the lagoon gradually let an obsession with public stability and security obscure individual liberty and entrusted authority increasingly to a hereditary ruling caste.

As they evolved a new way of life and a new political identity, so these new men, the Venetians, simultaneously established a new national vocation; islanders by misfortune, they became merchants by necessity. Because they possessed no agricultural hinterland they turned logically to the sea for their livelihood and became a nation of enterprising and guileful traders. They were common carriers, entrepreneurs, merchant venturers. Marco Polo was a Venetian trade scout, and Venetian merchant ships soon were familiar throughout the Mediterranean.

Everything about this developing nation was unique—its his-tory, its manner of living, its geographical situation. It stood on the borders of East and West, on the hazy dividing line between the two halves of the dismembered Roman Empire. Rome and Byzantium vied for its allegiance; its religion wavered between the Eastern and Western rites; even its architecture was made up of a stylistic mixture in which the domes of one world met the vaults of the other. Venice was a frontier station, and it was this central isolation that was soon to give the Venetian Republic its inde-pendence, its power, and its meaning.

In 809 Pepin, son of Charlemagne, made up his mind to annex Venice once and for all to the Western empire. His forces actually entered the lagoon, and the Venetians were obliged to concentrate their government offices upon a group of islands in its less vulnerable center—Rivo Alto, or Rialto, where one of the deep channels, the Canale Grande, wound a sinuous way through the archipelago. There they established a permanent capital, and there they successfully defied the greatest power of the day. Legend has it that Pepin's armies were undone by a patriotic old woman who deliberately misguided them into a quagmire. However simplistic the story may be, the invasion *was* defeated, and the Venetians were left cock-a-hoop. Not until the Napoleonic invasion would they acknowledge the suzerainty of any foreign empire, Eastern or Western. When the Byzantines, observing Pepin's humiliation, claimed the overlordship for themselves, the Venetians dismissed the claim out of hand. "This Venice," they said, "which we have raised in the lagoons, is our mighty habitation, and no power of Emperor or Prince can touch us."

Nor could it. Free, arrogant, and able, the Venetians were their own masters and soon grew rich in the Eastern trade. Commissioned to supply ships for the early Crusades to Palestine, they seized the chance to establish trading colonies in several cities of the Levant. Their Levantine warehouses served as terminals for the caravan routes from Persia, India, and China. Their city in the lagoon became an immense storehouse of Oriental commodities. Their ships distributed silks, spices, ivories, slaves, and precious stones throughout the countries of the West. Venice held "the gorgeous east in fee," as Wordsworth put it, and she became a half-Eastern place herself, a sensual and ostentatious city-state different in kind from any other. Her people discovered a taste for rich textiles, marbles, porphyries, damasks, and agates. Her style was tinged with that of Byzantium and even Islam; her colors were opulent golds, crimsons, and silvers.

This almost pagan profligacy was exemplified by the Venetian participation in the Fourth Crusade. In 1201 the pious leaders of that expedition, making one more attempt to free the Holy Land from the infidels, again asked the Venetians for sea transport. "We come in the name of the noblest families of France," said their emissaries to the doge Enrico Dandolo. "No other Power on earth can aid us as you can; therefore they implore you, in God's name, to have compassion on the Holy Land, and to join them in avenging the contempt of Jesus Christ by furnishing them with ships and other necessaries, so that they may pass the seas."

"On what terms?" was the characteristic Venetian reply, and, characteristically, the Venetians set their own immensely profitable

terms. Largely thanks to Venice, the Crusaders never reached the

Holy Land. First, at Venetian insistence, they conquered the city of Zara in Dalmatia. Then they decided to seize Constantinople, and instead of expelling the Moslems from Palestine, devoted themselves to toppling the doddering Byzantine Empire and looting its properties. The doge himself, ninety years old and nearly blind, led the assault on the towers of Constantinople, and a lion's share of the booty went to the Venetians. They proclaimed themselves to be "Lords and Masters of a Quarter and a Half-quarter of the Roman Empire" and sent shiploads of loot home to the lagoon, in a profusion never before seen in the West.

The Fourth Crusade gave Venice an empire. Not only did she consolidate her trading position in the Levant, but she acquired a whole string of islands and fortresses for the protection of her shipping routes. The Crusade made her a Great Power; and when, in the fourteenth century, she finally defeated the most stubborn of her maritime rivals, Genoa, to become the undisputed mistress of the Mediterranean, she had reached her high point. She stood at the summit of the world. She was immensely rich. She had a virtual monopoly of the Oriental commerce. She ruled possessions in Dalmatia, the Morea, the Aegean, and the Ionian Islands. From a straggling community of refugees she had developed into a grand sea-empire whose standards were familiar from Persia to southern England and whose ducats had filtered far to the east along the trade routes to Cathay.

An eye for the main chance had achieved all this—and a gift for self-advertisement.

In the Middle Ages Venice possessed a chimerical quality. She was fabulous among states, like a golden unicorn or a phoenix. She held herself aloof, calm, superior. Saint Mark the Evangelist, whose corpse she claimed to possess, was her protector, and his talismanic winged-lion appeared like a trade-mark on everything Venetian— coins, palaces, flags, the prows of galleys, the lead tops of drainpipes. Venice was essentially a great commercial concern, with an image deliberately designed to impress the customers and stamp itself upon the consciousness of the world. It was well known, at least in Venice, that Saint Mark had once been stranded on a sandbank in the lagoon, and the Venetian motto, the catchword of the republic, was retroactively converted to the words of reassurance the Almighty had given the saint on that occasion: "Pax Tibi Marce Evangelista Meus."

Like any business enterprise, Venice ruthlessly pursued her interests. Her affairs were run, in effect, by a board of directors, for

171

by now her government had become a highly efficient hereditary oligarchy. All political power was in the hands of a self-perpetuating caste—those whose names were written in the Golden Book of the Venetian aristocracy. In the great days of Venice their sense of public duty was high, and the system worked so well, and was so generally accepted, that it lasted, virtually unchanged, for four hundred and fifty years.

It was, however, a system hedged about with secrecy, counter-check, and inquisition. At its head stood the doge, a potentate of stunning magnificence, elected for life by his peers (in most ways, though, he was powerless, so careful were the rules that circumscribed his conduct, and little more than a figurehead). Below him were a cabinet, a senate, and a Grand Council representing all the patrician families; but as the years passed, executive power was put into the hands of a reticent body called the Council of Ten, the real check—secret, swift, and often sinister—upon personal ambition or corruption. These secular watchdogs were more powerful than any religious inquisitors and surrounded themselves with a calculated mystery. Conspirators would be found at dawn swinging from gibbets in the public square, or buried alive head downward among the flagstones. Unsuccessful admirals, swollen-headed *condottieri*, were strangled or jailed as examples. Venice was a police state, but instead of worshiping political power, she was terrified of it; the system was designed to forestall both revolution and personal dictatorship, to keep the state stable and competent, and to leave the field clear for profit.

Although Venice had a few manufacturing specialties, most notably glassmaking, she was primarily a republic of merchants, financiers, and middlemen. One of her great public ceremonials was the annual marriage of the Adriatic, when the doge, in his ornate state barge, attended by fleets of galleys, gondolas, and pleasure craft, sailed to the outer gates of the lagoon and threw a golden ring into the sea—allegorizing not only Venice's intimate union with the Adriatic but also her command of the Eastern profits. Her wealth flowed in with the tides, and the very title she gave herself—La Serenissima—suggested oceanic amplitude.

Venetian war fleets were the most formidable in the world, manned in their heyday only by freemen, and built within the high, shuttered walls of the arsenal, the first shipyard of Europe. In times of war the arsenal produced a galley a day, and as each new ship was towed out of the yard, it was victualed, manned, and equipped at the water gate, and then went to sea ready for instant

The winged lion of St. Mark displays the Venetian Republic's motto, "Peace to thee, Mark, my evangelist," in Carpaccio's 1516 canvas.

death or glory. The Venetian merchant fleets were built to a standard pattern, too, and although privately owned, were controlled by a department of state. Each year six principal fleets set out from the lagoon—to Constantinople, to the Black Sea ports, to Egypt, to Syria, to North Africa, and to western Europe. They were supported at home by all the organizational paraphernalia of international commerce—marketing agencies, banks, trade fairs, government departments of standards and measures. Venice was like an immense Eastern bazaar, except that the haggling that took place was of a supreme sophistication.

In her finest years she was a hard, unyielding, brilliant sort of state, like Victorian Britain in some ways, like contemporary Israel in others; an outsider state, never ordinary, never quite acceptable to, or trusted by, the comity of nations. She had brazenly traded with the infidel Turks and was notorious for her opportunism. She was, moreover, immensely pleased with herself. In the noblest days of the republic her people thought of themselves not so much as rich men or poor, patricians or plebians, but simply as Venetians, citizens of the best of states. They assumed that the Piazza San Marco—which Napoleon himself was to call "the finest drawing-room in Europe"—was the center of the world, and they looked upon themselves with narcissistic delight. Merchants, dip-

173

lomats, and sailors may have created the grandeur of the state, but it was immortalized by a succession of great Venetian artists— from the Bellinis of the fifteenth century, by way of Carpaccio, Giorgione, and Palma Vecchio, to Titian, Tintoretto, and Palladio in the years of climax. Though they mostly painted religious subjects, they were really celebrating the glory of their republic.

Before this noble spectacle the world stood astonished, for there had never been such a city—such a haughty hybrid of East and West, set so theatrically in the water like a sea creature behind its reef.

Consider the experience of a traveler arriving for the first time at this legendary destination toward the end of the fifteenth century. Through the sea gates of the lagoon his ship would sail, past the fortresses that protected the outer reefs and into the narrow, winding channel, marked with clumps of stakes, that led through the shallows into the great basin of St. Mark's. All the watercraft of Venice bustled up and down these waterways: the war galleys from the arsenal, the burly fishing boats of the lagoon, the high merchantmen, the florid ceremonial barges—and threading their way among them all, the lopsided hook-prowed gondolas, the familiars of Venice, with their oarsmen standing crookedly at the sterns. Amid this picturesque traffic our stranger passes wide-eyed, through the shimmering breadth of the lagoon, with its church-crowned islets all about and perhaps a distant glimpse of the snow-crowned Alps, until in the brilliant glare of noonday his ship drops anchor in the basin of St. Mark's, the esplanade of La Serenissima.

There before him extends the panorama of medieval Venice, one of the most extraordinary scenes in the world. The tall palaces of the patricians jostle down to the waterfront. The Grand Canal disappears in a lordly sweep into the heart of the city. In the foreground at the water's edge stands the cluster of buildings that is the architectural motif of Venice: the vertical Campanile, brick-red and genial; the horizontal Doge's Palace, gorgeous but severe; the domed Basilica, glittering and enigmatic. Flags fly everywhere; bells ring all day long; crowds stroll incessantly through the great Piazza or swirl about the quays. All is movement, color, dazzle. "The most triumphant city I ever set eyes on," decided Philippe de Comines in 1495, arriving in Venice as the ambassador of France.

Our traveler disembarks, and discovers that behind this façade Venice is unremittingly industrious. The city hums. In the glass factories the furnaces blaze; in the shipyards unfinished galleys lie skeletonic on their slips; in the street of the Frezzeria the bowmakers shape their yews; in the Merceria the silk vendors unwrap their splendid stuffs. Outside the office of navigation the merchants assemble before the great wall-chart to observe the progress of their distant argosies. In the banking houses around the Rialto bridge, halfway up the Grand Canal, the financiers manipulate their currencies or assess the condition of the indigo market.

Everywhere in the city, plastered to walls, embedded in pavements, gleaming in churches, is the loot of the Venetian centuries, culminating in the great gilded bronze horses of St. Mark's, stolen from Constantinople, which magnificently survey the Piazza from the façade of the Basilica. A sense of illicit luxury infuses Venice. Her buildings are inset with marble, her young men swagger in vivid striped hose, her women totter about on immensely high-soled sandals, as if they have emerged provocatively from a purdah. On the ground floors of the palaces that line the Grand Canal are stashed the material evidences of her wealth, the fabrics and the perfumes, the precious stones, and occasionally even the apes. It hardly feels like Europe.

There is another quality, too, a deliberate quality of the arcane or evasive—a mask of mysterious detachment, intended to keep people guessing about Venetian intentions and awe them with her enigma. Our stranger will be properly bewildered as he enters the dark portico of the Basilica, out of the brilliance of the Piazza, for this central shrine of the Venetian empire is like no other church in Christendom. Outside it looks like a Saracenic war-tent: a humped polydomed structure, with the four golden horses in resplendent contrast above its colonnaded porch and elaborate weather vanes like jewelry above its rooftops. Inside it is shadowy and intricate. Its tessellated floors dazzle the senses. Its balconies wind among the columns like ancient catwalks. Golden mosaics shine from high above, and the place is encrusted with queer baubles and reliquaries and vast jeweled screens. All is opulent confusion, and entering the Basilica from the bright sunshine is like walking into a cave, where inexplicable rituals are enacted in the middle of the afternoon and the independence of Venice is sanctified by a secret alliance with providence. "Redeem us O Christ," sings the celestial choir, somewhere in the shadows before the high altar, but the response from the opposite aisle is unorthodox: "To the Most Serene and Excellent Doge, Health, Honor, Life and Victory Perpetual!"

For the Basilica of Venice stands as an anteroom to the secular palace next door, the fount of Venetian power, where the puppet doge sits superbly above the Grand Council, silently disciplined by the councilors at his elbow. Out of the dim cathedral we may fancy our visitor threading his way through the tumult of the square, past the twin columns on the Piazzetta beside the dancing sea, one surmounted by the winged lion that symbolizes Saint Mark, the other by Saint Theodore with his foot on a crocodile—and so through the great carved gateway into the courtyard of the palace, where a ceremonial staircase rises in noble gradation to the state apartments above. Here is the laboratory of Venetian policy, the powerhouse of Venetian energy. Here the patricians rule their empire, and here, out of sight, are the prisons where the enemies of Venice—the disgraced commanders, the spies, the overambitious politicians—lie in the dark cells of their remorse.

At last, properly reduced in confidence and pretension by a surfeit of splendor, our traveler enters the presence of the doge. Here the awfulness of Venice awaits him in person. The councilors attend in their long robes, their grave Venetian eyes trained upon the visitor; and there upon his central throne, flanked by senators, sits the doge of Venice himself, Vendramin, Mocenigo, or Barbarigo, the great star of all this show, in the corned hat that is the ducal crown of Venice, and with the history of eight extraordinary centuries hanging around him like a nimbus.

Yet it is all a kind of bluff. All this queerness, this gaudiness, this secrecy, this ostentation, is not really alien or exotic at all. This, after all, is Venice, a Christian state of Europe, a well-known marketing concern and advertising agency, only a few days' journey from Rome or Paris. It is all a colossal act, sustained so long and so convincingly that the fiction has become half fact; and nobody enters more completely into the spirit of the charade, we may be sure, than the stranger himself, trembling with nervousness and historical awareness as he bends his knee before the doge and submits his credentials.

Europe was aware that there was chicanery here. Did not a Venetian bleed, laugh, and die like any other Christian? If the Venetian presence seemed ethereal in the lagoon, or among the distant islands of the East, on the mainland of Italy it was earthy enough. During the centuries of her overseas expansion Venice had acquired a hinterland empire. Even in the days of Byzantine hegemony she had established certain trading rights on the Italian mainland, and as she grew rich and powerful in the distribution trade, it became ever more important to secure safe access to her markets in western Europe and equable terms for her re-exports. If a superior fleet could starve her, hostile tariffs could ruin her.

So the Venetians became unavoidably embroiled in the rivalries of Italy and for several centuries were engaged in intermittent wars with their neighbors. By the middle of the fifteenth century Venice was one of Italy's most important land powers. Her frontiers extended to the Alps in the north and almost to Milan in the west. Padua, Bergamo, Vicenza, and Verona were all Venetian cities, and the republic's trading rights were protected throughout the Po valley by garrisons and fortresses. Some of the ablest of European mercenaries fought for Venice, and most of her soldiers were drawn from the mainland cities.

Jealous reactions were inevitable. Nobody likes the successful outsider, especially since the power of Venice (like the power of Britain three centuries later) was based not upon size or material resources but upon ability and chance. It so happened that Venice, on the frontier between two worlds, had mastered the commerce of the Levant and had become the dominant power of the Mediterranean. And it so chanced that her situation and her manner of life had obliged her to create a mainland empire, too. The Venetians' native gift of showmanship enabled them to confuse the world with persiflage and make the republic seem far more formidable than it really was. People were intoxicated by the form of it, and took the form to be the substance.

But it could not last forever. In April, 1498, news reached the Rialto that Vasco da Gama had taken his Portuguese caravels around the southern tip of Africa and had found a sea route to India and China. At once, we are told, several of the Venetian banks failed, so perspicacious were the financiers of the republic. They knew this was the beginning of the end, for eventually a sea route to the East would break Venice's virtual monopoly over Oriental commerce. Her occupation would be gone, and her power would vanish—for all her fleets, her diplomatic networks, her imperial possessions, existed only to safeguard her profits from the East.

After 1500 the story of Venice is one of almost unbroken decline, but the process was so slow, and so disguised with pageantry, that the world scarcely knew what was happening. In 1508 the exasperated European powers formed an alliance, the League of Cambrai, to suppress "the insatiable cupidity of the Venetians and their thirst for dominion." They feared that the growing land power of the Venetians would upset what they fondly supposed to be the natural balance of Europe. Yet for another three centuries Venice survived. Inspired artists still emerged from her studios, majestic

177

buildings still arose upon her mud flats, her manners and customs became ever more superb. During the seventeenth and eighteenth centuries Venice stood almost alone in resisting the expansion of the Turks, fighting a self-interested crusade on behalf of a distinctly unresponsive Christendom; Islam reached the western shores of Greece, but never crossed the narrow gap to Corfu, the defiant outpost of La Serenissima.

Gradually, almost imperceptibly, the fire died. The merchant princes lost their high sense of dedication. The profit instinct was blunted. The steel determination flagged. The arsenal, once the supreme armory of the world, became no more than a second-rate repair yard. The flag of Saint Mark was seen with decreasing frequency on the shipping routes. The Venetian caravansaries of the Levant closed one by one, and year by year the islands and enclaves of the overseas empire fell away, until by the early years of the eighteenth century nothing was left but the Ionian Islands and a few Dalmatian ports.

Now Venice, mistress of "a Quarter and a Half-quarter of the Roman Empire," became above all a carnival—"the Revel of the earth," as Byron put it, "the Masque of Italy." The pose became the reality; the façade, the state. In the overblown flower of her eighteenth-century decadence, stripped of her consequence and her possessions, Venice was the most dissolute, the most carefree, in many ways the most charming, place in the world. To her theatres, casinos, and salons the hedonists flocked from all of Europe. Gossip and license were her specialties now, and her gifts were devoted to pleasure. Almost anything went in this dizzily permissive society that was half boudoir, half bordello. The Venetians shamelessly played to the tourist gallery, and for the most part their visitors were less shocked than delighted. It may have been pathetic, but it was fun, and it still had style. Tiepolo the painter caught the rococo allure of it all in his guileless blues and pastry whirligigs of ornament; Goldoni immortalized the frothy humor; Goethe responded to the underlying innocence when he called the doge "the grandpapa of all the Venetians." La Serenissima no longer cared for power, politics, or war. In her heyday the city's population had been 190,000; by the end of the eighteenth century only 96,000 citizens remained.

For all the gaiety this was a melancholy spectacle, for Venice was still a part of Europe, part of the order of things. Her constitution still stood fast. In other countries kings had supplanted princes, coercion had capped rebellions, but in Venice the aristocratic system had remained virtually unchallenged. It was perhaps the most successful example of political consistency in history, and it gave to Venice, even in the poignancy of decline, an aura, however spurious, of natural permanence. "Venice has preserved her independence during eleven centuries," wrote Voltaire in the 1760's, "and I flatter myself will preserve it for ever"—so hard was it to imagine a world without the Venetian Republic.

Napoleon thought otherwise and looked upon La Serenissima and its oligarchy with disdain. His armies had contemptuously marched through the Venetian provinces of the mainland, fighting the Austrians as they went and requisitioning provisions right and left. By 1797 he was ready to sweep Venice into oblivion. To him the republic was no more than a depraved parody of a reactionary original, and like a scourge he fell upon the city that summer and ended its ancient order.

The sounds of carnival were silenced, and the tree of liberty was erected, like a poke in the patrician eye, within sight of the Doge's Palace. The loot that had come from the East passed now to the West. The golden horses of the Basilica went to Paris, for installation upon a triumphal arch, and diamonds from the St. Mark's Treasury were put aside, to be set a few years later in Josephine's crown. The dungeons of the Doge's Palace were thrown open, revealing only a solitary aged mute inside. For the words *Pax Tibi Marce* on the open book in the paws of the Lion of Saint Mark was substituted a slogan more proper to the times: "Rights and Duties of Man and Citizen." The last of the doges, whose visiting card was decorated with a nude Adonis asleep beneath a tree, abdicated without protest, handing his ducal hat to his servant with the listless comment: "Take it away. We shan't be needing it again."

Nothing is more frustrating for the historian than to have to deal with events and personages obviously of significance, yet of whom little is known. Portugal's Prince Henry the Navigator is a striking example. Despite his importance he remains a nebulous figure, an almost unknown personality. His aims and objectives remain obscure, though the results of his efforts were world-shaking. On a rocky promontory of southern Portugal he maintained for almost forty years what might be called the first center for research in applied science. Together with experts in geography and navigation whose aid he enlisted, he built a great library of books and charts, invented instruments, and improved ship design. The story of the expeditions planned by him and of the aspirations, religious and otherwise, that led the Portuguese along the African coast and eventually around the Cape of Good Hope is reviewed in this sparkling essay. The late Dr. Mattingly was Professor of European History at Columbia University and was well-known for his colorful account of the Spanish Armada.

NAVIGATOR TO THE MODERN AGE

GARRETT MATTINGLY

Five hundred years ago there died in a storm-battered little castle, perched on a cliff at the extreme southwestern corner of Europe, a medieval prince who was the father of the modern world. We have come to call him "Henry the Navigator," although he never sailed farther than the coast of Morocco just across from Portugal, and probably never navigated anything. He gave his father's house and the cheerful, comfortable, slightly backward little nation his father ruled, one of the most far-flung empires and one of the richest overseas trades the world had ever seen; but no progeny of his succeeded to that empire, and it seems doubtful whether trade or empire had much place in his plans. We can only guess at what those plans were, and what forces drove him to change the whole picture of the world.

We find him baffling, inscrutable. So did his contemporaries. The face which looks out from the "panel of Prince Henry" in the famous reredos at Lisbon is different from all the surrounding faces, not just because it is swarthier, not because the eyes are

Prince Henry of Portugal, by an unknown artist. This leaf from a Portuguese chronicle bears his motto, "The gift for doing good."   181

more brooding and the forehead more lined with thought, but because the whole countenance is marked by a deliberate stillness; withdrawn, aloof, it looks as if no one else existed, as if there was nothing at all except the vision or puzzle on which his attentive eyes are fixed. All we can be sure of is that he is seeing something no one else can see.

What it was he saw, he never said. His was a voluble, mercurial, self-dramatizing family, given to noisy quarrels and tearful reconciliations, to violence and rhetoric (after all, he and his brothers were half Plantagenets), to childishly magnificent display and childish cunning political charades. Amidst all this uproar, Prince Henry moved like an abstracted adult through the noisy play of children. Even his generosity had something absent-minded about it, so that while men respected him and served him gladly, it seems unlikely that many loved him. His family was literate, even literary, and for men of their time, unusually self-explanatory, but Henry wrote nothing, except perhaps a few prayers, that was not strictly utilitarian. His letters, for the most part, are as dry and business-like as if he were the bailiff of his own estates. Nowhere is there a line to tell us what he hoped and dreamed. The clues to that are in what happened.

What happened began like a tale in a romance of chivalry. The three eldest sons of King John I of Portugal—Duarte, Pedro, and Henrique (Edward, Peter, and Henry)—had grown up during an uneasy truce with Castile which only the year before had been converted into a permanent peace. Now, in 1411, they were, respectively, twenty, nineteen, and seventeen, and it was high time they should be knighted. But there was no enemy against whom they might win their spurs; so their father planned a series of magnificent tournaments to which all the best knights of Europe would be invited and where the three princes might exhibit their prowess at the risk of nothing more than a few bumps and bruises. The king had no more than begun his plans when his sons sought an audience and knelt at his feet. Let not the wealth of the kingdom, they implored, be squandered on vain displays and mock battles. Let them, instead, flesh their swords on the enemies of Portugal and of the Christian faith. Portugal had been born of the Crusade. With their new dynasty, let the Crusade begin again. And since the lands of Castile lay athwart the way to the nearest infidels, the Moors of Granada, let them requite the old insults of past invasions and strike at the paynims, this time on their own African soil. Let them attempt the conquest of Ceuta.

It was a surprising suggestion. People still talked about the Cru- sade but seldom did anything more. In general, throughout Europe, Christian princes preferred to pursue their vendettas with one another while they wrangled over which of the three current popes best deserved their allegiance. Christendom seemed to be shrinking and breaking up. The Ottoman Turks, quickly recovering from the awful blow dealt them by Tamerlane, pressed forward again on its eastern flank. Even in Portugal, which from one end to the other had been carved out of Moslem territory by the swords of cru- saders, nobody had done any serious crusading for a hundred and fifty years.

Nevertheless, when he came to think of it, King John could see merits in his sons' suggestion. Ceuta, lying just across the strait from Gibraltar, was the chief port of the Barbary corsairs. It could watch all the shipping that went to and fro in the strait. From Ceuta swooped the swift galleys to seize Italian merchantmen making for Lisbon or to raid the little villages of the Portuguese Algarve and carry off men, women, and children to the slave mar- kets of Africa. Moreover, Ceuta was the favorite staging area and jumping-off-place for the hordes of desert fanatics who from time to time had swept into Spain. To hold it was to hold one of the chief keys to the whole peninsula. Finally, Ceuta was the chief terminus west of Algiers for the caravan trails which came up across the great desert from the wealthy black kingdoms of the south. The bazaars and warehouses would be stuffed with monkeys and parakeets, ostrich plumes and elephants' tusks, rare woods and Guinea pepper, and there would be leather bags of gold dust and wedges of reddish-yellow gold tucked away in the strong rooms of every prosperous merchant. At the very least there would be rich spoil, and if the caravans would keep coming, the trade of Africa might fill the coffers of Portugal. When his spies reported that Ceuta might prove vulnerable to determined assault, King John began to make his preparations.

There was a great deal to do. Portugal had to buy cannon and gunpowder abroad, and even ordinary arms and armor. It had to hire ships. And it was impossible in a poor little kingdom to keep these expensive preparations secret; so all of Portugal's neighbors got justifiably nervous. There was grave danger that Castile might take alarm and, thinking these preparations were meant against her, strike first. There was even graver danger that Ceuta might smell the threat and strengthen her defenses. A properly prepared Ceuta would be, against any possible Portuguese effort, impregnable. But by an elaborate comedy of misdirection, King John actually succeeded in persuading observers that what he was preparing was an invasion of—of all places—Holland, so that when the Portuguese armada turned south from Lisbon, the watchful Moors were astonished and dismayed. Even though a tempest blew the invasion fleet off station before a surprise attack could be mounted, Moorish vigilance and Moorish valor could not stop the wild rush of the Portuguese who came boiling off their little ships and splashing through the shallows with Prince Henry at their head. There was savage fighting in the narrow, twisty streets, but before nightfall the last Moorish defenders had fled, and King John was able to knight his three sons in the first city, outside Europe, taken from the infidels in almost three hundred years.

The loot of Ceuta was richer even than had been anticipated. This was a city as stuffed with treasure as Venice, and though most of the gold and precious stones seem to have vanished into the pockets of seamen and archers and men-at-arms, the immediate profit to the crown made the venture a success. But for the long pull, Ceuta was a liability. No more caravans brought the wealth of Ghana across the Sahara to its bazaars. No more merchants from Cairo came with the silks and spices of the East. The wooded hills behind Ceuta were full of Moorish partisans, and the place was under virtual siege except when its former ruler found enough allies to make the siege close and actual. In either case, a strong Portuguese garrison had to be maintained, and the whole town, Christians and Moors alike, had to be fed by sea by convoys escorted by war galleys. For a little country like Portugal, the drain of such an outpost was heavy and the advantage doubtful. No one expected in 1415, when the eyes of Europe were fixed on Agincourt and Constance and on all the internal squabbles which were weakening Christendom against the advancing Turk, that the capture of Ceuta marked the reversal of a trend and that, henceforward, instead of contracting, as it had done for the past two hundred years, Europe would begin to expand again until its civilization circled and dominated and began to unite the globe. It was for no such reason that the Portuguese hung on to Ceuta; they did so simply because it seemed shameful to abandon a city won from the infidels.

The burden of its defense was laid on Prince Henry. Some months after the taking of the city, when he was only twenty-two, his father appointed him Governor of Ceuta and, a little later, Lieutenant-General of the Kingdom of the Algarve, the southernmost province of Portugal, and Grand Master of the crusading Order of Christ. Entrusting the actual command of the garrison at Ceuta to a deputy, the prince himself undertook the harder task of maintaining the line of supply. At first he lived mostly near the sleepy little port of Lagos on the south coast. Later he spent more and more time on the wind-swept headlands of Cape St. Vincent looking out south and west over the tumbling Atlantic. And sometime in those years he saw the vision and accepted the mission to which, with monklike dedication, he devoted the rest of his life. In an ominous waxing crescent, the great world of Islam, stretching from the Russian steppes to the Atlantic coast of Morocco, hemmed in and threatened the smaller Christian world. But beyond the barrier of Islam to the east and south were non-Islamic peoples, some of them (nobody knew how many) Christians. If Islam could be outflanked, the old enemy could be taken in the rear and the Crusade resumed. There was only one way to do it—by sea.

The thing to do was to sail south down the African coast. Henry's earliest chronicler, Zurara, sets forth the prince's objectives as if they had been analyzed by a staff for a command decision. The date, he implies, was about 1419, when Henry was first setting up his court at Sagres. A scientific objective: to explore the coast of Africa beyond the Canary Islands and Cape Bojador because at that time nothing was known by experience, or from the memories of men, or from books, of the land beyond that cape. An economic objective: to seek beyond the cape countries with whom it would be possible to trade. A military objective: to find out by reconnaissance how far south the country of the Moors extended, since a prudent man tries to learn the strength of his enemy. A political objective: to seek a Christian kingdom as an ally. A religious objective: to extend the faith. More than thirty years later, Duarte Pacheco told a somewhat different story. "One night," he said, "as the Prince lay in bed it was revealed to him that he would render a great service to our Lord by the discovery of the Ethiopians . . . that many of them could be saved by baptism . . . and that in their lands so much gold and other riches would be found as would maintain the king and people of Portugal in plenty and enable them to wage war on the enemies of our holy Catholic Faith." There is at least a poetic truth in Pacheco's version, for what turned out to be the greatest series of scientific experiments ever conducted up to that time by Western man, a series which changed the face of the globe and introduced the modern age, began in the haze of a medieval dream. The dream is explicit in the fourth of Zurara's dryly

Lerrelte ma

Arabia sterilis

Mare rubru

Barnacais. r.

Abeschi. r.

India maior ethiopi. Preste

mero
et saba

Louame
.R.

stated objectives: to seek a Christian kingdom as an ally. That could only be the kingdom of Prester John.

Probably the first Prester John heard of in Europe was some Turkish chieftain of the Eastern steppes, some sort of Buddhist or, perhaps, Nestorian Christian, a priest and king at enmity with neighboring Moslems. Later, Prester John became identified with the Coptic Christian overlord of the Abyssinian highland, some of whose priests had chapels at Jerusalem and Bethlehem and some of whose envoys, or persons representing themselves as his envoys, occasionally found their way to Rome and the courts of the West. Medieval Europe was able to transfer the same king, with the same legend, from central Asia to northeast Africa with a minimum of trouble, for both lands lay "somewhere toward the Indies" on the borders of myth and fable. Here unicorns strayed and griffins guarded gold. Here were cannibals, and men whose heads did grow beneath their shoulders, and other men who hopped about on one leg with an enormous foot which, when they took a noonday siesta, they used as an umbrella. Here was a nation of giants who hunted dragons, using lions as hunting dogs. In the midst of these wonders, Prester John dwelt in a high-perched impregnable castle, its moat a constantly flowing river, not of water but of precious stones, and in its throne room a magic mirror in which the Priest King could see at will any part of the world. Seven kings served at his court, sixty dukes, and three hundred and sixty counts. Seventy-two kings obeyed him. Thousands of war elephants marched at his command and hundreds of thousands of horsemen, to say nothing of a special division mounted on ostriches and another on camelopards. His foot soldiers were as innumerable as the sands of the sea. The legends of Prester John vary. In one he was John, the Beloved Disciple, who could not die before the Second Coming and so sat, meditating on his mountain, guarded by hosts of the faithful, awaiting the day of the Last Judgment. But however the legends vary, there is one common factor: in all, the Priest King is very wealthy and very powerful, a reputation which, one may be sure, such subjects of the Ethiopian emperor as reached the West did nothing to diminish. To reconnoiter the Moorish left flank, and perhaps to divert to Portugal the trade which the Moors had diverted from Ceuta, to increase knowledge and convert the heathen, these were all worthy objectives, but the grand objective was to

The Prester John legend persisted long after Henry's death. Diego Homem's 1558 map pictures the fabled king enthroned in Ethiopia.

find Prester John and reunite the broken halves of Christendom in a renewal of the Crusade.

The only way to get in touch with Prester John was by sea. And by sea there were, geographically, two possibilities. Either Africa was a peninsula, almost an island, or it was not. Herodotus said it was and that a bold crew of Punic seamen had once sailed down its west coast and emerged, after three years, at the head of the Red Sea. Nobody was known to have repeated their feat since, and certainly not all of Herodotus's geographical information was thoroughly reliable; but some Greek, some Arabic, and some Western geographers spoke of Africa as a peninsula, though they differed about how far it might extend to the south. The contrary opinion, however, was sustained by the great authority of Ptolemy—an authority never greater than in the first years of Prince Henry's mission, for the first complete Latin translation of Ptolemy's geography had just been published in 1410. Ptolemy was sure that the land masses north and south of the equator must be roughly equal, otherwise the globe would be overbalanced. So the great world map constructed from his gazetteer shows Africa curving round until it joins with Asia, making the Indian Ocean a vaster Mediterranean.

Nevertheless, Prince Henry thought the best chance of reaching Prester John was to sail south past Cape Bojador. For even if Ptolemy were right, and the way by sea was blocked, there might be another way to the fabled kingdom. Some Arab sages said that the Nile which flowed through Egypt rose in a great lake amidst the Mountains of the Moon. And out of that same lake, they said, flowed another mighty river, the Western Nile, which took its course through the land of the blacks and emptied into the Atlantic. At least one fourteenth-century map showed both rivers with, right between them and near the shores of the lake in the Mountains of the Moon, the magic castle of Prester John. Now it was well known that through wealthy Ghana flowed a great river (the Niger, really) with rich cities on its banks. It was not unreasonable to assume that the kings of these cities, like the Ethiopians farther east, were the subjects and vassals of the Priest King, and that the ascent of their River of Gold might lead directly to the Priest King's court. So Prince Henry said to his captains, "Go south!"

Nevertheless, for fourteen years none of them got south of Cape Bojador. Their resources were somewhat limited. Most years, there were at sea in the prince's service not more than two or three *barcas*, the kind of ships the Portuguese used in fishing for tunny or haul-

Before the development of the caravel, Henry's sailors explored in clumsy barcas of the type shown on this fifteenth-century bowl.

ing wine and grain along the coast—half-decked vessels shaped like butter tubs with one stubby mast and one clumsy great square sail amidships, commanded by daring, impecunious fidalgos and manned by fishermen from the neighborhood of Lagos. They were not afraid of blue water, however, and they knocked about a good deal in the Atlantic, perhaps looking for the islands, real or imaginary, with which all medieval maps dotted the Ocean Sea, perhaps testing Ptolemy's hypothesis that India was, after all, not very far west of Spain. In the course of their voyages they touched the Canaries and discovered, or rediscovered, the Madeiras and the Azores. And every year one or more of them went down to Cape Bojador, took a good look, and came away again. In spite of Prince Henry's repeated exhortations to go farther south, that was as far as any of them went.

It is not that it is so hard to round Cape Bojador. It's an insignificant little bump on the coast of Africa, and once you have reached it, the difficulty is *not* to round it. Most of the time a wind blows steadily from the northeast—the wind Yankee sailors called, hundreds of years later, "the Portygee Trades"—a wind capable of shoving even a tubby Portuguese *barca* along at a stiff clip while the current tugs at her keel with a force of another knot and a half. But out to seaward, as far as the eye can see, there is brown shoal water with here and there a tumble of breakers. Once past this cape, with no sea room to maneuver and the wind and current against you, how would you ever get back? Rounding Cape Bojador was like entering the mouth of a trap. That is what men were convinced it was, a death trap, for the wind and current would be thrusting you on into the Green Sea of Darkness.

The legend of the Green Sea of Darkness begins with the theories of the Greek geographers. Basically, they said, the globe was divided into five zones. At either pole there was a Frigid Zone, where men could not live because it was too cold. Its outer ring was merely inhospitable, gradually becoming incapable of supporting life. Nearer the pole, the air was so mixed with frozen water that it was opaque and unbreathable One Greek traveler actually claimed to have seen this interesting phenomenon. Then there was the Temperate Zone, with the best climate, of course, in Greece, getting gradually too hot in Egypt and too cold in Scythia. In the Southern Hemisphere there was another Temperate Zone, the Antipodes, where, some said, everything in the north Temperate Zone was exactly reproduced. But it would be impossible to find out because between the two lay the Torrid Zone. In it the heat of the sun grew so fierce that no man could hope to cross the Torrid Zone and live.

To this symmetrical Greek picture, the Arabs added horrors of their own to describe the sea beyond Cape Bojador. As the sun grew hotter, the steaming sea became a thickening broth coated with a scum of green weed and infested with loathsome monsters. Near the equator the sea boiled, the tar would boil in a ship's seams, and the brains would boil in a man's skull. But it was unlikely that any ship could get that far. Long before, it would have been dragged to the bottom by the huge sea serpents which abounded in the region, or crunched up like a biscuit by a crocodile bigger than the biggest whale. Allah had placed the Green Sea for a barrier across the southern ocean. Even to attempt to enter it was blasphemy.

Only the most ignorant believed that the world was flat and that men who sailed too far would fall off the edge, but geographers, Arab and Latin, took the Green Sea of Darkness seriously. Nobody knew just where it began, and many must have rejected its more spectacular terrors, but there was considerable agreement that the ocean south of Cape Bojador was dangerous. At least no one had sailed it and returned. In 1291 two Genoese brothers had rounded Bojador, making for India by sea. They were never heard of again. Half a century later, an adventurous Catalan expedition on the same course, looking this time for the River of Gold (the Western Nile?), also disappeared without a trace. Understandably, even brave Portuguese fidalgos hung back. But Prince Henry still said, "Go farther south."

Then, in 1434, after these probes into the vast spaces of the ocean had gone on for fourteen years, one of the prince's captains, Gil Eannes, rounded Cape Bojador and returned. The sea and the wind and the sandy desert shore seemed much the same on one side of the cape as on the other, and the next year Eannes went farther, and the next year one of his companions went farther still, four hundred miles into an unexplored ocean along an unexplored coast. Then came a pause. A disastrous campaign in Morocco and serious domestic disorders distracted Henry's attention, and without the prince's driving will nobody went exploring.

In that interval a great step forward must have been taken in the development of the vessel which made possible the conquest of the ocean. According to Zurara, Gil Eannes rounded Bojador in a *barca*. Nobody says what ships made the next two voyages, and no record survives of how the new type was developed; but when exploration was resumed in 1441, only caravels were used, caravels built in Prince Henry's port of Lagos, expressly, one assumes, for the prince's captains. Caravels continued to carry the explorers until almost the end of the century. They were longer, narrower, more graceful ships than *barcas*, with lateen sails—the primitive form of the fore and aft rig—on two or three masts. They could lie close to the wind and were capital for inshore work. "The best ships in the world and able to sail anywhere," wrote the Venetian Cadamosto after he had commanded one for Prince Henry. For some years, only the Portuguese built caravels, and they sedulously cultivated the legend that no other type of ship could make the African voyage.

We know nothing, except by inference, of Prince Henry's role in the development of the caravel. And we know almost as little of the famous "school" which he set up at his villa at Sagres. He early drew there Jaime of Majorca, prince of cartographers and instrument makers, a man learned in everything that concerned the stars and the sea, the son of the great Abraham Cresques who designed the Catalan Atlas, and possessor, probably, of his father's books and maps. But Henry was always drawing learned men to Sagres, and experienced pilots and far-wandering travelers. It was not so much a school, really, as a sort of scientific congress in continuous session, working out for the first time the problems of navigating the trackless ocean and of charting unknown coasts by using what the northerners knew of tides and the lead line, what the Italians knew of stars and compass piloting, what could be learned from the Arabs, and what from the ancient Greeks—all to be tested by continuous experiment at sea.

Henry died in 1460, just as his captains began reporting that the African coast was trending to the east. He must have died hoping that Prester John and the fabulous Indies were now not far off. They were more than a generation off, actually, but the back of the problem was broken. By compass and quadrant, Portuguese pilots were finding their way across the trackless ocean, standing boldly out from the Cape Verdes to make a landfall at the Azores, harnessing the great wind systems of the Atlantic—the trades and the westerlies—confidently to their purpose. The African coast was mapped as far as the beginning of the Gulf of Guinea. So were the islands. And sugar from Madeira and cargoes of slaves from Negroland were helping to finance the exploring voyages. Men had seen a new heaven and a new earth, the lush green land beyond the Sahara and the rising constellations of the Southern Hemisphere. And, best of all, the superstitious terrors of the Sea of Darkness, the scientific terrors of the Torrid Zone had been dispersed forever. The ocean south of Cape Bojador was like the ocean north of it. There were no clinging weeds, no horrendous monsters, and a man on the deck of a ship off Sierra Leone, less than ten degrees from the equator, was no more uncomfortably hot than he might have been on a July day in the streets of Lagos. To the south, anyway, there were no unnavigable seas, no uninhabitable lands.

More than forty years of patient, probing experiment had at last made Europeans free of the ocean. From this the voyages of Vasco da Gama and Columbus and Magellan, the European settlement of the Americas, the European commercial dominance of Asia and Africa necessarily followed, and with these things followed too the revolutions, in men's ways of thinking and of making a living, which ended the Middle Ages. The monkish ardor of a medieval prince, his long quest for a mythical kingdom, made inevitable the modern world.

*The Church Fathers who hammered out the tenets of the Christian
religion also constructed an administrative system for the Church,
based on Roman institutions but adapted to the needs of the
"barbarian" society. More than most religions, Christianity was
strictly organized and intolerant of all deviation. The very rigidity of
what might be called the Establishment, however, made heresy almost
inevitable. The Church fought dissenters and subversives continually,
the more so as they usually called for a return to primitive, simple,
communistic Christianity. In this essay Professor Trevor-Roper
discusses the various categories of dissent and suggests that it
appeared and spread chiefly among the economically more advanced
areas, where opposition to feudalism, in society as in the Church, was
almost endemic. And so it happened that in Protestant Europe, that is,
in the area where the greatest offensive against dissent was attempted
and failed, the most striking progress was made in scientific thought
and industrial development.*

*Mr. Trevor-Roper is Regius Professor of Modern History at Oxford
University and an outstanding authority on sixteenth-century history.*

FOUR FACES OF HERESY

H. R. TREVOR-ROPER

An account of religious heresy, in a single essay! What an undertaking! Only once in history, to my knowledge, has so vast a
subject been comprehended in one work, and that was in the *Im-
partial History of the Church and the Heretics*, published by the
Lutheran pietist Gottfried Arnold in 1699. The example is not entirely propitious. Arnold's two volumes, which consisted of twenty-
three hundred double-column folio pages—and there were fewer
heresies then than now—raised a storm that lasted a generation.
He was denounced by his contemporaries as an infamous falsifier of
history; the most judicious of Lutheran historians described him as
an ignorant, impertinent disturber of the peace of the Church; and
one critic declared that he had written "the most wicked book
since the birth of Christ." From this it will be easily deduced that
Arnold, on the whole, took the side of the heretics.

But Goethe (and who would not wish to be on the same side as
Goethe?) thought differently. When Arnold's book fell into his
hands, he was enchanted by it. It had, he wrote, a great influence
on him. Now he saw the heretics of history in a new light. "I had
often heard it said," he wrote, "that every man came in the end to
have his own religion, and now it seemed to me the most natural

193

thing in the world that I should devise my own; which I did with great comfort. . . ."

To devise one's own religion—that is, in fact, exactly what heresy is. It is the literal meaning of the word. Heresy is private choice, the opposite of orthodoxy which is not chosen but imposed and accepted. For this reason there is a great difference between heresy and schism, for schism does not necessarily imply choice, or if it does, it is not private choice. A schismatic church is a church that has broken away, en bloc, as the Eastern Church broke away from the Western in the Middle Ages and the Protestant Church from the Catholic at the time of the Reformation. Schism may begin in heresy, just as orthodoxy may (Christianity began as a Jewish heresy), but it need not. The Roman Catholic Church regards the Anglican Church as schismatic, not heretical. And a schismatic church soon builds up its own orthodoxy and begins to persecute its own heretics. The pure heretics are those who never created an established church or an orthodoxy and whose members came to it by personal choice.

Even so, what hundreds of them there are! Every generation in the two thousand years of the Christian church has produced them, and their recondite doctrines have never ceased to enrage the orthodox and amuse the infidel. Turn up any century at random: it is like turning up a stone in a well-kept formal garden. Above, all is smooth and quiet, but underneath there is a scurrying of disturbed wood lice and trotting centipedes that cause the orthodox nose to wrinkle in disgust but delight everyone who enjoys the rich variety of Nature. In the third century we will find the Ebionites, the Basilidians, the Valentinians, the Marcionites. In the fourth, the Donatists, with their extremists the Circumcellions, divided Africa from Europe, while the Arians divided East against West. In the fifth, the Nestorians, the Eutychians, the Apollinarians, and the Monophysites convulsed the Byzantine Empire with their metaphysical speculations. There is no end to the list. If we are to make an end, we must select, or we must find some principle of continuity, reducing the multitudinous species to a few intelligible families.

This is not easy, for the history of heresy is subject to a general obscurity. Most of it has been written by outraged champions of orthodoxy, more eager to condemn than to understand. The works of the heretics themselves have been destroyed. Nevertheless, if we keep our heads, we may be able to restore the distinctions which indignation has blurred and see the continuity which has been hidden under a multiplicity of names.

For in fact, when we look closely at these heresies, we soon find that for every dozen names there is only one idea. The great heresies are not the fanciful notions of underemployed monks, each trying to be more original, or more absurd, than the other; they are recurrent ideas which break through the continually sealed crust of orthodoxy because they contain an important truth or an irrepressible human aspiration. They are not confined to one religion. Pre-Christian ideas cropped up as Christian heresies, pre-Islamic ideas as Islamic heresies, and some Christian and Islamic heresies have been interchangeable. Some heresies have been absorbed into orthodoxy, at least for a time; very few have been permanently excluded from it.

Let me give a few instances of the process. Consider Arianism, the doctrine that the Father is a good deal more important than the Son, let alone the Holy Ghost. This doctrine was declared heretical at the Council of Nicaea in 325, and after half a century of ding-dong struggle (for some of the emperors were Arians), it was stamped out of the more sophisticated provinces by the first of the Spanish Inquisitors, the emperor Theodosius the Great. But it survived for a time in remote frontier provinces and was embraced by the Goths and Vandals who carried it to Spain and Africa; and, though bruised, it survived even longer in the East. There, in the fifth century, it took a new shape as Nestorianism. Suppressed by the Byzantine emperors, it did not entirely perish: with the Moslem conquests it merely took on a new, Moslem color. Whatever the pundits might say, the doctrine that God is one, not three, continued to seem more plausible to simple-minded barbarians, and if they were not allowed to believe it of Jehovah, they would change his name and believe it of Allah. Later the idea crept back into the Christian church and was held, in even more extreme form, by some less simple-minded barbarians of remote provinces: by Servetus, who discovered the mechanism of the heart, and was burned alive by Calvin amid universal applause; by Joseph Priestley, who identified oxygen, and whose house was burned down around him by the orthodox citizens of Birmingham; and by Sir Isaac Newton, who rearranged the universe, and, after dying in his bed at the age of eighty-five, was carried to his tomb in Westminster Abbey by competing earls and dukes and the Lord High Chancellor of England. (But this transformation came about because of an important new fact, to which we will turn our attention later.)

Or again, consider the two doctrines that competed with Christianity for the soul of the young Saint Augustine—Manichaeism and Neo-Platonism. Manichaeism was a Persian heresy maintaining that the world was governed by the interplay of two independent positive forces, the spirits of good and evil. Neo-Platonism was a late Greek mixture of mysticism and mathematics, in which the Platonic doctrines of the divinity that pervades the universe and the human soul were preserved by allegorizing all that was inconvenient in them. When Christianity prevailed, these defeated rivals did not perish: they became movements within it and enjoyed a long Christian history. Manichaeism was ruthlessly put down in the Eastern Empire in the sixth century by that great lawgiver, builder, and persecutor, the Louis XIV of Byzantium, the emperor Justinian. It then reappeared in Armenia as the Paulician heresy, and after it was crushed there, turned up in the Balkans where it flourished, especially in Bulgaria, under the name of the Bogomil heresy. Extirpated once again in the eleventh century, it moved still farther west, and cropped up in southern France as the Albigensian heresy, the heresy of the Cathars (the pure). This was perhaps the most hated of all heresies until the Reformation; it was the heresy par excellence, the first to be legally punished by death. By crusade and Inquisition, it was exterminated, but it has left some traces in modern languages. The word "Cathar" became the German word for heretic *(Ketzer)*, while the word "Bulgar" was adapted in other languages to denote a less speculative form of nonconformity.

The history of Neo-Platonism is much less sanguinary, partly because the ideas of Neo-Platonism were much more abstract: they were embraced by conservative philosophers, not radical prophets. Consequently, once Christianized it was never officially declared a heresy. Still, some incautious Neo-Platonists, especially after the Reformation, found themselves heretics, and some, like the philosophers Giordano Bruno and Giulio Cesare Vanini, were even burned as such. As a Christian movement Neo-Platonism cropped up in fourteenth-century Germany, in fifteenth-century Florence, in seventeenth-century Germany and England. It had a great influence on the development of science from the last days of antiquity to the eighteenth century, and also on the romantic movement in literature. Goethe wrote that Neo-Platonism lay at the basis of his own religion; it was the religion also of William Blake.

A sixteenth-century fresco shows Arius humbled before the Council of
Nicaea, which declared his Arian doctrine heretical in 325.

Once we recognize that the heresy of twenty centuries, though as infinite as private choice, is not random but keeps to certain well-defined channels, it becomes possible to see past the multitudinous polysyllabic names to a few constant forms. If we do this, we may be able to go further: we may discover that these swarming individualists were not merely, as the orthodox have always maintained, the miscellaneous maggots which it has been necessary from time to time to stamp or steam out of the majestic fabric of the Church, but also, as Gottfried Arnold supposed, people with continuous traditions of their own to which we may owe a debt.

Almost all the recurrent heresies of the Christian church have fallen, basically, into four main categories. They have been puritan and evangelical; or they have been millenarian and messianic; or mystical and quietist; or rational and critical. These four categories are not by any means mutually exclusive: the great periods of religious ferment have always seen a merging of types and thus the pullulation of intermediate heresies. But they are, it seems to me, the four main sources from which, or from whose intermixture, all particular heresies are derived, and so I will say something of all of them. All of them look back, in different ways, to the teaching of Jesus and the primitive Church. All of them oppose, or at least ignore, the far more elaborate church structure built up in the days when the Church had triumphed in the Roman Empire and become a great department of state. All of them were considered "heretical" because of this fact: because they presumed to "choose" between the real, solid, bureaucratic, political church of their own time, and the simple, imaginary church of the "unforgettable age of the apostles." When it came to a showdown, the real church, with its fire and fagot, was real; the imaginary church was imaginary.

Let us take the puritans first. Undoubtedly the early Church was puritanical. So were its Old Testament models. The prophets, from Elijah to John the Baptist, had been puritans, denouncing the gay polytheism, the local cults, the jolly beanfeasts of the Syrian tribes that surrounded and seduced the grim people of God. All through the first three centuries after Christ, the Church had kept itself pure from similar contamination. The early Christian writers had denounced such unedifying pagan habits as the burning of incense, the "impious and detestable" practice of sprinkling holy water, the absurd use of candles and votive pictures, the "profane, damnable, impious" cult of images, etc., etc. Such practices, the Christians thought, were exactly the kind of things which the

prophets had denounced and which Christ had ordered them to ignore, saying that mercy was better than sacrifice, evangelical
poverty and mutual charity better than sophisticated profusion or
pharisaical ritual. So the early Christians kept themselves apart
from society, trying to live like the first disciples, without compromise, in "apostolic poverty" and "primitive communism," a
self-contained, puritan "out-group" in the secular, pagan world.

Unfortunately the virtues of a sect can rarely be preserved in an
established church, and when Constantine made Christianity the
official religion of the Empire, the bishops soon yielded to the
temptations, or the necessities, of power. Little by little the Christian clergy took over some of the methods of the pagan priests
whom they had replaced. With the pagan temples they adopted
the pagan sacrifices. Pagan gods became Christian saints. "Apostolic poverty" was forgotten. And the puritan virtues were left, as
the unvalued relics of an outworn chrysalis stage, to the heretics
who refused to move with the times.

The first "puritan" heretics were the Donatists of the fourth
century. They were strong in rural North Africa—always (even
when it became Islamic in religion) a puritan area. They believed
that corrupt, or time-serving, priests—the priests, in fact, who had
complied with the persecuting edicts of Diocletian—invalidated
the sacraments which they administered, a moral view no established church can afford to hold. In eighth-century Byzantium
there was another puritan revolt—this time headed by puritan emperors—against the "images," the costly pagan magnificence of
the Church. And this "iconoclastic" movement has recurred often
since. We think especially of Reformation Europe and Cromwellian
England, when preachers, distinguishing between "the living
images of God," mankind for whom Christ died, and the "dead
images" of the Church to which they had been sacrificed, led
mutinous crowds to topple the statues, slash the pictures, hew
down the organs, and shatter the stained-glass windows of the
Gothic churches.

With puritanism—the hatred of hierarchy and wealth—went
evangelical poverty and community of property; sometimes also
refusal of military service or of infant baptism. The established
church always distrusted these subversive ideas, but in every century little communities of heretics clung to them. The monasteries
—at least in their beginnings—were "communist" bodies within
the Church, and the friars—again in their beginnings—were exponents of apostolic poverty. But monasteries and friars soon be-

came rich and corrupt; their original doctrines were condemned; and the communities which clung to them were denounced as heretics. Nevertheless, such communities have continued to appear, from the Waldenses of the twelfth century to the Shakers and other utopian communist sects of nineteenth-century America. The fifteenth-century Bohemian Brethren, the seventeenth-century Quakers, and other sects refused military service, just as the early Christians had done under the pagan empire. Infant baptism was rejected by numerous sects, of which the sixteenth-century Anabaptists were by no means the first. Such rejection emphasized that church membership was not hereditary or automatic but a rational "choice"—a heresy.

Puritanism, evangelical communism, came direct from the Bible. So did the second heretical tendency, messianism. The first disciples of Christ held several extravagant notions popular among the persecuted Jews of his time. In particular, they believed—Christ himself had said it—that the end of the physical world would come in their own time; and they looked forward to the Last Judgment, the thousand-year reign of the saints, and the violent destruction of the profane world. These doctrines, a mixture of Old Testament and Christian prophecies, were brought into sharper focus after the death of Christ by the great Jewish revolt and the destruction of the Temple of Jerusalem by Vespasian. Their most famous expression was in the book of the Apocalypse, in which the pagan Roman Empire was clearly designated as the earthly Babylon, ripe for destruction.

But, once again, the fourth century brought a change. When Rome became a Christian state, and the Christian church began to enjoy secular power, the orthodox gradually lost the taste for revolutionary doctrines. If the secular state were to blow up, the established church would blow up, too, and that did not now seem so desirable. So the old texts were reinterpreted. The Apocalypse was omitted from the canon of Scripture by the Council of Laodicea; Saint Augustine afterward explained it away as a pious allegory; and in 431 the whole idea of the millennium was condemned at the Council of Ephesus as a superstitious aberration. Those who insisted on clinging to the pre-Establishment ideas of Christianity found themselves heretics; and convincing themselves (as heretics do) that they were the only true Christians, they still looked on Rome, though now Christian, as Babylon and on its ruler as the betrayer of Christ, Antichrist.

When Biblical interpretation could lead to such practical incon-

veniences as this, clearly something had to be done about the Bible. *Four Faces* One answer which, as we have seen, was found useful, was to evade *of Heresy* inconvenient or unedifying texts by representing them as allegorical. Unfortunately allegory is a game at which two can play, and before long the established church would find that while its tame theologians were using it to explain away subversive texts, impertinent heretics were using it to explain away useful and orthodox texts. In the end the Church would come to the view that the best thing to do with the Bible was to suppress it altogether: to keep it firmly locked up in dead languages and to dole out to the people only such texts, and such interpretations, as could not possibly raise any doubts about the divine basis of the established church and all its practices.

The heretics who dodged the inconvenient texts of Scripture by allegory and symbolism relied ultimately on mysticism. Not all mystics, of course, were heretics: it depended on which texts they dodged. But the basic theory of mysticism was always heretical, for it implied that direct personal inspiration could undermine the literal meaning of the Bible. This not only gave a dangerous latitude of interpretation, which might be misused; it also implied that the individual could have access to God without availing himself of the costly apparatus of the Church. Naturally the Church looked askance on such ideas. In order to retain control of Biblical interpretation, it built up the concept of "tradition"—i.e., the collected, mutually consistent body of its own reinterpretations—to which, in the end, it gave equal authority with the Bible, and in which, though always with some hesitation, it incorporated the visions of the more conservative mystics. To the less conservative mystics it showed no mercy. Alumbrados were burned in Catholic Spain, Pietists persecuted in Lutheran Germany. As a consequence, these sects became more radical. At certain times extremists appeared who claimed that their direct relations with God exempted them from all common beliefs and justified them in the most outrageous actions. Such were the egomaniac messiahs who captured control of radical religious movements in the Middle Ages and in the sixteenth and seventeenth centuries. Such also were the adepts of "the Free Spirit," who believed that "to the pure all things are pure" and scandalized the orthodox by behaving accordingly: Bohemian Adamites, French Libertines, German Anabaptists, and English Ranters.

However dangerous, an injection of mysticism was necessary to the Church. Periodically it reinflated the sagging body. It also lifted it over some of the jagged texts of Scripture which might otherwise have punctured it. But not everyone is capable of skipping lightly over solid difficulties, and there have always been some men, even within the Church, who insist on facing them, even if they are thereby forced to disturbing consequences. At first such men were few. Critics could stay outside the Church, and converts, when they swallow, swallow whole. But with the rise of learning in a Christian society, Biblical critics arose who were not afraid of following their rational conclusions even into heresy. They were never very many, but their impact was great. It was they, for instance, who, in the sixteenth century, refloated the long-wrecked hulk of Arianism and converted the simple, puritan intolerance of barbarian tyrants into the rationalized belief of a Servetus or a Priestley. It was they who, slowly and painfully, built up the irreversible science of Biblical criticism, and thereby devalued orthodoxy and heresy alike.

Puritanism, millenarianism, mysticism, rationalism—these, then, are the four permanent sources of heresy. None of them are necessarily heretical; all of them, at times, have been contained within the Church. Nor need they be radical. All have been held, at times, by fundamentally conservative men. But at certain times, and in certain places, something has happened to swell these streams into a flood, threatening the whole structure of the Church and society. One of these floods occurred in the twelfth and thirteenth centuries in Western Europe; another during the Reformation and the religious wars of the sixteenth and seventeenth centuries. By studying these periods we may come to some conclusions about the significance of heresy and its contribution to society.

The remarkable thing about the twelfth- and thirteenth-century outburst of heresy was its universality. In the Byzantine Empire there had been some spectacular heresies. Government had been convulsed, archbishops had hurled anathemas at each other, and armies of barbarous monks had been thrown into action to decide between the single or the dual nature of Christ. But these recondite heresies, more often than not, had been slogans in the long struggle for power between the churches of Constantinople and Alexandria. The really important heresies—the permanent heresies which had their roots in the Bible and in society and would recur again and again—had risen sporadically: the Donatists in fourth-century Africa, the Paulicians in seventh-century Armenia, iconoclasm in eighth-century Constantinople. But now a whole crop of such heresies occurred at one time, and all over Christendom. In Lyons a rich merchant, Peter Waldo, gathered a congregation of Waldenses, or Poor Men of Lyons, and preached a crusade to restore the Law of Christ. In Lombardy a puritan sect, the Umiliati, similarly preached and practiced the evangelical virtues; in Umbria Francis of Assisi created the cult of Holy Poverty; in France, Germany, and Italy Arnold of Brescia, a pupil of the learned Abelard, denounced the temporal power of the pope; and in Paris, in 1209, a prophet was burned for declaring the pope to be Antichrist. Meanwhile, in southern France the most ascetic, most highly organized of all heretics, the Albigenses, openly challenged the Church by setting up a rival organization. They had their own clergy, the *perfecti*, and their own laity, the *credentes;* they had their own theology, based on Manichaean dualism, which refused any compromise with the forces of evil, and among the forces of evil they numbered, especially, the established church of Rome.

Finally, at the same time there was a recrudescence of those millenarian doctrines which the Church thought it had allegorized out of existence. In the toe of Italy a studious abbot, Joachim of Floris, extracted from the Scriptures "scientific" prophecies which proved that the last great age of the world was about to begin (it would begin, said his more exact commentators, in 1260). Then all institutions, including the church of Rome, would wither away, and the kingdom of saints, without clergy or sacraments, would be established on earth, to endure till the Last Judgment. As if to illustrate these theories, a crop of messiahs also appeared. Two were Tanchelm of Antwerp, who began by denouncing clerical vices and exactions and ended by claiming the properties of Christ and distributing his bath water as a sacramental beverage to his followers, and Eon de l'Estoile, who declared himself King of Kings and partner of God and swept through the woods of Brittany destroying churches and monasteries in order to maintain his "court" of rapacious peasants. Such lunatic messiahs would crop up in every great period of heresy. The most famous was "John of Leiden," who in 1534 put himself at the head of the Anabaptist revolution in Münster and inaugurated scenes of license that were to curdle the blood of the Establishment for generations.

Naturally such an epidemic of heresy alarmed the papacy. At first the popes tried to contain the movement. They cultivated Joachim of Floris and tried to make use of his prophecies. Though they hanged Arnold of Brescia and then burned his body, they sought to win over the Umiliati and the Waldenses. With the Umiliati they succeeded, but the Waldenses would not be con-

English heretic John Wycliffe suffered the posthumous indignity of having his bones dug up, burned, and cast into the river.

trolled: they retired to the mountains of Bohemia, to merge with later heretics, and to the Alps, where they were periodically massacred by orthodox peasants. The most famous massacre, in 1655, inspired Milton's sonnet:

> *Avenge O Lord thy slaughter'd saints, whose bones*
> *Lie scatter'd on the Alpine mountains cold,*
> *Ev'n them who kept thy truth so pure of old*
> *When all our fathers worship't Stocks and Stones.*

But Rome's most signal triumph was the winning over of the Franciscan movement. Although there was always a "spiritual" party among the Franciscans, which resisted the worldly embrace of the Establishment, the order itself was tamed: the early biographies of Saint Francis, which emphasized his dangerous doctrines, were burned, and ultimately, in 1322, the doctrine of apostolic pov-

erty was itself condemned as heretical. By that time the Franciscans
were rich and powerful, firmly on the side of orthodoxy and even
reaction.

These were important victories; but it had been a near thing.
The greatest danger had been in the early thirteenth century, when
all these heresies, which formed a subversive International throughout Europe, nearly found a territorial base. For the toughest of all
the heretical movements, the Albigensian Church, was patronized
by a rich and independent dynasty, the counts of Toulouse. It was
to scotch this danger that the greatest of medieval popes, Innocent
III—who had already launched the Fourth Crusade, which brought
the "schismatic" Church of Constantinople back into the fold, and
parceled the ruins of the Byzantine Empire among greedy Frankish and Italian princes—now proclaimed another and bloodier crusade against the heretical Cathars and parceled the rich but ruined
lands of Languedoc among the predatory noblemen of northern
France. Thereafter the new order of Saint Dominic was fashioned
into a shock corps of orthodoxy and the Roman Inquisition was
established to prevent heresy from ever reaching such proportions
again.

For three centuries these measures were successful. Admittedly
heresy was not extinguished: the very remedies devised against it,
by increasing the abuses of the Church, intensified the protest
against them. In 1260—the year in which, according to Abbot
Joachim, the rule of the saints was to begin—troops of messianic
puritans appeared in Italy and scourged themselves throughout
the towns, calling on all to repent. From Italy the movement
spread to other countries. Unable to control it, the Church condemned it in 1349. Later in the fourteenth century Wycliffe led a
puritan "Lollard" revolt, and popular preachers in England and
elsewhere advocated a return to primitive equality. In the fifteenth
century Wycliffe's ideas created revolution in Bohemia, which
nearly became the territorial basis of a new international revolution. But in the end all these protests were effectively silenced; the
Bohemian radicals, the Taborites, were crushed as the Albigenses
had been; Wycliffe's revolt, in Milton's words, was "but a short
blaze, soon damped and stifled"; and the radical heresies frequently
ended in mystical resignation. For mysticism, whether heretical or
not, is often the refuge of defeated radicalism. The messianic Taborites of Bohemia, after their defeat, became pacifist, mystical
Bohemian Brethren just as, afterward, in defeat, the messianic
German Anabaptists would become pacifist, mystical Mennonites,

and the messianic English "Fifth-Monarchy Men" would become pacifist, mystical Quakers. The fourteenth and fifteenth centuries, the years when heresy was crushed and yet the Church was not reformed, were the great centuries of European mysticism: the Neo-Platonic mysticism of the Germans Suso and Tauler, the Dutch mysticism of Ruysbroeck and Thomas a Kempis, the English mysticism of Margery Kempe and Richard Rolle.

Then came the great new outburst of heresy in the sixteenth century. Against the background of the previous centuries, there is little that is new in the Reformation. Only this time international heresy obtained a secure territorial basis and prevailed. At least some forms of it prevailed, and by prevailing became orthodoxies, established churches themselves. But others did not. Anabaptism, Socinianism, and a dozen other varieties of "permanent" heresy struggled along, outside the reach of Rome, in the interstices of protestant societies. Sometimes they made a bid for power, as the Anabaptists did in Münster in 1534 and again in England in 1653. Because of their numerical weakness, such heretics always needed the support of messianic doctrines and so fell under the control of fanatics and were destroyed. More often they contracted out of the established society and cultivated evangelical virtues in private corners, hoping that one day their time would come.

Has their day ever come? In a sense, I think that it has. For the modern world owes far more to these heretics than it is aware of. Exactly how much it owes is uncertain, and not everyone would agree with my argument; but I believe that modern society, this extraordinary society which, from its basis in Europe, has transformed the whole world, was created in large part by the heretics. They did not create it intentionally—no doubt they would be horrified if they saw it—but nevertheless it was largely their work. Certainly it was not the work of orthodoxy.

Consider the orthodox world. From the days of Constantine, Christian orthodoxy attached itself to the Roman world, a world of solid, hierarchical, bureaucratic power; and from that world it acquired its own character: the character which the heretics regarded as a betrayal of the real inheritance of Christ. In the Dark Ages the solidity of the Church served society well, but by the twelfth century, in a period of great economic growth, the tensions appeared; and they appeared, especially, in the areas of economic activity: in Lombardy, in the Rhineland, in Flanders, in Bohemia, and in the rich commercial cities of Languedoc. Moreover, it is notable that the "primitive christian" communities were generally communities of textile workers or miners. The Albigenses were also known as *Textores* (weavers). The Flemish heretics were mostly weavers. The Umiliati worked in the textile industry of Milan. The Waldenses were recruited in Lyon by a cloth merchant. The Taborites were mostly Bohemian miners, and the other centers of Central European heresy were Saxony and Silesia, the mining areas of Germany. Now cloth-working and mining were the only two great industries of the Middle Ages. Altogether the heretic International of the twelfth century can be seen, in part, as a general rejection of the institutions of feudal society by the laity, and the solid cells of resistance were to be found in the small, scattered units of European industry. Moreover, when the established church triumphed, what happened? It doubled and redoubled its own feudal bureaucratic structure, absorbed more and more of Europe's wealth and talent, and became a heavy burden on Europe's economy. The years from 1300 to 1450 in Europe, the years of the medieval counter-reformation, are generally admitted to be a period of economic decline, in which the great promise of the earlier centuries came to nothing.

The same thing can be said of the sixteenth-century Reformation. The heretics of the Reformation came largely from the economically advanced areas. Many of their leaders came from the merchant classes; the most stubborn of their martyrs were Anabaptists in the clothing towns of England, Flanders, and the Rhineland, and in the mining towns of Germany. When the established church triumphed over the Reformation, it was once again by doubling its "bureaucratic" structure. Just as the Catholic Church of the thirteenth century triumphed over heresy by the creation of new orders (the friars) and the Roman Inquisition, so in the sixteenth century it triumphed by the creation of new orders (the Jesuits) and the Spanish Inquisition. And the result was the same. Just as the years from 1300 to 1450 were years of economic stagnation in Europe, after the promise of the twelfth century, so the years 1600 to 1750 were years of economic stagnation, after the promise of the Renaissance, in those countries of Europe from which heresy was driven out.

For the Counter Reformation of the sixteenth century, unlike that of the thirteenth century, was not complete. Over a large part of Europe—Protestant Europe—it failed; and in those Protestant countries where it failed, economic expansion was continued. It was continued not so much by the orthodox, even there, as by the heretics, and particularly by the heretics squeezed out from the

Catholic countries. It was Calvinists and Mennonites driven from Flanders who founded the industries of the Ruhr. It was Baptists and Quakers who made the industrial revolution in England. It was the Pietists of Saxony who began the industrialization of eastern Germany. And the greatest industrial power of today, America, lived in its formative period on the heretics of all Europe.

But our debt to heresy does not stop there. The advance of science also owes more to heresy than to orthodoxy. For at every stage, orthodoxy has tended to restrain intellectual speculation and new steps forward have been taken either by bold heretics or by mystics, happily emancipated from the constriction of literal dogma. Neo-Platonic mysticism—then still pagan—was a powerful force in the science of the late Roman Empire: in its Christian form it was even more powerful in breaking the watertight system of obsolete knowledge fabricated by the late medieval Schoolmen. Many of the Neo-Platonic mystics of the Reformation period seem unintelligible to us: the writings of Paracelsus, the sixteenth-century Swiss physician, and Jakob Boehme, the mystical shoemaker of seventeenth-century Silesia, can seem to us pure gibberish. But new scientific conceptions tend to spring out of metaphysical visions which they then discard. Isaac Newton and many of his contemporary scientists began as heretical mystics. Newton himself may have been inspired by the unintelligible Jakob Boehme. Out of the mysticism of the Neo-Platonists and the Quakers the heresy of English deism was born, and deism was the matrix of the Enlightenment of the eighteenth century. And it was Neo-Platonism, again, which inspired the advances in biology at the end of the eighteenth century.

More intelligible to us than Neo-Platonism, but also more heretical, was the most rational of all Reformation heresies, Socinianism. The real founder of Socinianism was Erasmus, who was the first to prove that the only text in the New Testament which could be used as evidence for the doctrine of the Trinity was a late and fraudulent interpolation. He did this in 1516. The Socinians drew the obvious conclusion that God was one, not three, and thus revived, in an uncompromising form but on purely intellectual grounds, the old Arian heresy. They also believed in the complete disestablishment of the Church and in toleration. The established churches—Protestant and Catholic alike—expressed horror at such monstrous ideas, and, between the two, the Socinians had a thin time of it. They found a refuge, first in Poland, then, when the Jesuits came to Poland, in Holland. From Holland, in the seventeenth century, they exercised great influence in England, sometimes even within the Established Church. Whether he was a disciple of Boehme or not, Newton was certainly a Socinian. So was John Locke. In the seventeenth and eighteenth centuries the Socinians were regarded as the intellectual leaders of the English dissenters. Ultimately even the established churches have caught up with them. Since the eighteenth century, Protestants have generally believed that Erasmus was right about the New Testament references to the Trinity. Even the pope has not tried to deny it since 1898. But neither the pope, nor the Archbishop of Canterbury, nor the Lutherans, nor the Calvinists, nor the Greek Orthodox Church has yet come to the more radical "Socinian" conclusion that God is not three but one. That, at this time of day, would be too difficult.

Such is our debt to the long tradition of European heresy. The heretics have been, if not the makers, at least the pacemakers of industrial society, scientific advance, disestablishment of the Church, and religious toleration. But those who prefer orthodoxy can at least make one boast. Heretics have done nothing for art. One reason is no doubt economic. The wealth and patronage which spends itself in art has always been at the disposal of the established church, not of its persecuted critics, and this economic fact has often become a moral attitude: heresy, which is essentially intellectual, disdains appeals to the senses. Moreover, the puritan spirit, which is so powerful in heresy, is positively opposed to art. Magnificent churches, to heretics, have symbolized only the wealth and corruption of the Church, religious pictures have been falsifications of the Gospel, statues have been "dead images," "idols" only fit for destruction. Erasmus, seeing the elaborate Certosa di Pavia, could only exclaim that all that cost might have been spent on the poor. Zwingli, seeing the splendid abbey of Einsiedeln, was roused to hatred of the rich, corrupt church which preferred magnificence and magic to piety and humanity. The English puritans hewed the heads off statues, shivered stained-glass windows, and threw a painting by Rubens into the Thames. The artistic product of two thousand years of heresy is nil. On the other hand, as Gibbon remarked, "the Catholic superstition, which is always the enemy of reason, is often the parent of the arts." Only a rich, established church, which appeals to the senses as well as the conscience, can afford to patronize, or wants to employ, a Giotto, a Fra Angelico, a Greco, or a Rubens.

*This essay should be of particular interest today because, like Erasmus
four hundred years ago, many liberally minded intellectuals find
themselves caught between extreme pressures from both right and left.
Activists on the one side will provoke retaliation and repression on
the other, and the man of moderation, the man of reason, tolerance, and
compromise, can hardly hold his own. The tragedy of Erasmus lies in
the fact that, with his great knowledge, his keen critical sense, his high
ideal of Christian virtue, and his faith in human potentiality for good,
he and his fellow humanists were preparing the way for fundamental
reforms in the Church when Luther and other radicals, men with the
same aims but entirely different temperaments, threw down the
gauntlet to the Establishment and presently rent beyond repair the
society that might have been transformed with less ruction.
Unfortunately, men of the Erasmus type seem to be always out
of season.*

*Dr. Bronowski, of the Salk Institute for Biological Studies, and
Professor Mazlish, of the Department of Humanities at the
Massachusetts Institute of Technology, are the authors of
The Western Intellectual Tradition.*

ERASMUS:
A MAN OUT OF SEASON

J. BRONOWSKI AND BRUCE MAZLISH

Desiderius Erasmus is more than any other man the symbol of
humanism. This powerful movement, which had begun in the
Renaissance, culminated in Erasmus: his personality was formed
by it, and for a lifetime he expressed humanism for all men. He was
born about 1466 in Holland, but his mind was cosmopolitan, and it
dominated intellectual Europe in his age as the mind of Voltaire
was to dominate a later age. One of his friends confessed: "I am
pointed out in public as the man who has received a letter
from Erasmus."

The movement of humanism which Erasmus personified was (if
one must find a single phrase for it) a liberal movement. Its history
and its defeat, therefore, have a special interest for our time. The
life of Erasmus has a modern moral and, indeed, a very modern
ring. He had the respect of thoughtful men and, like his friend Sir

*Erasmus was fifty-six and his prestige was in decline when his friend
Hans Holbein the younger painted this portrait in 1523.*   211

Thomas More, for a time he had the ear of princes. Then, in 1517, the Reformation divided Europe into two religious camps, and soon each side outdid the other in dogmatic bitterness. Erasmus was helpless between two forms of intolerance, and the last years of his life (he died at the age of seventy in 1536) are marked with his own sense of failure.

Thomas More had lived the tragedy of an individual martyr. Erasmus lived the tragedy of a whole generation of intellectuals—and of later generations too. His rise showed that a movement of tolerance, such as humanism was, can inspire men only so long as it confronts a single intolerance. And his decline showed that tolerance as an ideal no longer moves men when two opposing intolerances clamor for their loyalties. This has been the dilemma of the liberal spirit in every age since Erasmus.

Humanism was a movement in which many strands were woven together: the strand which leads directly to Erasmus was the new interest in the classical writers of Greece and Rome. This interest, which was strong throughout the Renaissance, goes back in its beginnings at least to the fourteenth century in Italy. It was first clearly expressed at that time in the works of Petrarch, whose poems already showed the characteristic coupling of ideas in humanism: classical literature was thought of, not as an end in itself, but as the expression of a wider love for man and nature.

In one sense, humanism was a pagan movement. It was impatient of the narrow asceticism which the Church laid down; it was not willing to abhor nature as a beautiful snare, to think the flesh evil, and to find virtue only in a monastic renunciation of life. The doctrine of the medieval church was original sin—the belief that the soul and the body are sharply divided and that, because man cannot express his soul except through his body, he carries an unavoidable sin. The doctrine of humanism was original goodness —the Greek belief that the soul and the body are one, and that the actions of the body naturally and fittingly express the humanity of the soul.

Just as the Churchmen leaned on the Bible and the Church Fathers, so humanists turned for support to the pagan classics. The literature of Greece and Rome, therefore, came to be regarded as a golden ideal in all things. Aeneas Silvius Piccolomini, an early humanist who later became pope, wrote: "Literature is our guide to the true meaning of the past, to a right estimate of the present, to a sound forecast of the future. Where letters cease, darkness covers the land: and a Prince who cannot read the lessons of his-

tory is a hopeless prey of flattery and intrigue." In the same spirit
Machiavelli found it natural to support his realistic advice on the
conduct of politics by references to Livy's *History of Rome.* But the
appeal to classical literature was, at its best, an appeal to its spirit.
Humanism was not a literary but an intellectual movement, a
shifting of values and an awakening to a new self-consciousness of
the human spirit.

In the setting of those times it was, of course, impossible for
humanists to think of themselves as anti-religious. Like all reformers, they felt their protest to be a protest only against abuses of
religion. They criticized Churchmen and scholastic philosophers;
but in this, they felt, they were not opposing Christianity, they
were merely correcting the errors which the medieval church had
put on it. When Lorenzo Valla, a papal secretary, wrote a book
which he called *Pleasure as the True Good,* he insisted that its
moral was to show that elegant living was an expression of
Christian virtue.

The theme of Christian virtue ran through Renaissance humanism, all the way from Petrarch to Erasmus. The splendid flesh
tones of Raphael and the lyrical treatment of naked muscle in
Michelangelo were, to these humanists, elements in a devotional
art. The greatest architectural monuments of the Renaissance are
churches; its greatest books take moral virtue as their theme. The
clearest note in Renaissance literature is a constant wish to show
that virtue in the Greek sense and in the Christian sense are one.

There were, indeed, elements of Greek Stoicism in the model of
Christian virtue which the medieval church had set up. But, at
bottom, the link which the humanists tried to find between the
medieval Christian vision and the vision of the Greeks was false.
The Church idealized the ascetic and monastic virtues and allowed
man the pleasures of the flesh only because man was by nature
weak. By contrast, the pagan vision glorified the flesh, and for a
time the humanists converted at least some leaders of the Church
to accepting this vision. For a time, humanism persuaded the
Church to take as its ideal the complete, the universal man.

In doing so, humanism had to attack the monastic virtues, and
therefore had to represent these as false doctrines imposed on the
true structure of Christianity. The work which made the reputation of Erasmus was a bitter satire on this theme, *The Praise of
Folly,* in which he mocked both the monastic life (he had spent six
unhappy years in a monastery) and the indulgences and abuses
of the Church.

213

An attack on abuses is always an attractive refuge for those who do not want to be deeply involved in principle. By making fun of superstition, by showing the bigot at his most absurd, the critic can keep aloof from the deeper issues which drive men to commit themselves. But the critic deceives himself if he thinks that an attack on an established way of life can stop at what seem to be its accidental faults. What Erasmus said about the corruptions of the Church in fun, Luther soon said in earnest. And for Luther these corruptions became not accidents but essentials—evils that grew out of the structure of the Catholic Church itself. Humanism undermined the belief in medieval tradition and practices, and inevitably Luther turned its attack into a new theology.

Even the scholarship of the humanists had the effect of destroying respect for the medieval church. When Lorenzo Valla studied the *Donation of Constantine*, he proved it to be a papal forgery; other critics uncovered the spurious history of other Christian texts. Research in history and in languages, which followed naturally from interest in classical literature, unexpectedly turned out to throw doubt on the authenticity of much that was revered in the Church. As a result, the authority of the Church came to be doubted in other fields, and Aristotle and the Christian Fathers were no longer accepted as infallible. Luther took advantage of these infectious doubts although, ironically, the new dogmatism that he created soon sustained itself by means no more scrupulous than the old.

Erasmus was an illegitimate child, as Leonardo da Vinci had been; and like Leonardo, he seems to have felt the slur. As a young monk, he believed that because of his birth he could hope for no great career in the Church. And when he was at the apex of his fame, in 1516, he wrote to the pope in some embarrassment to ask him to lift the bar by which he, as an illegitimate child, could not legally hold church office.

Erasmus's childhood, however, was not unhappy or isolated. His parents lived together and had another son, and Erasmus went to a school run by the lay society of the Brethren of the Common Life. Here the stress was on the spiritual teachings of Christ, the Bible, and the good life.

These years of simple piety ended when Erasmus was fourteen; his mother died of the plague and his father died soon after. His guardian was anxious to be rid of responsibility for the two boys and had them prepared for the monastery. There was no escape; reluctantly, Erasmus became an Augustinian monk at the age of twenty-one. Even in the monastery the writers he cared for most were Aeneas Silvius Piccolomini and Lorenzo Valla. His first book, which he called *The Book Against the Barbarians*, was modeled on Valla, and argued that the new learning of the pagan writers was not opposed to Christian virtue.

If 1492 Erasmus became a priest and was able to move from the monastery to the court of the Bishop of Cambrai; and at last, in 1495, he was able to go to the University of Paris, the most famous school in Europe. But here, where he had hoped for a new spirit, he found that the theology again shocked and disappointed him: the scholastic arguments were empty. As Erasmus wrote privately: "Those studies can make a man opinionated and contentious; can they make him wise? . . . By their stammering and by the stains of their impure style they disfigure theology, which had been enriched and adorned by the eloquence of the ancients. They involve everything while trying to solve everything."

The Schoolmen, who repeated the traditional philosophies either of Plato or of Aristotle, were bitter opponents of the new learning. Erasmus describes their bigotry in his *Letters:*

It may happen, it often does happen, that an abbot is a fool or a drunkard. He issues an order to the brotherhood in the name of holy obedience. And what will such an order be? An order to observe chastity? An order to be sober? An order to tell no lies? Not one of these things. It will be that a brother is not to learn Greek; he is not to seek to instruct himself. He may be a sot. He may go with prostitutes. He may be full of hatred and malice. He may never look inside the Scriptures. No matter. He has not broken any oath. He is an excellent member of the community. While if he disobeys such a command as this from an insolent superior, there is stake or dungeon for him instantly.

And Erasmus saw that the formalism which withered the minds of these men also withered their lives. If thinking was merely an arrangement of traditional arguments, then living was merely an arrangement of traditional observances. In 1501 he wrote *Handbook of a Christian Warrior*, in which he contrasted this mechanical worship with true piety:

Thou believest perchance all thy sins and offenses to be washed away at once with a little paper or parchment sealed with wax, with a little money or images of wax offered, with a little pilgrimage-going. Thou art utterly deceived . . . !

It was the abuse of indulgences which tipped over Luther's patience in 1517; and the sentences of Erasmus are, therefore, the prophetic rumblings, sixteen years before the thunderclap, of the storm which was drawing together over Rome.

When the *Handbook of a Christian Warrior* was written, Erasmus had already made, in 1499, a visit to England which deeply changed his life. There he had met Thomas More and other English humanists, among them Grocyn, Linacre, and Colet. They were devout and even ascetic men, but their virtues seemed to grow naturally out of their personalities, and their lives and their minds were of a piece. Among these English idealists, Erasmus felt, Christianity was truly an expression of the spirit, and of the classical spirit. Argument and worship were not brittle forms here; the search for truth was generous and faith was not, as he had felt it to be in Paris, a dead superstition.

Erasmus had always longed for the liberal and humane vision of the classics and had always believed that it expressed the best in Christianity. Now, having seen that best in action, he felt that Christianity could be an expression of broad and tolerant virtues, of the whole man. In the houses of Sir Thomas More and his friends, Erasmus could feel that his longing was realistic and that he in his own person could bring this vision to Europe. This, he saw, should be his life's work: the reconciliation of the classics with Christianity. To a later age the noble savage became the model for a natural morality; to Erasmus the simplicity of the classics spoke with the same inspiration. The classics were a natural gospel; reading Cicero and other moralists, he was carried away: "A heathen wrote this to a heathen, and yet his moral principles have justice, sanctity, truth, fidelity to nature, nothing false or careless in them. . . . When I read certain passages of these great men I can hardly refrain from saying, Saint Socrates, pray for me."

All this Erasmus believed, but believed in part on hearsay, from his English friends. For in fact Erasmus, like others trained in the monastery, did not at this time read Greek. Yet his belief was so strong that he at once began to learn Greek when he went back to Paris, though he was already thirty-four, in need of money, and often ailing. He wrote: "I am determined, that it is better to learn late than to be without that knowledge which it is of the utmost importance to possess. . . . We see, what we have often read in the most weighty authors, that Latin erudition, however ample, is crippled and imperfect without Greek." And he mastered Greek in three years.

He now began to translate, to edit, and to popularize the works of antiquity. He had already published, in 1500, a collection of about eight hundred *Adages*, or tags, from the Latin classics, which, like the collection of wise saws which Benjamin Franklin made later, went through countless popular editions. He enlarged this to more than three thousand sayings, many now drawn from Greek authors. He translated Aristotle, Euripides, Plutarch, Lucian, and Seneca.

At the same time, it was part of Erasmus's sense of his own mission that he should also translate and edit Christian documents. His work here has been called "the foundation of modern critical study of the Bible and the Fathers." He published editions of a number of Church Fathers, among them Saint Jerome and Saint Augustine. His great edition of Saint Jerome was printed by the famous Swiss printer Froben in nine volumes in 1516.

Saint Jerome had translated the Greek Bible into Latin, and this translation was the accepted Vulgate. This was the center of Erasmus's interest in Saint Jerome, and in the same year, 1516, he printed his own translation of the Bible, in Greek and Latin together. On one page stood the Greek text as Erasmus had revised and edited it, and on the opposite page his translation into Latin, which differed markedly from the Vulgate of Saint Jerome. Erasmus felt that he was giving the Bible freshly to common men, as the Brethren of the Common Life had given it to him. He wrote in his preface: "I wish that all women might read the Gospel and the Epistles of Paul. I wish that they might be translated into all tongues of all people, so that not only the Scots and the Irish, but also the Turk and the Saracen might read and understand. I wish the countryman might sing them at his plow, the weaver chant them at his loom, the traveler beguile with them the weariness of his journey." In a few years Luther broke tradition still more abruptly by translating the Bible into the everyday language of his country, German.

For some years from 1504 on, Erasmus had traveled through Europe and in particular had spent time in Italy. In those years some of the greatest Renaissance painters were pouring out their work: Raphael and Michelangelo in Rome, Giorgione and Titian in Venice, and many others. It is an odd quirk of character that the humanist Erasmus took no interest in their art. With so subtle a gift of thought, with so rich a gift of words, he plainly had no gift of visual imagination; like another great humanist and satirist of a later age, George Bernard Shaw, he had no sensuous appreciation of the color, the texture, the shape of things. He may also have been lacking in sensuality in his private life.

When Henry VII died in 1509, Erasmus's English friends urged

217

him to come there in the hope that he might find advancement under the new king, Henry VIII. He left Italy at once; and it was while he was crossing the Alps on his way to England that he conceived the idea of writing his famous satire on monkish life. He wrote the satire in a week in the house of Sir Thomas More, with whom he again stayed in England; and by way of acknowledgment he gave it a title which was meant as a pun on the name of More: *Moriae Encomium*, or in English, *The Praise of Folly*.

The Praise of Folly was published in 1511 and was at once read with delight everywhere. It was printed in many languages and editions, and in 1515 Hans Holbein the younger, who was then eighteen, added a set of marginal drawings to it. It inspired many other satiric books, among them those of Rabelais.

The satire in *The Praise of Folly* seems oddly lacking in humor to us now. The attack on the formalism of Churchmen and the greed and stupidity of monks is not noticeably gayer than it had been in Erasmus's serious books. For example, Erasmus writes in *The Praise of Folly:*

Perhaps it were better to pass over the theologians in silence, and not to move such a Lake Camarina, or to handle such an herb *Anagyris foetida*, as that marvelously supercilious and irascible race. For they may attack me with six hundred arguments, in squadrons, and drive me to make a recantation; which if I refuse, they will straightway proclaim me an heretic. . . . They are protected by a wall of scholastic definitions, arguments, corollaries, implicit and explicit propositions. . . . The methods our scholastics pursue only render more subtle these subtlest of subtleties; for you will escape from a labyrinth more quickly than from the tangle of Realists, Nominalists, Thomists, Albertists. . . .

There is little to distinguish this from the earlier text by Erasmus on the dreary disputation of the Schoolmen. Yet, to his own generation, Erasmus in *The Praise of Folly* seemed somehow nimbler and more carefree; it was possible to side with him in laughter without being committed to a more profound criticism. The fool was a familiar device in the tales of the times; and by speaking in the universal person of the fool, Erasmus made himself one with all his readers.

Erasmus was speaking the discontent of his age, in his satire as much as in his serious translations. The monks and the Schoolmen had ceased to be a vital intellectual force; they no longer reached the minds of their hearers, nor did their own minds give anything fresh to their doctrines. Thus the Churchmen no longer commanded intellectual respect. But since they claimed that their doc-

A drawing by Holbein for the 1515 edition of The Praise of Folly *satirizes an indulgence in self-love.*

trine spoke to men's minds, there was no other form of respect that could be given to them. They were, therefore, seen simply as figures of pomp, offering empty words of superstition.

The age had had enough of clerical pomp and of obedience without respect. In fun and in earnest Erasmus voiced the discontent of the powerful minds of the age; and princes and popes heard him with pleasure and were his friends. The simple minds of the age felt the same discontent; but for them it was voiced more dramatically by Martin Luther.

Martin Luther nailed his Ninety-five Theses on indulgences to the door of the church at Wittenberg on October 31, 1517. With that gesture he turned discontent into action. The Church could no longer smile at its own weaknesses, as the popes who befriended Erasmus had done.

Luther had studied the works of Erasmus and had been guided by them—by the *Adages*, by *The Praise of Folly*, and above all by Erasmus's edition of the Greek New Testament, which Luther used as the basis of his own lectures. In 1516 he had prompted a friend to write to Erasmus to criticize his interpretation of Saint Paul's Epistle to the Romans—characteristically a text on which the liberal and the zealot would fall out. Luther sensed from the outset that Erasmus was not, either in temperament or in opinion, radical enough for him. Six months before he nailed up the Theses, Luther already wrote about Erasmus that "human considerations prevail with him much more than divine."

Erasmus was a supporter of the Ninety-five Theses, in principle; he sent copies of them to Thomas More and to Colet in England, with a letter of approval. But Erasmus was not—and this again both by temperament and by opinion—a man to push the criticism of the Church so far that both sides would find themselves committed to positions which allowed no movement. A year after the Theses, in October, 1518, Erasmus wrote to a supporter of Luther, John Lang, approving them but pointing out that their result was likely to be just this: that those who were allied to the Church would be forced to take up an inflexible position. "I see that the monarchy of the Pope at Rome, as it is now, is a pestilence to Christendom, but I do not know if it is expedient to touch that sore openly. That would be a matter for princes, but I fear that these will act in concert with the Pope to secure part of the spoils."

Luther had now been commanded by the Church to recant, and had refused. In general, the humanists supported him. Erasmus's Swiss publisher, Froben, printed a book of Luther's pamphlets. Their violence alarmed Erasmus; he was both more timid and more farsighted than others; above all he saw that humanism itself, the revival of learning, the cause of "good letters" which he had nursed so long, would be threatened. He wrote privately to Froben to advise him not to publish Luther's writings, "that they may not fan the hatred of the *bonae literae* still more."

Meanwhile, Luther in his first struggles needed what support he could get, and he particularly needed the open support of Erasmus. He therefore wrote to him in March, 1519:

Greeting. Often as I converse with you and you with me, Erasmus, our glory and our hope, we do not yet know one another. Is that not extraordinary? . . . For who is there whose innermost parts Erasmus has not penetrated, whom Erasmus does not teach, in whom Erasmus does not reign? . . . Wherefore, dear Erasmus, learn, if it please you, to know this little brother in Christ also; he is assuredly your very zealous friend though he otherwise deserves, on account of his ignorance, only to be buried in a corner, unknown even to your sun and climate.

But Erasmus was not to be drawn. In his reply he carefully dissociated himself from Luther's writings:

Dearest brother in Christ, your epistle showing the keenness of your mind and breathing a Christian spirit, was most pleasant to me. I cannot tell you what a commotion your books are raising here [at Louvain]. These men cannot be by any means disabused of the suspicion that your works are written by my aid and that I am, as they call it, the standard-bearer of your party. . . . I have testified to them that you are entirely unknown to me, that I have not read your books and neither approve nor disapprove anything. . . . I try to keep neutral, so as to help the revival of learning as much as I can. And it seems to me that more is accomplished by civil modesty than by impetuosity.

What Erasmus wanted from both sides was moderation. He did not want Luther to be wronged: on the contrary, he tried to guard him from persecution, and he even wrote to the Archbishop of Mainz to plead for Luther's safety—and this though the indulgences which Luther had attacked in his Theses had been preached precisely for the coffers of this Hohenzollern archbishop.

At the same time Erasmus wanted Luther to be moderate. In encouraging John Lang, he wrote in a tone which is wishful to the point of being absurd: "All good men love the freedom of Luther who, I doubt not, will have sufficient prudence to take care not to allow the affair to arouse faction and discord." It was, in fact, absurd to believe that in such a quarrel either side could be reasonable. And Erasmus knew that Luther was a less moderate man, indeed less a humanist, than many Church dignitaries. What made Erasmus helpless was that he believed Luther's criticisms of the Church to be just, but that he also knew they would merely entrench in the Church the uncompromising men, the monkish bigots whom the humanists had worked so hard to displace. If Luther was defeated, then the reactionaries would also sweep away all that the humanists had gained. "I am deeply disturbed about the wretched Luther. If they pull this off, no one will be able to bear their intolerance. They will not be quiet until they have utterly ruined the study of languages and 'good letters.'"

In the summer of 1520 a papal bull declared Luther a heretic, giving him sixty days to recant or be excommunicated. Luther's answer was to burn the papal bull, and the canon law with it, in public. After this, in spite of further searches for a compromise, there was in effect no going back. Erasmus was already under attack from the University of Louvain, where he had lived since 1517, and where the Churchmen now accused him of double-dealing. The Church was making it clear that those who were not openly against Luther must be counted to be for him. Albrecht Dürer made a last appeal to Erasmus to take the side of Luther, at a time when Luther was thought to be dead or in hiding: "O Erasmus of Rotterdam, where will you be? Hear, you Knight of Christ, ride forth beside the Lord Christ, protect the truth, obtain the martyr's crown. . . . I have heard you say that you have allowed yourself two more years, in which you are still fit to do some work; spend them well, in behalf of the Gospel and the true Christian faith. . . . O Erasmus, be on this side, that God may be proud of you."

Luther had recently appeared before the Diet of Worms, in April, 1521, but had refused to retract anything of his doctrine. Duke Frederick of Saxony, with prompt political foresight, had had him seized on his return from Worms and hidden from the coming storm. It was this defensive stroke which had set off the rumor that Luther was dead. And indeed, as the Duke had foreseen, the emperor almost at once gave in to papal persuasion and signed the edict which outlawed Luther and commanded his books to be burned.

Erasmus knew that he was not the man for such heroics, and in his view the heroics had already done harm to his cause. With that unposturing simplicity which gives all his writings their modest personal air, he wrote sadly: "All men have not strength for martyrdom. I fear lest, if any tumult should arise, I should imitate Peter. I follow the just decrees of popes and emperors because it is right; I endure their evil laws because it is safe."

It was not only his temperament that made Erasmus retreat from the side of Luther. He found Luther's opinions more and more distasteful. He did not care for Luther's German nationalism, for his fanaticism, his intolerance, and above all for his belief in the essential helplessness of man under the divine will. For Luther was now outspoken in beliefs which we should call Calvinist, and which left no room for the humanist belief in the goodness of man. To Erasmus, Luther's belief in predestination was no better than the medieval belief in original sin.

Therefore when the Church pressed Erasmus to speak out against Luther, he chose an issue, free will, on which he was indeed intellectually opposed to Luther and to the rising shadow of Calvinism. Luther replied by writing *The Bondage of the Will*, and left no doubt that there was no longer common ground between them. He sent a copy of *The Bondage of the Will* to Erasmus, with a letter which at last stung Erasmus to speak his mind:

Your letter was delivered to me late and had it come on time it would not have moved me. . . . The whole world knows your nature, according to which you have guided your pen against no one more bitterly and, what is more detestable, more maliciously than against me. . . . The same admirable ferocity which you formerly used against Cochlaeus and against Fisher, who provoked you to it by reviling, you now use against my book in spite of its courtesy. How do your scurrilous charges that I am an atheist, an Epicurean, and a skeptic help the argument? . . . It terribly pains me, as it must all good men, that your arrogant, insolent, rebellious nature has set the world in arms. . . . You treat the Evangelic cause so as to confound together all things sacred and profane as if it were your chief aim to prevent the tempest from ever becoming calm, while it is my greatest desire that it should die down. . . . I should wish you a better disposition were you not so marvelously satisfied with the one you have. Wish me any curse you will except your temper, unless the Lord change it for you.

Alas, Erasmus had not succeeded in mollifying the Church either. He left the Catholic University of Louvain and went to Switzerland. Catholic hotheads insisted that he was the man who "laid the eggs which Luther and Zwingli hatched." Although Erasmus protested that "I laid a hen's egg; Luther hatched a bird of a different breed," the eggs were all broken together. *The Praise of Folly* was placed on the index of forbidden books; his work on the New Testament was expurgated; and Erasmus himself was condemned by the Council of Trent as "an impious heretic." His cause had failed; he was at home in neither of the two camps now at war; and he had lived beyond his time.

What had failed when Erasmus failed was not a man but an outlook: the liberal view. He gave his life to the belief that virtue can be based on humanity, and that tolerance can be as positive an inpulse as fanaticism. Above all he believed in the life of the mind. He believed that thoughtful men would become good men, and that those who knew and loved the great writings of all ages must live more justly and more happily in their own age.

When Erasmus was appointed to the court of the young Emperor Charles V in 1516, he wrote for him *The Education of a Christian Prince.* The word "Christian" in the title points the contrast to *The Prince,* which Machiavelli had written three years before, and so do the opening words of Erasmus's dedication, ". . . no form of wisdom is greater than that which teaches a Prince how to rule *beneficently.*" But the sense in which Erasmus used the word "Christian," his longing for universal good, could not survive the violence of both sides in the coming struggle.

Part of that struggle was national: Luther was very German, and the Reformation of Henry VIII was very English. In this also Erasmus was out of place; he had hoped to make humanism a movement of universal peace from one end of Europe to another. And in his great years he had traveled Europe as if this empire of the mind, this free Christian community, had already been created. For a time the courts of Italy and England, the universities of France and Spain, the houses of cardinals and reformers, were open to him. But the time was short, and it has not returned.

Adrian Collaert sculp.

The naval victory of the Holy League against the Ottoman Turks in October, 1571 is memorable not only because it was the first major naval engagement since the Battle of Actium in 30 B.C., nor yet because it was a decisive event in the Christian defense of Europe against the encroaching forces of the sultan by land and sea. Actually the huge armada of Don John of Austria barely escaped encirclement and was saved only by the six galleasses, or Venetian dreadnaughts, with their vastly superior power. Yet the victory was celebrated throughout Europe with endless tolling of bells, religious processions, and festivities of all kinds; after a long period of Turkish advance it was a welcome relief and, as was to appear later, did in fact presage the decline of Turkish power. Mr. Warner, a well-known naval historian and biographer, gives a colorful account of the desperate clash of hundreds of galleys and the hand-to-hand fighting as soldiers boarded each others' ships.

THE BATTLE OF LEPANTO

OLIVER WARNER

There is scarcely a great city in western Europe—Rome, Madrid, Vienna, Genoa, and Venice notable among them—without its proud memorials of the mighty clash at sea between Christian and Moslem forces that took place near Lepanto on October 7, 1571. It was not only a terrible encounter in itself, it was one of the most picturesque in all sea history. Painters, weavers of tapestry, carvers of trophies-of-arms, engravers of commemorative medals, and jewelers vied with one another to do honor to the Christian victory, the most extraordinary of its kind ever won.

Sea battles may be great in showing the sea commander at his most skillful or resolute; they may be tame and even indecisive as battles, yet important in their effect; or they may be both. Lepanto was great in every sense of the word. It was a milestone in the grim and protracted struggle between the Cross and the Crescent.

It was fought off the shores of Greece, at the entrance to the Gulf of Patras, and it led to a wave of renewed hope and vigor among the Christian nations. A fleet made up of the forces of the Holy League—Spain, the Papal States, and the Republic of Venice —all under the command of Don John of Austria, defeated the principal fleet of the Turks under Ali Pasha. On the victor's side,

This detail from a contemporary engraving captures the confusing tangle of close-in fighting that marked the Battle of Lepanto.

notable leaders were the Marqués de Santa Cruz, a Spaniard; Andrea Doria, leading a Genoese squadron; and Marc Antonio Colonna, who commanded the forces of Pius V. It was, in fact as in name, a company drawn from most of Catholic Europe, France excepted.

Lepanto, coming as it did after the repulse of the Turks at the siege of Malta six years earlier, made it certain that the Mediterranean would not become a Moslem lake. Henceforward no sultan would in fact exercise paramount sea power, and although this result was slow to make itself apparent, any further Moslem expansion into the Europe that they had invaded with such success would be mainly at the expense of Poland and Russia. It would be by land. By sea, Spaniards and Italians, with the example before them of the island Knights of Malta, had shown that with leadership, courage, and the help of a new weapon (in this case the heavily gunned galleass) they could withstand the ancient method of fighting solely with oared galleys manned by slaves.

Don John of Austria, who in the year of Lepanto was not yet twenty-five—though he had already served with distinction against the Moors in Granada—was the bastard son of the Emperor Charles V by Barbara Blomberg, the daughter of a wealthy Bavarian. He was thus half brother to Philip II of Spain, one of the pillars of the Holy League; and he had long been, in name at least, the principal Spanish admiral. Fair-haired, eager for fame, Don John proved a good leader for a mixed and quarrelsome fleet.

Among the Italian forces the Venetians, led by Augustino Barbarigo and the veteran Sebastian Veniero, were smarting under the recent loss of most of Cyprus to the Turks, and they bore no love toward the Genoese, their ancient rivals at sea, led by Giovanni Andrea Doria, nephew of one of Genoa's greatest men. In Doria's squadron a Spanish volunteer was serving whose fame was destined to outshine even that of the commanders. He was Miguel de Cervantes, later to become the author of *Don Quixote*.

The League had been formed in May, 1571, through the tireless efforts of Pope Pius V. This pontiff, who held the See of Rome for only a few years (1566–72), was one of the most memorable figures in an age renowned for great men. Portraits and medals show him with a high forehead, rather sunken eyes, a strong, curved nose, and a pointed beard. He was of humble origin, and even as pope he

Don John of Austria, the astute commander of the Holy League forces
at Lepanto; a portrait probably done to commemorate his victory.

preferred to continue the ascetic habits of a Dominican monk. His personal piety, zeal, and devotion to the Church have never been exceeded, but he had a gift for diplomacy rare in the saintly. Through his skill and patience he was able to form the first effective combination of Christian forces at a moment that was critical for Europe. His aim was twofold: to bring help to the Venetians, who were losing ground in the eastern Mediterranean, where they had long been the great traders and where they held outposts and possessions; and to prevent the power of the warlike Turk from spreading any closer to the Papal States.

Ever since the tenth century the Turks had been steadily eroding the power of the ancient Christian empire of Byzantium, with its capital at Constantinople. Checked at first by the Crusaders, they became established in Anatolia as early as 1300. Then, crossing first the Black Sea and later the Sea of Marmora into Europe, they began to advance upon the nearer territories of Christendom. The crowning humiliation came in 1453, when Mohammed II took Constantinople itself.

The Turks moved south as well as west. In 1517 Egypt was occupied by Selim I. His successor, Suleiman I, whom men called the Magnificent, extended his sway in the course of a long and splendid reign to Baghdad, to Rhodes, to Belgrade, to Budapest, and almost to the gates of Vienna, capital of the Holy Roman emperors who ruled most of western Europe. To this day Hungarians remember the defeat of Mohács, fought less than half a century before Lepanto, as one of the saddest in their history, although much later they had their revenge on the very same field.

The Turks were united. They were bred to arms. They upheld the great cause of Islam. Only by following their example of unity and devotion, only by reviving a spiritual fire that seemed to have been damped since the Crusades, could the Christians hope to stem the tide.

If the Christians found the necessary inspiration in the noble and determined character of the Pope, they were hardly less fortunate in their tactical leader. Don John of Austria was one of those rare men who seem to have been born with a gift for war. He had been brought up in Spain, and was recognized very early as a young man to whom responsible posts could be entrusted; and his age, his birth, and his experience against the corsairs of North Africa and the Moors in Granada all seemed to fit him to lead the great armada which the efforts of Pius V had assembled.

Don John's original rendezvous was to be at Messina. When he arrived there, he found himself in charge of more than three hundred ships, two thirds of them known as royal galleys, each with a nominal complement of one hundred soldiers in addition to the rowers who toiled at the oars.

The Spanish contingent was the largest: eighty galleys, twenty-two other vessels, and no less than twenty-one thousand fighting men. The Venetians contributed more than a hundred vessels, but most were poorly manned, and their six heavily armed galleasses were in fact the Republic's most important asset. These galleasses, which were towed into action by lighter vessels, were broader in the beam than the galley; the additional depth allowed the erection, forward, of a structure, fitted with swivel guns, that anticipated the modern armored turret.

In the galleass the usual ornamental stem of the galley was replaced by a formidable point, while lower down the solid cutwater, or prow, was effective against anything of smaller size that could not get out of the way. Sides and stern were also heavily armed, while the rowers were protected by a deck that served as a platform for the fighting men. In battle the rowers were yoked in both directions, some pulling and some pushing at the fifty-foot oars.

The Pope himself fitted out twelve galleys, hired many more, and supplied the necessary troops. No less than eighty thousand men assembled at Messina with his official blessing. Of these, some fifty thousand volunteers, impressed men, and slaves labored at the oars. The rest were soldiers. Don John, with the aid of a blackboard, explained his methods to representatives of the fighting men, gave the captains of his fleet detailed information as to how he would meet the most likely tactical contingencies, and arranged for appropriate signals.

While he was surveying and ordering his fleet, he got news that the Turks, who were believed to have massed about three hundred ships, were roving the Ionian Sea and attacking the islands therein. On September 16 the Christians put to sea, and the first precise news of the enemy came before the end of the month, when Don John anchored off Corfu. There he learned that the Turkish commander, Ali Pasha, had recently landed, burned some churches, failed to subdue the island's fortress, and had then retreated to the anchorage of Lepanto, which was far up the eighty-mile stretch of water now known as the Gulf of Corinth.

At a council of war, characterized like many such councils by acrimony and dispute, those who were for instant attack carried the day. They included Colonna, Barbarigo, Santa Cruz, and Don

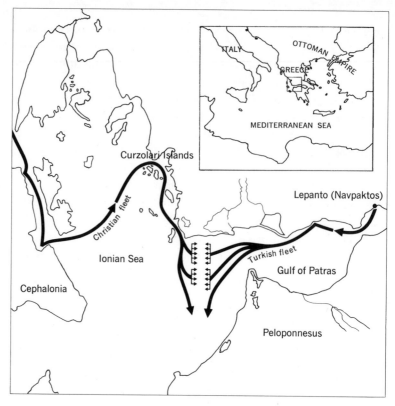

The position of the two fleets at the mouth of the Gulf of Patras is shown here, as well as the outflanking maneuvers of both.

John himself. The season was growing late, and the differences between the Allies, never far from the surface, were increasing. Spaniards and Venetians had already come to blows, largely due to the fact that Spaniards had to be drafted into the Venetian ships to bring them up to strength.

Off Cephalonia, on October 6, a ship from Crete brought news of the fall of Famagusta, the last Venetian stronghold in Cyprus, and of the torture and death of its noble defenders. A wave of horror spread through the Allies, and an immediate advance was ordered into waters where the enemy was known to be waiting. One further item of news was not altogether cheering. It appeared that Ali Pasha had been reinforced by the ships of Uluch Ali, once a Calabrian fisherman but now the dey of Algiers and known to be a daring corsair by many in the Christian fleet.

During the night of October 6 the Turks, with a favoring wind, advanced westward toward the Christians. At dawn on October 7 the most powerful forces that had ever met at sea came within sight of one another at the entrance to the Gulf of Patras, which is west of the larger Gulf of Corinth.

Here, as at most earlier naval battles, fleets met like armies. Their formation was rigid; the commands were military; and tactics were based upon experience by land. The sailors got the ships where they were wanted, while the "generals" and their soldiers fought it out.

Before he drew up his formal line of battle, Don John gave two orders. The first was to remove the iron beaks which protruded ten or fifteen feet from the bows of certain of the fighting ships. The second was that no one should fire "until near enough to be splashed with the blood of an enemy." Both directives were wise. The battle would not be won by ramming, but by close fighting, in which the Spaniards' armor, together with their arquebuses, might prove a decisive advantage.

Barbarigo and his Venetians were placed on the left wing, Barbarigo himself sailing as close as he dared to the inshore rocks and shoals, in the hope that his flank could not be turned. Andrea Doria was on the right wing, where papal galleys were mingled with the Genoese. In the center was the flagship of Don John, conspicuous by its high, carved poop and triple-stern lanterns, its green pennant at the forepeak, and its Holy Standard at the maintop. Near him were Veniero and Colonna. In reserve were thirty-five Spanish and Venetian galleys under Santa Cruz, ready to apply their strength where most needed.

As the fleets neared each other the six Venetian galleasses, the spearhead of the Christian attack, were towed into position. Two, in line ahead, were placed in front of each main squadron. When every preparation had been made, Don John boarded a fast vessel and sailed behind the three-mile front across which his forces extended, heartening his men and, in his turn, being cheered.

By the time Don John had returned to his own galley, the wind had changed in his favor. He was now able to see that the Turks had their fleet arrayed in the form of a huge crescent, but this was altered, almost at once, to conform to his own dispositions. There were many Christian galley slaves in the Turkish fleet. To them Ali Pasha said: "If I win the battle, I promise you your liberty. If the day is yours, then God has given it to you."

First blood was drawn by the galleasses of Don John's center. Their guns, heavier than anything the Turks possessed, did their execution at long range, sinking several Turkish galleys even before the main forces were in contact. Partly as a result of this

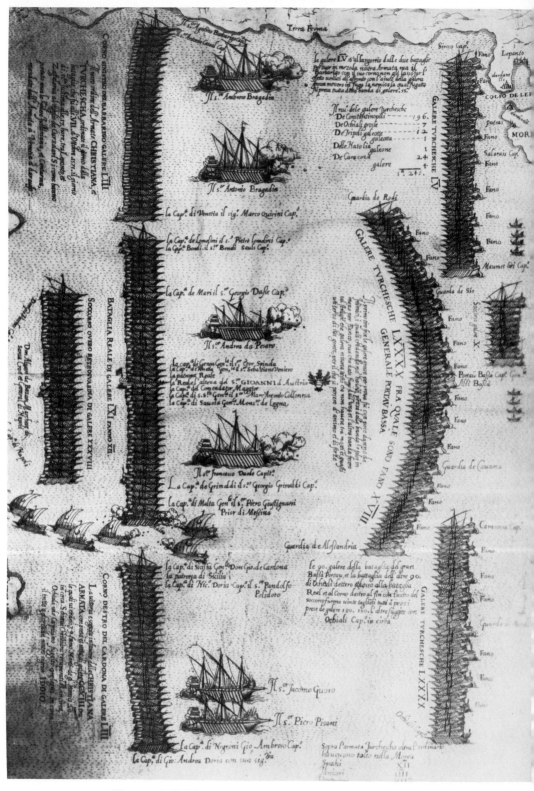

The tactical disposition of the opposing fleets, Christian at left, Turkish at right. In the center are the six Venetian galleasses.

initial setback the left and right wings of the Moslems separated
from the center. Uluch Ali made a wide sweep toward the southern
shore in an attempt to outflank Andrea Doria, while Mohammed
Sirocco held a similar course toward Barbarigo and the northern
shore. Ali Pasha's center squadron, eluding the powerful galleasses
as best it could, drove on to meet that of Don John. By midday, or
shortly after, the two flagships were locked together, crossbow and
arquebus being exchanged for sword and scimitar, the decks slip-
pery with blood from close fighting. And by that time, all three
squadrons were at grips.

Against the Christian left, Sirocco's maneuver succeeded. His
knowledge of the shore line enabled him to sail even closer to it
than Barbarigo, and to surround him. The Venetian admiral was
attacked by eight Turkish galleys, and he himself was killed by an
arrow. Twice the Venetian flagship was stormed; twice it was re-
taken. At last, when help came from Canale and others, Sirocco's
ship was sunk and he was thrown into the water. Although by then
badly wounded, he was rescued, only to be beheaded on the spot
by his captors.

On the Christian right the battle had at first gone equally badly.
Although Uluch Ali had not been able to outflank Andrea Doria, he
had at once doubled back to a gap that had opened in the Allied
line and had taken part of Don John's squadron in the rear. Among
the ships attacked was the *Capitana* of Malta, commanded by
Giustiniani, Prior of the Order of Saint John. The Prior fell with
five arrows in his body, and the *Capitana* was made prize. At the
most critical time Santa Cruz, seeing the Maltese in tow of the
enemy, moved to the rescue, and Uluch Ali, relinquishing his capture, made haste to retreat.

The issue was decided in the center. Here, from the first, the virtue of Don John's order to dismantle the iron beaks had been
clear. The Turkish admiral had not done this, and though the
forepeak of his flagship towered over the Christian decks, his fore-
castle guns fired into the air. Those of Don John, placed at a lower
level, riddled the Turkish galley with shot just above her water
line. The armored Spanish arquebusiers soon decimated the Turkish ranks. Not for nothing were the Spaniards reckoned the steadi-
est soldiers of their time.

The climax came when Don John gave the order to board: once,
twice, parties were driven back, but at last they carried the Turkish poop. There Ali Pasha, already wounded in the head, tried to
buy his life with a promise of treasure. It was in vain. Even his

An unknown Venetian artist's view of the action. Crescents mark Ali Pasha's ships; Don John's vessels fly a variety of colors.

protective talisman, the right canine tooth of Mohammed contained in a crystal ball, did not avail him. A soldier cut him down, hacked off his head, and carried it to Don John. The admiral, recoiling in horror, ordered the man to throw the grisly trophy into the sea. But the Spaniard disobeyed him and mounted it on a pike, which was then held aloft in the prow of the Turkish flagship. Consternation spread among the Moslems, and within a few mo-

ments resistance was over. The Ottoman standard, inscribed with
the name of Allah twenty-nine thousand times and never before
lost in battle, was lowered from the maintop. Don John was then
able to turn his attention to his right wing, where all was not well.

No less than five of Doria's galleys had been stricken. On the
San Giovanni and the *Piamontesa* virtually everyone was dead.
The *Doncella* was not much better off, while in the *Florence* only
the captain and seventeen seamen survived out of two hundred.
The *Marquesa* was also hard pressed. It was in this ship that Cer-

vantes was serving. He had been ill with fever before the battle, but he had risen from his sickbed and had volunteered for a place of danger. There he remained throughout the battle and received the wound that disabled his left hand for life.

Uluch Ali, whose Algerians had done most of the damage on the Christian right, retreated to the shelter of Lepanto where he learned of the death of Ali Pasha, although sixteen of his galleys turned on their pursuers and fought one of the bloodiest encounters of the entire day with Don Juan of Cardona. But as the four-hour fight came to a close, with the enemy center and right almost totally destroyed and the left in gradual retreat, Don John at last had time to survey the action as a whole and to begin to reckon his gain and loss.

Nearly eight thousand of the bravest men in Spain and Italy were dead; double that number were wounded. The Turks and Algerians lost at least three times as many killed, and some twelve thousand Christian slaves were rescued from their galleys. Never again did the Turkish sultan contrive to assemble so powerful a fleet. Christians and Turks had been roughly equal in numbers, and had fought with equal courage. Victory went to the side with better weapons and better leadership; here the galleass and the person of Don John proved decisive.

Lepanto was Don John's first and last major sea battle. He died in the Low Countries at the age of thirty-one, a man of one paramount success and many disappointments. Like the galleys he commanded, he belonged to an old order of sea warfare, one whose history went back to the days of Actium, Salamis, and beyond. The future was with sail, with the broadsides of the future ships of the line.

The "tumult and the shouting" died, the "captains and the kings" departed, the fleet dispersed, the squadrons on regular service took up new dispositions, the wounded went home to die or to be cared for; and then, slowly but surely, the news of the action spread far and wide. In the sixteenth century events took a long time to fit into a proper perspective—yet there were compensations. Great happenings made more impact than anything we hear as news today, except in the rarest circumstances. Men and women gave every episode and incident its full value, and survivors of Lepanto would tell their tales to enraptured audiences in every corner of Europe.

The cumulative impact was both astounding and permanent.

The victory may be said to have begun a spirit of revival—in war,

diplomacy, the arts, and architecture—which was in time to bring
Europe to the proud splendor of the flowering of the Baroque
age. Vaults, cupolas, and arches, which had originated in the architecture of Imperial Rome and been modified in Byzantium, reappeared in great buildings, replacing the slender, mystical dreami-
ness of later Gothic buildings. There was a new, rich solidity of
horizontal planes, and polychromatic exuberance in metal and
marbles. All betokened renewal of belief in life, religion, art, and
politics.

To be sure, Lepanto did not end Turkish power and aspiration,
or even destroy Turkish sea power. More than seventy years later
the Turks mounted an invasion of Crete, which was one of the
main Venetian outposts. The siege began in 1645 and continued
over two decades, Candia holding out against all attacks until at
last attrition and hunger took their toll and the fortress fell. The
Turks continued their struggle with the Holy Roman emperors of
Vienna, the capital being once again endangered in 1683 and saved
only by an astonishing rescue march by John Sobieski, Poland's
hero-king, who rendered a unique service in the old chivalrous
spirit to a fellow Christian ruler.

What Lepanto proved was that Turkish power could be contained, and that the Crescent was not invincible. It was as profound in its effects as, for instance, were the battles of Stalingrad
and Midway in World War II. It was the beginning of a long and
lasting revival. Christendom had found the will and strength to
push back the invader; memories of the Crusades came flooding
back; and as Cervantes grew older, more mature, and more experienced, he wrote that affectionate monument to Christian
chivalry, *Don Quixote.*

*A difficult problem confronting the art historian is the identification
and definition of styles. Any survey of the arts in their various aspects
reveals the change of dominant forms, recognizable, for example, as
Gothic, Renaissance, Rococo, or Romantic. Among the different
modern styles, the Baroque of the seventeenth century was long
despised only to be now highly appreciated. Despite its extravagances
it is now recognized as an outgrowth of the Renaissance and as a style
more expressive than any other of man's thirst for power, his yearning
for action, his elation and his depression. Professor Friedrich, who
has written a book on the Baroque period of European history, in this
essay reviews the expression of the Baroque spirit in the various art
forms and stresses the immense contributions made by its leading
exponents. What is more, he relates the development of the arts to the
political history of the period, with particular reference to the decay of
medieval institutions and the emergence of modern state forms.*

THE BAROQUE AGE

CARL J. FRIEDRICH

T he architecture of the Baroque speaks the same language as
that of the Renaissance, but a brutalized version of it." So
wrote the great Swiss art historian Jacob Burckhardt just over a
century ago. The idea spread and persisted for many a year that
not only in architecture but in all the arts the Baroque was little
more than an ugly, perverted, overdone excrescence of the Renaissance. This is still the judgment of many who have a reasonably
clear notion of the Gothic and the Renaissance itself, along with
the Classic and the Romantic, but for whom the Baroque remains
a confused, uncertain concept.

Much nearer our own time, however, the historian Oswald
Spengler went to an opposite extreme in speaking of the Baroque.
The gigantic, if wrong-headed, portrait of Western man and his
civilization that Spengler painted a generation ago celebrated the
Baroque age as the high point of our culture; ever since that time,
he thought, the decline of the West had progressed rapidly.

Between such opposing views, a middle ground of new interest
in the nature and scope of the Baroque has spread. Today, no past
period is the subject of so much debate and, perhaps, of so much
curiosity. Men of our time have developed a better grasp than the

*The Baroque love of curves and illusion enriches the Clementinum
Library in the Jesuit college in Prague, begun before 1600.*   239

classicist Burckhardt ever had of a period that embraced Bernini and Rembrandt, Descartes and Spinoza, Milton and Bach. A sense of kinship is felt with it today, not only in the fine arts but in poetry and music as well. Contemporary composers find more inspiration there than in works from later periods, and the same holds for poets and dramatists, even for philosophers. Many critics now recognize and celebrate the Baroque as a great and distinct age, although not necessarily calling it the highest point of our culture as Spengler did.

How shall we define and delimit the Baroque? Its beginnings reach far back into the sixteenth century, but its first great manifestations appear in the last quarter of it. The seventeenth century is, however, its true domain, with further extensions (especially in music, often a late arrival) far into the eighteenth. Styles are like mountain peaks merging into each other in the valleys between; the peak of the Baroque ought perhaps to be placed around the year 1650.

Like all styles, it has no uniform set of traits, but can be better described by an anology to two magnetic poles operating within a common field of ideas and feelings. This common field was focused on movement, intensity, tension, force. As contrasted with the debonair worldliness of the Renaissance, reflected in the luminous harmony of the paintings of Raphael, the Baroque was tormented by doubts, shot through with conflicts and extremes. Not a happy and unreflective pleasure of the senses, but gross sensuality alternating with pangs of conscience becomes the dominant note. The Baroque age was torn between extremes. The warm-blooded *Sinnenfreude* of the previous age turned into coarse materialism and carnal debauch, while the philosophical and scholarly inquiries of humanism led to skepticism and scientific discovery.

Tension and intensity are natural to music and, to some extent, to painting, but they produce seemingly insoluble problems for the static arts of architecture and sculpture. The word "Baroque" suggests the grotesque, the overladen, the extravagant. Baroque is all that. But it has a beauty of its own which is missed when viewed from the canons of classical aesthetics. Such canons had ruled supreme during the Renaissance. But by 1600 they were dead. Painting, sculpture, and music had exhausted the possibilities of that approach. Something new was needed.

Why was it needed? What overpowering drive gives a new style its meaning and significance? This is and remains a mystery. We cannot penetrate the inner sanctum of the creative impulse, but we may enter into the courtyard. Here we find new experiences which shape the feeling and thinking of men as they enter upon a new age. The style that results is the outward projection of such new experiences around one central, shattering explosion. In the age that ushered in the Baroque, the explosion was partly cosmic and partly social. Cosmically, it was an experience begot by the Copernican discovery that the earth is not the center of the universe, but only a fragment of it, and not a particularly significant one at that. The comfortable notion of man in the middle of an earth-centered universe gave way to the lonely vision of man lost in the vastnesses of infinite space. But this discovery was accompanied by a sense of incredible new power born of the same new science—the power to see what is very far away, and the even more startling power to interpret the harmony of the spheres as an order obeying laws which man can know and manipulate to extend his dominion over nature.

To this exciting experience of power reaching into the infinite, beyond all dreams of former ages, was added another in the world of politics. The modern state was emerging from the chaos of the religious wars of the sixteenth century and supplanting the feudal order which had disintegrated. With its central bureaucracy and standing army or navy, this modern state was indeed a new order. As it organized and directed ever larger masses of men, and encircled the globe in the empires of Spain, France, and Britain, the new state again embodied power of a magnitude never before experienced. The close-knit community of the town behind its walls crumbled, along with the independence of the nobility in their castles. And once again, as the ancient bulwarks of local pride and power sank into ruins, there was also a sense of utter helplessness in the face of such new might. Here, too, man was seized by a novel feeling of loneliness, of isolation and despair.

Some great styles are characterized by a profound polarity—an inner contradiction that springs from the experience upon which they are built. These are the styles of "open" form—the Gothic, the Romantic, as well as the Baroque. The experience of power on one hand and of utter lack of it on the other, of potency and impotence, was at the core of man's new attitude to the world around him. Artists and writers, musicians and philosophers sought to express it. Was there ever a more power-haunted face than the portrait Frans Hals painted of René Descartes? Was ever a more dramatic paean sung to power than the challenge Satan issues to God in Milton's *Paradise Lost?* One philosopher whose life spans the

Baroque age as if he were to be its symbol is Thomas Hobbes. Born in 1588, not long after the completion of the pioneer Baroque church of Il Gesù in Rome, he lived until 1679, brooding over man's life as "a restless desire for power after power that ceases only in death."

But the drama of power and of man's despair in striving for power is not the complete story. It is merely the Baroque's vital center. Around it are grouped the fantastic possibilities which artists, scientists, and men of politics discovered when "attempting the impossible." This fascination with power and the despair over man's impotence created Baroque man's deep concern with death and the dreamlike quality of life. Shakespeare, in the Baroque mood of his late work *The Tempest*, calls the world a stage, as does the utterly Baroque Spaniard, Calderón. So strong was the era's feeling for the delusive, theatrical nature of man's existence that the great men of the age had themselves portrayed as players of dramatic roles. The large paintings of Richelieu by Champaigne and of Olivares by Velázquez testify to this sense of ever-present drama. It is no wonder that the wig was in fashion in the seventeenth century. Although originally merely a device for hiding Louis XIII's baldness, the wig spread very fast among people who saw themselves as actors in the *Theatrum Mundi*—the title of a seventeenth-century Who's Who and Encyclopedia rolled into one.

There was, however, one escape from the tension between power and despair. The Baroque age shares with the Gothic age the distinction of having produced Christianity's deepest mystics. In Spain, in France, in Germany, in England, everywhere, people confronted with the finite in man and the infinity of spirit and cosmos sought refuge in relinquishing completely the cares of this world. Saint Theresa and John of the Cross in Spain, François de Sales and Pascal in France, Angelus Silesius and Jakob Boehme in Germany, John Donne, Sir Thomas Browne, and John Bunyan in England—these are only the most remarkable among a host of spiritual thinkers and doers. The mysterious figure of Richelieu's *"éminence grise,"* Père Joseph, a mystic and yet a devoted servant of the ruthless struggle for power, was the very Baroque link between the two worlds of the mystic and the statesman.

Two symbolic figures recur in Baroque literature and court ballet: the peacock and Circe. The peacock is the traditional symbol of vanity and display; Circe, of course, is the beautiful enchantress who transformed Ulysses' companions into pigs. The strutting and play-acting of Baroque man is peacocklike indeed. The way of the

women who lend color to the seventeenth century is feminine in
the old-fashioned sense: charming, deceitful, intriguing—and certainly capable of turning men into pigs. The great ladies of France,
from the Queen to the fabulous Duchesse de Chevreuse, spun their
plots, played with men and kingdoms. To this day, the parks of
the great castles which the Baroque age has left us are appropriately
inhabited by stately, preening peacocks. Circe and the peacock
figuratively greet us as we enter the Piazza Navona in Rome—
one of the high points of Baroque art, with its fountains by Bernini
and the façade of the church of Sant' Agnese by Borromini—and
beckon us to delve more deeply into the elated and yet tormented
souls that erected these masterworks.

There was a time when, stimulated by the Swiss-German art historian Heinrich Wölfflin, it was the fashion to assert that the
Baroque was the radical opposite of the Renaissance. Such a view
grew out of seeing the Baroque style as a corrupted Renaissance
style. Styles rarely stand in such antithesis to each other. They
evolve naturally out of each other and bear close resemblance,
particularly in periods of transition. It is easy to describe the
stylistic difference between Raphael and Rembrandt; it is not so
easy in the case of Correggio and Caravaggio. Raphael has clear,
contrasting colors and linear, sharply defined outlines presenting
separate and distinct figures or objects in harmonious relation,
whereas Rembrandt, especially in his late period, paints in chiaroscuro; thus browns, grays, and black, contrasted with yellow,
predominate, the outlines merge with the background, and typically
either *one* figure or a mass of figures composes one scene. To
heighten contrast, Rembrandt very often lets the light fall upon
the focal point of interest, while Raphael's pictures are so fully "in
the light" that the beholder is not really conscious of a source of
light at all.

But in any case, we cannot say of stylistic periods that one begins where the other ends. While the builders of Il Gesù were working, in the decade around 1575, on their novel design of what was
to be the first Baroque church, much building in clear Renaissance
style was going on all around them, and the great Palladio was
flourishing as the last crowning glory of Renaissance architecture.
The story of the Baroque, as of all styles, is the history of its spread
from a center, in successive waves that produced new and distinctive national and regional variations. Rome and Italy were for the
Baroque what the Ile-de-France was for the Gothic, the heart and
inspiration of a style that helped to shape all art and life through-   243

The psychological depth of Rembrandt's work, and his striking use of light, are exemplified in his canvas titled The Supper at Emmaus, *painted in 1629.*

out Europe to the end of the seventeenth century.

What, then, are the characteristic features of the Baroque style? Like all styles, it has no simple, single trait by which it can be characterized, but rather a cluster of them, grouped around antithetical poles. Like the experience of power from which it sprang, Baroque art is limitless; its protagonists attempt the "impossible." In their concentration on movement and force, they were great experimenters with untried forms and materials. Many interpreters have stressed the Baroque artists' preoccupation with time, as against space alone. It has been said that they gave even spatial relationships a temporal dimension. You can walk into Baroque paintings: they draw you into their landscapes with the distant views, the misty horizons, and setting suns beloved by Claude Lorrain, one of the greatest Baroque painters. It is the infinite which these horizons hint at; Lorrain, who at the same time was preoccupied with light, somehow succeeded in painting time. Of him, Goethe could say to Eckermann: "There is not a trace of reality in his pictures, but the highest truth. . . ."

In Baroque poetry, too, a sense of the passage of time and of the inexorable destruction it brings is very prominent. It dominates the work of such poets and writers as Góngora, Lope de Vega, and Calderón, the mature Shakespeare, Donne and Milton, Corneille, Grimmelshausen, and others too numerous to mention.

Was it an accident that a great American writer of our time should choose Donne's immortal words about the tolling of the bell as the title of one of his most moving novels? The symbol of the bell speaks of the passage of time, and of the death that comes to all. Indeed, in Donne's prose and poetry almost all the great themes of Baroque writing—from fleshly lust to the most mystic metaphysics—are intoned. Of Donne it has been said that he was "more medieval and more modern than the Renaissance." That is to say, he was Baroque. For, in a sense, the Baroque is the impossible effort to unite the spirit of the Gothic with that of the Renaissance in a new synthesis.

This concern with time and death caused the preoccupation with such symbols as the skull and the skeleton. "The men of the Baroque differed from those of other epochs . . . they liked an art that harps on death and corruption," Aldous Huxley has remarked. Yet at the same time they liked an art that was also sensual and profoundly worldly, such as that of Rubens. Baroque artists and writers were forever going to the extreme while probing the depth of human emotion.

*Examples of the Baroque spirit in opera and architecture. Above is the
set for the final scene in Marazzoli's "Il Trionfo della Pietá,"
performed in Rome for Sweden's Queen Christina in 1656. At right,
Fischer von Erlach's extravagant Karlskirche in Vienna, which
features a Pantheon-like dome and freestanding columns.*

But we are still speaking of *what* they did. Which forms did the
Baroque favor?

Baroque art found its richest fulfillment, it seems to me, in the
opera. It was this age which invented the form, Claudio Monteverdi's *Orfeo* (1607) having been called the first opera—although
Euridice by Peri and Caccini predated it by seven years. *Orfeo* was
followed by many others, among which Monteverdi's *The Coronation of Poppea* (1642) is outstanding. Written in the monodic style,
they are markedly different from what we today think of as opera,
as embodied in the work of Mozart, Verdi, and Wagner. But the
opera remains at its outset a Baroque creation, blending many
different arts into a harmonious whole—architecture with paint-

ing, sculpture, poetry, and music, not to speak of acting and the *grande toilette* of the ladies attending. The dramatic descriptions of great opera performances fill today's reader with nostalgia as he realizes that he can never hope really to relive the world of the Baroque in all its sumptuous, if fleeting, pomp and splendor.

That such a style should have given rise to much that was ugly and even horrible goes without saying. In trying to break all bounds and accomplish the impossible, the Baroque artist often achieved merely the ludicrous. This is particularly evident in certain extravaganzas of church architecture, in the gilded interiors of chateaux which were bad copies of Versailles, and in the more fearsome elaborations of Baroque poetry, especially in Italy. It is therefore rather easy to recite bad verses or to portray bad architecture as typical of the Baroque, and to forget the magnificent procession of superb achievements which the age produced.

In architecture, it brought forth the richly ornamented façade, the sweep of flowing staircases, the ornamental garden opening out toward a distant view. Reflect for a moment upon the staircase. The Renaissance sought to hide it, as did Jefferson with his classicist leanings. For the staircase suggests movement and, in doing so, portrays the flux of time. This dramatic feature of the staircase endeared it to Baroque architects who, without question, created the most beautiful staircases of the Western world, which nothing before or since can rival. As for façades and dramatic detail, there is such a wealth of Baroque marvels that one can hardly choose, but Saint Peter's Colonnade in Rome, Versailles and its many rivals, more especially the Bishop's Palace at Würzburg and the cloister churches of Wies, Vierzehnheiligen, and Melk, and finally, Saint Paul's at London are among the most outstanding. The names of the great architects of this era range from Bernini and Borromini through Mansart to Balthasar Neumann and Wren. To them one is tempted to add Michelangelo, the man who in some of his most remarkable work, like the Sistine Chapel, seems to transcend the Renaissance and herald the coming stylistic revolution.

In painting, the same dramatic preoccupation can be seen. Hard outlines and sharp color contrasts yield to the merging of object and background in chiaroscuro, and instead of the primary colors, the many-hued browns, grays, and greens become predominant in most Baroque masters, especially Rembrandt, Champaigne, and

The Baroque painters' goal of seizing and enlisting the viewer's emotions is inherent in this Crucifixion altar by Rubens (1620).

A quality of rich realism pervades the portraiture of Philippe de Champaigne; witness his study of Omer Talon at left. Another celebrated Baroque painter, the Frenchman Claude Lorrain, seemed intent on exploring the limits, or the limitlessness, of space in such canvasses as Landscape with Merchants *(above).*

Claude Lorrain. There are Baroque painters, such as Rubens, Poussin, and Velázquez, who only occasionally display the twilight shades; they achieve similar infinitudes by massive movement and dramatic posture as well as by the distant perspective. In the great landscape painters of the Low Countries, from Rubens to Ruysdael, the sky often becomes predominant. Again and again one feels the wind blowing, one is chilled by the fast-drifting clouds. In not a few paintings, a storm is raging: a drama of destruction that conveys the feeling of the passage of time. Torn and uprooted trees, abandoned ruins, and the driftwood of the seashore touch the same chord. And yet it is equally Baroque to descend to the common depth, to the lusty peasant, drinking and making merry, as portrayed by Teniers, or more gently by the Brothers Le Nain.

Closely connected with this sense of time and movement is the preoccupation with individuality in man and nature. Portraiture had been a key concern of the Occident for several centuries, but the earlier faces have a timeless quality of eternal youth or manhood. Baroque art produced its greatest masterworks in the portrayal of the old and the very young: Velázquez's children and Rembrandt's old men and women represent the pinnacle of this new way of seeing the human being in its temporal setting, where the now and here is merely a parable of what has been and is yet to come.

Theater and the drama, more especially the heroic tragedy, really came into their own during the Baroque period. Whether or not we should call Shakespeare "Baroque" may be argued, but the structure of his plays, bursting the bounds of established canons, is stylistically in line with Baroque conceptions; and in dramas like *King Lear* (1609), he surely attempts the "impossible" in the portrayal of human emotions. In any case, recent scholarship inclines to claim at least the Shakespeare of after 1606 for the Baroque—and certainly Lope de Vega, Calderón, and the host of other Spanish dramatists of the generations after 1570 are Baroque to the core. They in turn inspired Corneille, who in many ways founded the French theater. He was followed by Racine and Molière, and finally by Lully, the man who transformed Italian opera into something very French, even though he himself was an Italian.

French historians of literature and culture have only recently begun to acknowledge the intensely Baroque quality of their great classicists. Even now, the conventional view is that French classicism is something special unto itself, not only in literature but in architecture as well. And indeed it is. It is the French version of the Baroque. But classicism, rightly understood, is not a style, but a particular way of treating any style. Goethe, the classicist, was a leading figure of the Romantic age. Unquestionably, some styles, like that of the Renaissance, have a particular affinity with the worked-out rules of Greek art. But that is all. Let us take *Le Cid* of Corneille. It is a drama of honor, not only of Spanish honor but of French and universal honor; all other values must be sacrificed to this highest good. It challenges even the most sacred taboo of the age, the authority of the monarch. Throughout this drama, written

in rigid Alexandrine verse, there pulses an all-engulfing passion.
The work displays the unique power of formalized representation
of the emotions. To a later age such scenes as those between the
two lovers in *Le Cid* seem stilted and stagy, as indeed they are
compared with Shakespeare's. But this view fails to appreciate the
cult of form, which achieved its greatest triumphs in the classicist
versions of the Baroque.

Yet form dissolves amid the favorite theme of life's illusion. It
appears frequently in Shakespeare, but perhaps the most perfect
Baroque creation embodying it is Calderón's *La Vida Es Sueño*
(*Life Is a Dream*). Here we find the parallel to Hamlet's "To be or
not to be": "*Que toda la vida es sueño; Y los sueños, sueños son*"
(that,all life is a dream, and the dreams are dreams as well).

The clear, sharply defined surfaces of Renaissance bodies melt
into the twilight of ever-changing, illusory shadows: "What is
life? Frenzy! What is life? An illusion, a shadow, a fiction!" The
spaces of church interiors, once luminous and sharply defined, become ever more complex and agitated—the walls seem to vanish as
they become more wavy and curving, and the ceilings rise and soar
into the infinite as the great Baroque painters provide ever more
distant vistas of heaven and of God Almighty. It is a world of
beauteous sheen, of semblances and the effervescent foam of passing forms.

Of all the means of expression which man has developed to give
vent to his feelings in beautiful and communicable form, music is
the most inward, and at the same time the most intensely emo-
tional. It is also usually the last to achieve stylistic fulfillment in
any given age. The greatest musicians of the Baroque—Bach,
Handel, and Vivaldi—all belong to the end of the seventeenth and
the first half of the eighteenth century. The work of these towering
geniuses has until recently made music lovers forget the magnificent achievements with which Baroque music was ushered in by
Gabrieli, Monteverdi, and the other exponents of the *stilo nuovo*.

It was these extraordinary Italians of the early seventeenth century who abandoned the formal approach of Renaissance music, as
it had been written by Palestrina and Sweelinck, for the more expressive monodic style which animates their operas and oratorios
and the vast body of organ music written by such masters as
Frescobaldi, Gesualdo, and Carissimi. It is also the Baroque that
brings the full flowering of instrumental music, in many ways the
most unique cultural achievement of the West. And among all the
instruments invented and perfected in this musical age, the organ

was the most important. The organ, with its infinite variety of voices and moods, embodies the Baroque spirit at its best and most creative. Only recently has the superiority of these great instruments with their vast tonal potentialities been appreciated again, and the early art of organ-building been restudied and revived. The D minor Toccata and Fugue of Bach has rightly been proclaimed the pinnacle of organ form, building as it does an infinite range of musical expression out of the simplest elements.

But the organ was only the most mighty of the instruments that the Baroque age perfected. The unique achievement of Bach was his exploration of the furthest potentialities of all instruments, keyboard and string. One loves the great Italians from Frescobaldi to Vivaldi and Scarlatti; yet it was Bach who composed, especially in his solo suites, what was destined to become "the final page," so to speak, for each instrument. In his Brandenburg concertos he also achieved the ultimate in polyphonic wealth of contrast of instruments, although his highest accomplishment remains the combination of these instruments with the human voice, both singly and in choral masses, in his great Passions. Only the *Messiah* of Handel can be compared to them. Yet it is too often forgotten that Bach in these works, too, was a master at perfecting what others had begun. Of one of these early oratorios, written in 1628 by Orazio Benevoli, it has been said that it is "as if Bernini's Spanish staircase and his gigantic colonnades before St. Peter's had been transformed into music."

In contemplating the six generations from 1570 to 1750 who lived and created the Baroque style in the arts, music, and letters, one always goes back to the historical setting. At the beginning of the age, men could and did still believe that the medieval world might be revived. The Counter Reformation, no less than the political ambitions of the house of Hapsburg, suggested the possibility of re-establishing the unity of Christendom. By the end of the seventeenth century, all this world was dead. The Holy Roman Empire had been declared a monstrosity by Grotius, one of the greatest jurists of the day, and the Church had ceased to be a primary factor in European politics.

Long in the making, the modern state now became firmly and irrevocably established in Europe and, above all, in France, where Richelieu, Mazarin, and Louis XIV—three of the greatest actors who strutted across the stage of the *Theatrum Europaeum*—built the *Etat* which was to dominate Western thought until constitutionalism, spreading from England, triumphed in the nineteenth

century and foreshadowed the world of today. Three primary
events which filled the first half of the seventeenth century mark
this emergence: the Thirty Years' War (1618–1648), the victory of
France over Spain as the predominant power in Europe, and the
English revolution and civil war (1642–1660). Later, the successful turning back of the Turks and the entrance of Russia into the
European concert mark the end of the century. The emergence of
great powers follows the emergence of the modern state, and between them they provide the political setting for this marvelous
age. Throughout runs the obsessive struggle for power—the era's
libido dominandi, as the pale language of psychoanalysis calls it in
our day. John Milton's Satan was perhaps as striking a portrait of
Baroque man as any the age created: "aspiring / To set himself in
glory above his peers, / He trusted to have equalled the Most
High. . . ." Yet he was hurled to the depths, and at last he seems to
echo Shakespeare:

> "We are such stuff
> As dreams are made on, and our little life
> Is rounded with a sleep."

Even the Spanish historians of today tend to devote their attention and energy to the study of Spain's golden age, that is, to the sixteenth century when Spain, having discovered and conquered huge empires in the New World, employed the resources of those empires to make itself the leading power in Europe. Charles V, though Holy Roman Emperor, was first of all king of Spain and based his immense power on that country. But Spain's greatness was to prove ephemeral. Its decline was as rapid as its rise had been. The glorious victory of Lepanto (1571) was soon followed by the disaster of the Armada sent against England in 1588.

The author of Don Quixote *was a hero of the golden age who, on his return to Spain in 1580, found himself thrust into a new, deflated generation. As this essay so effectively argues, it was because he spanned the periods of greatness and of decline that Cervantes was able to make Don Quixote so plausible and sympathetic. Professor Trevor-Roper here pays tribute to one of the world's greatest writers and to his famous masterpiece.*

THE TWO SPAINS OF DON QUIXOTE

H. R. TREVOR-ROPER

The only good book in Spanish literature, said Montesquieu, is the one which proves all the others bad. He was referring, of course, to that incomparable, irresistible, unique work, *Don Quixote*, whose first part was published in 1605, and which, it is said, killed by ridicule the "romances of chivalry" that had been the staple literary diet of Spaniards for a century. Certainly they did not survive it. The most famous, most persistent of them all, *Amadis de Gaul*, was last reissued in 1602, three years before *Don Quixote* appeared; and thereafter, in America as in Spain, the whole literary genus was practically extinct. But whether *Don Quixote* really killed them, or merely appeared as their epitaph, is a difficult question, a question to be solved, if at all, rather in the field of social than of literary history. In this essay I wish to consider the social background to Don Quixote and seek in it, if possible, the key to its unique quality and marvelous success.

Don Quixote's disastrous tilt with the windmills, as portrayed by Gustave Doré. A despairing Sancho Panza surveys the scene.

Of course no masterpiece is completely explained by circumstances. By definition, a masterpiece proceeds from the human genius of its author, not from the material which he uses. But it is undeniable that Cervantes, though his work has transcended the age which it described, was—perhaps more than any other great writer—a child of his time. No other of his works has gained immortality. Only in this did his happy spirit attain perfection. And even in this he showed himself essentially a recorder, not (like Dickens or Tolstoy) a critic or reformer of his own age. A great Hispanist, A. Morel-Fatio, has called *Don Quixote* "the great social novel of early seventeenth-century Spain"; but he has added, "No writer has been more of his time than Cervantes; he is not ahead of it by one line." Therefore, in considering its character, we are justified in looking carefully at the material out of which it was made: the personal experience of Cervantes in sixteenth-century Spain.

First of all, what is the essential quality of *Don Quixote?* The plot of the book is soon told. Don Quixote is a middle-aged Castilian hidalgo—that is, a poor but proud rustic gentleman—who for many years has lived in his decrepit manor house in La Mancha, a seedy, remote province of Spain, alone with his niece and his old housekeeper, reading "romances of chivalry." Of these romances of chivalry we shall have something to say in a moment: at present it is enough to say that the constant reading of them has, by the beginning of the story, unhinged Don Quixote's mind, and so he sets out, with his equally decrepit and equally engaging horse Rozinante, in order that he too may seek similar adventures, opposing giants, rescuing damsels from dragons and enchanters, and challenging rival knights-errant to single combat to prove the superior beauty of their respective ladies. For such a purpose Don Quixote needs a lady, and so he idealizes, as the Lady Dulcinea del Toboso, a local farmer's daughter. He also, like all knights-errant, needs a trusty squire. For this function he impresses a devoted but hard-headed, earth-bound local peasant, the perfect foil to his own high, chivalric fantasies, Sancho Panza.

Once the dramatis personae are assembled, the action seems almost automatic. Don Quixote and Sancho Panza set out: the former boldly, with all his bees buzzing in his exalted bonnet, and the latter reluctantly, awed by his master's high language, but thinking primarily of incidental cakes and ale and ultimate material reward. To Don Quixote the real world hardly exists. To him inns are castles, innkeepers their constables, windmills giants, flocks of sheep rival armies, funeral processions troops of en-

258

chanters carrying off their spellbound victims; and whenever these majestic misconceptions painfully conflict with the real world, he explains the real world away with yet more ingenious rationalizations. But to Sancho Panza, though he takes his master's theories on trust, there is ultimately only one real world, and that is the world which he has left behind in his village, exchanging it not for ideal adventures but, as he discovers, for solid bumps and bruises, the price to him of his master's chivalry.

Don Quixote and Sancho Panza are inseparable: they are the joint heroes of the book, and the book owes its character to this constant duality. But it is not a crude duality. It may begin as such, but little by little, as we read on, we find that it becomes increasingly subtle. For the contrast is not really *between* the knight and his squire, it is *in* them both. Don Quixote may be mad when conversation is of knights and ladies, dwarfs and enchanters, but in other matters he has remarkable good sense, which breaks disconcertingly through his follies. Sancho Panza may be, at bottom, a hard-headed, prosaic peasant, but periodically he too is carried away into the world of fantasy, fitting himself into his master's world and imagining himself rewarded with the government of an island. To the firm overtones there are always subtle undertones: the whole world of Cervantes is schizophrenic, and the men in his novel merely participate, in differing degrees, in both the reality and the make-believe.

Consider their attitude toward the books of chivalry, the clearly convicted source of all the make-believe. At first it seems that Don Quixote alone takes seriously what other men regard merely as foolish novelettes. But soon we realize that this is not so. Everyone may agree that these "lying histories" are pernicious works which have made the poor knight mad; but everyone, it transpires, is as deep in them as he, and perhaps just as affected by them, though in other ways. When Don Quixote has set off on his adventures, there is dismay in his home, and his housekeeper and his niece, together with the barber and the curate, as pillars of sanity, resolve to burn all the wicked books that have disordered his mind. But what is the result? As each book is identified, they all remember it, discuss its merits, argue about its fate; and half of them are ultimately saved from the burning.

Later, when the same barber and curate pursue Don Quixote to the inn in the Sierra Morena, which is the theater of his follies, they explain to the innkeeper the origin of his madness, only to discover that the innkeeper, his housekeeper, his daughter, and his maid are all passionate readers of such romances: How then, they exclaim, can such delightful reading, which keeps them alive, make anyone mad? Later still, when the curate and the barber bring Don Quixote back to his village in a cage on an oxcart—a wonderfully comic episode—they are overtaken by a canon of the Church, whom Don Quixote gravely informs that he has been bewitched and encaged by jealous enchanters. Having then heard the true story from his escort, the canon expresses indignation against those pernicious books which the Church has constantly but ineffectively condemned. But as the conversation proceeds, we soon discover that the same indignant canon has not only read as many of these pernicious books as Don Quixote but has even written one as well. And so it is with everyone: goatherds and plowmen, dukes and duchesses, all are as deeply involved as Don Quixote—whom they presume to think mad—in the same ever-expanding world of make-believe.

For as the book progresses, so does the world of make-believe. The barber and the curate, who set out to cure Don Quixote's follies, end by becoming participants in it, actors in his imaginary history. Sancho Panza starts talking his master's language. The Duke and Duchess, who receive the pair, adjust their whole dukedom to his follies, so that Don Quixote is no longer any madder than his surroundings, and Sancho, with perfect gravity, gives laws to his imaginary island. Well might a bystander cry out, on seeing our hero, "The Devil take thee for Don Quixote of La Mancha! Thou art a madman; and wert thou so in private, 'twere less evil; but thy property is to make all that converse or treat with thee madmen and coxcombs!" Finally, by an exquisite piece of fancy, Don Quixote himself becomes the champion of truth against falsehood. For in 1614, nine years after its publication, the success of Cervantes's first part had prompted a rival novelist to publish a continuation of the story. Cervantes was indignant at this plagiarism, and in his own second part, which appeared the following year, he showed Don Quixote, now made famous by the first part, continually meeting and confuting the misguided readers of "the false second part." Thus the genuine first part and the false second part of the story become additional elements in its last phase, complicating still further the delicious and now inextricable confusion of reality and make-believe.

Such, very briefly, is the character of this incomparable work. I have described it as a "schizophrenic" book because of the duality of heroism and disillusion, make-believe and reality, which so completely pervades it. It is this duality which makes the book, sustaining and animating it throughout its great length—indeed, so animating it that Dr. Johnson could describe it as the only book which one wishes were longer. And it does so because the duality is genuine. Cervantes himself, we feel, is schizophrenic; he is on both sides at once: on the side of Don Quixote and on the side of Sancho Panza. The duality, in fact, is in his own mind, and—since he is so completely "of his time"—in the society in which he lived, late sixteenth- and early seventeenth-century Spain.

In what sense was Spain, in those years, schizophrenic? If we look at it closely, I believe we can find an answer. In Cervantes's lifetime, Spain had two very different moods. They were the moods of two successive but antithetical generations. The generation of the fathers was bound together by one set of experiences which created one kind of mood, a mood of fantastic confidence, heroic tension, intoxicating romance. The generation of the sons had different experiences, and consequently a different mood. Immune from their fathers' experiences, they knew only defeat, disappointment, disillusion; and their mood was one of cynical realism, passivity, emptiness. Now the life of Cervantes straddled both these generations, and in his own person he experienced, directly, both the heroism of the fathers and the disillusion of the sons. In his book, which is in some ways an autobiography, or at least a self-portrait, he expressed—sympathetically, because he had left them both—the two mutually opposing moods, moods which met in his lifetime and, particularly, in him.

Let us look at these two generations, so close in time, so opposite in character. First, let us take the generation of the fathers, the men who grew up during the reign of Charles V, "the Emperor"; for he was Holy Roman Emperor while king of Spain. Under the Emperor, Spain found itself suddenly a world power. Not long before, it had been a poor, rural appendix at the back end of Europe; now its armies fought and conquered on the Rhine and the Danube, in Italy and Africa, against German heretics and Turkish infidels. Spanish adventurers were conquering huge empires (and huge estates for themselves) in new-found America; and the wealth of America, spent on armies, fleets, and the imperial court, sustained and inflated an archaic feudal society, with chivalric notions imported from the magnificent Burgundy of Froissart and Comines.

It was an astonishing change, astonishing in its suddenness, comparable with the great Arab conquests of the seventh and eighth centuries; and the Spaniards who witnessed or achieved it

Few works have inspired as many varied artistic interpretations as *Don Quixote. Above is Daumier's sketch of the gaunt knight on his shambling horse, trailed by Sancho. On the opposite page, a woodcut by the American Antonio Frasconi depicts the Don charging a windmill under a spectacular sun and star. In a Japanese view below, the samurai-like knight braves a tigerish lion in its den.*

were inspired by a sense of divine mission and superhuman power. God was behind them, they felt, and nothing beyond them. They flinched before no obstacle, accepted no authority except that of their own king. Even the Pope received scant respect from them: when he was tiresome, the imperial court, inspired by the exciting, liberal doctrines of Erasmus, did not hesitate to strike at him, and the imperial armies seized and sacked the Holy City itself. Only the Emperor himself commanded unconditional respect; and he commanded it the more because, from a foreigner, a Fleming who knew no Spanish, he had become a Spaniard: *"esta figura tan española!"* ("this truly Spanish figure!") as a great historian has called him, who refused, even to the Pope's ambassador, to speak any language but the Spanish which he had lately learned.

It was this mood of exaltation in the time of the Emperor which found its popular expression in the famous "romances of chivalry." Throughout the sixteenth century, but particularly in the Emperor's reign, they were the best sellers of Spain, the equivalent of our "science fiction"; for though absurd in content, they symbolized a boundless new confidence which found nothing impossible. The adventures of Amadis de Gaul, Policisne de Boecia, Palmerin de Oliva, and their descendants were published and republished in serial form—scholars have counted 316 editions in the sixteenth century—and there is scarcely a famous Spaniard of "the golden century" who was not an avowed or secret reader of them: for the condemnation of the Church was powerless to suppress them. Wounded at Pamplona, the young Ignatius of Loyola spent his convalescence reading them, and when he became a missionary saint, his activities read like one of them: he became a knight-errant of religion. Saint Teresa of Avila confesses that in her youth she was never happy unless she was secretly reading them.

The Emperor himself, ignoring the protests of his clergy, was a constant reader and even wrote a sequel to one of them. They were the favorite reading of his soldiers in Italy. In spite of an official ban they poured into the Indies. When the companions of Cortes looked for the first time on the lake of Mexico, studded with Aztec cities, "we were amazed," says one of them, "and said that it was like the enchanted things related in the book of Amadis de Gaul." The passion of the Spanish soldiers in America for these "lying histories" has left its traces today: California in the Northern Hemisphere, Patagonia in the Southern, are both named after heroines of these trashy novelettes.

Charles V abdicated the Spanish throne in 1556, retiring (with two books of chivalry in his luggage) to the monastery of Yuste, and three years later his son and successor, Philip II, came to Spain. Later historians have seen Philip II as a great ruler, but it is worth noting that this respect for the uniformly unsuccessful bureaucrat-king did not begin until the reign of his grandson, when few could remember him. To contemporaries he was a poor figure, mean, jealous, and suspicious. In his reign the old liberalism of Charles V was finally crushed, the last of the old "Erasmians" burnt; the Empire was frayed at its edges and rotted at its core. But this decline was not at first apparent. For a decade, at least, after 1560, the heirs of Charles V kept his spirit alive. Particularly it lived on in Italy, away from the stuffy bigotry and waspish intrigues of the new court. There all eyes looked south and east to the great crusade which Charles V had conducted from Italy, the defense of the Mediterranean against the Turk. In 1571 the dead Emperor seemed to live again when his bastard son, Don John of Austria, of whom his legitimate son was so jealous, won a resounding naval victory at Lepanto (for which the church bells were rung even in Protestant England) and went on to occupy Tunis, ending forever the Turkish domination of the Mediterranean.

But if Lepanto echoed the imperial age, it was the last echo. In the 1570's Don John was undermined by his royal brother and died, and meanwhile Spain itself was being slowly ruined by a gigantic, ill-conceived, desk-dictated policy of religious and political reaction in northern Europe. By 1590 the new generation had grown up: a generation with no memory of the imperial days and their buoyant mood. Instead it had experienced only disillusion and defeat. For the last twenty years it had seen Spain mobilizing massive efforts which only disintegrated in humiliating disaster and squalid recrimination. All the wealth of America had been poured out in vain. The long revolt in the Netherlands was still unquenched. The Invincible Armada had been shattered. The attempt to conquer France had failed. In the years that followed, the disasters pressed nearer home. In the 1590's there was both plague and famine in Spain. The Crown was bankrupt, the nation impoverished. The political and military scandals were great and public. In 1596 an English force, under Queen Elizabeth's Earl of Essex, actually landed in Spain and seized and sacked its greatest port, Cádiz. Two years later, after a long and terrible illness, as slow and agonizing as his reign, Philip II died, and with his son, Philip III, was enthroned the new spirit of Spain—the spirit of cynicism and disillusion, the negation of all heroism, the cult not of religious crusades but of passive, superstitious piety.

The contrast between the new spirit and the old is remarkable. Wherever we look, it is there. In politics a wooden defensiveness replaces adventure; in literature satire replaces bombast. Social values are different: the old aristocracy had been military leaders; the new give themselves up to the giddy pursuit of official status and expensive pleasure. And religion reflects the same change. In the sixteenth century the Spanish Church had been active, crusading, missionary: its heroes had been Las Casas, Loyola, Saint Teresa; in the seventeenth, it is dull and passive: its only great figure is Molinos, the founder, appropriately, of religious quietism.

Perhaps the most striking illustration of this new spirit is the sudden change which took place, early in the seventeenth century, in the patron saint of Spain. For centuries that saint had been *Santiago*—Saint James, who was reputed to have come to Spain, and who was there transformed into a fighting saint, the patron of holy war. He was known as *Santiago Matamoros*, "Santiago, the killer of Moors." All through the Middle Ages, Santiago inspired Spanish Christians fighting against the infidel. Again and again, in the critical moment of battles, he appeared to them, mounted on a white horse in the sky, to give them fresh courage and turn defeat into victory. In America, too, fighting far from home against overwhelming odds, the conquistadors often saw Santiago, sometimes alone on his white horse, sometimes at the head of an ethereal army, doing battle for them in the clouds. More than two hundred places in Latin America still commemorate his name. But then, quite suddenly, in Spain and America alike, his authenticity was challenged. The doubters—Cervantes himself among them—raised their voices; there was a brief struggle, conducted in full legal form; and in 1617, Santiago, the saint of crusade and victory, collapsed. He was replaced, in Spain, by Saint Teresa of Avila—or rather by an imaginary Saint Teresa, not the real saint, that "gad-about nun," social, energetic, practical; but a gaping *beata*, as we see her in Bernini's effigy, the personification of passive, inexhaustible female credulity. In America, having appeared at least ten times in the sixteenth century, Santiago showed himself only once in the seventeenth and then disappeared. He was replaced in Mexico by the creole San Felipe de Jesús, in Peru by another female *beata*, the half-caste Santa Rosa de Lima. This sudden change of saints symbolizes a change in the whole religious character of Spain.

I have dwelt upon this sudden shift, in one generation of Spanish life, from heroic tension to empty disillusion, because it was the essential background to Cervantes's own life, the background to *Don Quixote*. Cervantes, in a sense, fell between the two generations, sharing the moods of both. Born in 1547, in the reign of Charles V, he was brought up in Spain by an old Erasmian teacher who still breathed the confident, liberal air of imperial times; and then, as a young man, he went to Italy and was intoxicated by the ebullience, the vitality of Italian life. He read Ariosto, the poet of gaiety, chivalry, and enchanted romance. He enlisted as a soldier, fought and was wounded in Don John's great, victorious battle of Lepanto, served in the campaign against Tunis and Goletta, and in 1575 set sail, full of honor and pride, and with letters of recommendation from Don John and the Spanish governor in his pocket, for Spain, promotion, and further glory. He was a hero, a self-conscious hero, living fully and investing heavily in that (as he was to discover) last twilight of the heroic age. Nor did his heroism end there. On his way home, off the coast of France, his ship was captured by Algerian corsairs. Seeing his letters of recommendation, the pirates presumed him to be a man of mark who would command a high ransom. Cervantes was taken to Algiers and there remained for more than five years, a prisoner and a galley slave.

266 In his captivity at Algiers, Cervantes continued his heroic ex-

ploits. He never forgot them. Long afterward, in *Don Quixote*, he recalled them. There, a captive, escaped from the Moorish galleys, meets Don Quixote and tells the story of his captivity. In it he refers to a fellow captive "called something-de-Saavedra" (Cervantes's full name was Miguel de Cervantes Saavedra), who achieved such a personal ascendancy over the Moorish governor that although "we all feared that he should be broached on the stake for the least of many things he did . . . yet he never struck him nor commanded him to be stricken, nor said as much as an evil word to him." Cervantes's own account is borne out by a contemporary who, in a history of Algiers written before *Don Quixote* had made its author famous, tells us that "of the captivity and brave deeds of Miguel de Cervantes one could write a whole history. Four times he narrowly avoided death by impaling, hanging, or burning for having set fellow captives free. And if fortune had aided his courage and ingenuity, Algiers would be in Christian hands today, for he aimed at no less." And indeed, while still a captive, Cervantes wrote to King Philip's secretary urging the conquest of Algiers. If only he were ransomed, he wrote, he would throw himself at the King's feet and say, "Great monarch, you who have enslaved a thousand barbarian peoples, who receive tribute even from the blacks of India, how can you tolerate the resistance of a miserable hovel? Ah, could you but complete the work begun by your valiant father!"

"Your valiant father"—always, in his heroic dreams, Cervantes, like other Spaniards, looks back to the Emperor Charles V. Later, in the preface which he wrote for his collected short stories, he gave a brief autobiographical sketch of himself, which compresses into two sentences his cult of heroism, his pride in his own heroic life, and his veneration for the Emperor. The author of these stories, he says, "was a soldier for many years, and a captive for five and a half years, and so learned patience in adversity. He lost his left hand from an arquebus-shot at the sea fight of Lepanto: an ugly wound, which, however, he thought comely because he had received it in the greatest, most memorable event that the past has seen or the future may hope to see, fighting under the triumphant banners of [Don John of Austria] the son of that thunderbolt of war, Charles V of happy memory."

Such was the Cervantes who, in 1580, returned from captivity to the Spain of Philip II. We can recognize him perfectly: he is a true, if somewhat belated, representative of the first of our two generations, the heroic, romantic, chivalrous generation of Charles

V. But when he returned to Spain, what did he find? Already, while he had been breathing the heady air of Italy, fighting at Lepanto, braving his infidel captors in Algiers, the new generation was taking over in Spain, and now, instead of a grateful hero-king promoting him, accepting his advice, and leading an enthusiastic people into new crusades, he found only an atmosphere of growing weariness and disillusion. Year after year Cervantes struggled to make a livelihood, first by poetry, then as a government purchaser, finally as a tax collector. None of these callings prospered. Economically—though not in spirit, for he retained, in every hardship, his own inexhaustible optimism—he sank down and down: bankrupt for small sums, excommunicated for trying to tax the clergy, finally imprisoned. In 1596, the year of the sack of Cádiz, he reached his lowest ebb, and wrote a wry, sardonic poem on that national humiliation. Two years later the death of Philip II drew from him an even more sardonic epitaph. Clearly the days of heroism were over: the days of disillusion had come. It was in those years of lowest ebb that Cervantes, in prison, conceived the idea of Don Quixote, the hero, the reader of romances, the Erasmian (for *Don Quixote* has many sly "Erasmian" touches which were duly pounced on by the Inquisition), who discovered that the real world—the world of narrow, materialist common sense—thought him mad.

For of course Don Quixote is Cervantes. This is well pointed out by one of the most perceptive writers on Spanish literature, Gerald Brenan. "I think we ought to take note," he says, "that the famous knight had many features in common with his creator. We learn, for example, that Don Quixote was of the same age as Cervantes when he set out on his adventures, and that he had the same physical appearance: we read of his wits being dry and sterile and his head turned by too much reading, just as we are told in the preface that his author's were. Moreover, he was the incorrigible optimist and idealist who set out to reform the world by force of arms and instead was beaten by it. Must not this, or something like it, have been Cervantes's view of his own history? . . . I suggest therefore that one of the sources of Don Quixote's power to move us comes from his being a projection of a discarded part of Cervantes himself: that is to say, of the noble intentions and failure of his life. It is for this reason that the irony in this most ironical of books has often the deep and searching quality of self-irony."

No doubt it is self-irony, but also it is a delicate self-irony: that is why it is so attractive, why it makes so great a book. When a man makes steppingstones of his dead selves, he is very likely (as Samuel Butler once wrote) to jump upon them to some tune. But Cervantes did not jump. If he is disillusioned, there is nothing vindictive or cynical about his disillusion. How could there be, when half of his own life had been invested in those illusions which he now found himself, with all Spain, forced to mock? A generation would come which had made no such investment and which could afford to be severe against the fantasies of the past. But Cervantes could not, for he had a foot in either world. And so he wrote essentially not for the future (though the eighteenth century would rediscover him and set him among the immortals), but for his own generation, the generation of the disillusioned, which could yet regret its illusions: for they were its own.

*One reads of the greatness of the Dutch Republic only with amazement,
not to say incredulity. How this small, none-too-well endowed corner
of Europe should, for more than a century, have attained such wealth,
such eminence in almost every field of human endeavor, will forever
remain something of a mystery. The long struggle against Spanish
rule, inspired by religion, seems to have released energies that then
found expression in commerce, literature, and the arts, achievements
immortalized by the great Dutch genre painters as few other phases
of European culture have been recorded. Yet the period of Dutch
greatness was relatively short, coincident with the decline of Spain,
the religious conflicts in France, the civil strife in England, and the
Thirty Years' War in central Europe. It remains, then, as one of
the bright spots in the history of European achievement, brilliantly
reviewed by one of the leading historians of the seventeenth century.*

THE GOLDEN AGE OF THE DUTCH REPUBLIC

C. V. WEDGWOOD

On a narrow, low-lying strip of coastal country in northern
Europe, scarcely two hundred miles long—a country so water-
logged that enemies and rivals spoke of it as a mud flat—there
arose in the seventeenth century one of the great civilizations of
the world. The Golden Age of the Dutch Republic stands out as
one of the most comprehensive, most astonishing, and most admirable achievements of mankind, a monument alike to human
industry and the human spirit.

From this little country, with its windy sand dunes and its damp
pastures, ships went out to sail the farthest seas. On the mud flats
large, solid, prosperous cities came into being. Their quays received the goods of all the world, which their merchants exchanged
and distributed again to all the world. Their great banking houses
financed the sovereigns of Europe. Thanks to its geographical position and the enterprise and energy of its people, the Dutch Republic was—only two generations after its founding—the richest commercial community Europe had yet seen.

*This unknown officer, portrayed by Frans Hals, typifies the sturdy
citizen-soldiers who maintained the Dutch Republic's independence.*   271

Such a civilization, built on trade and industry, on hard work and financial acumen, might have been wholly materialist in all its manifestations. The Golden Age of the Dutch Republic might have been a golden age only in the narrowest and hardest sense. It was not so. The mercantile people, with their code of self-reliance and hard work, of enterprise, courage, and good craftsmanship, gave much more to the world than mere material gain. Scientists, thinkers, and poets flourished among them. The works of their great painters, luminous, tranquil, and profound, shine out among us still. Spiritual and material greatness were deeply, inextricably interwoven in the great achievement of the Dutch.

No precise bounds can be set to the epoch of their glory, but the generation from 1625 to 1648, during which Frederick Henry, Prince of Orange, guided their affairs, is usually taken as the high noon of the Golden Age. Rembrandt was painting, Frans Hals was at the height of his powers, Hugo Grotius was laying down the foundations of international law, Vondel was composing his great poetic dramas, Abel Tasman was exploring the far Pacific, and the great Dutch admirals Piet Heyn and Martin Tromp were sweeping the Spaniards off the seas. But this golden summer had already been preceded by a wonderfully promising spring and was to be followed by a fruitful autumn. The last of the harvest was not gathered until the end of the century.

The political story of the free and independent Dutch had begun a hundred years earlier. The Netherlands had come by a series of dynastic marriages to form a part of the great Hapsburg dominions, and in 1555 they were assigned to King Philip II of Spain as his share in the family inheritance. At that time the Reformation had shaken and divided Europe, and Philip II saw it as his mission to reunite Europe within the fold of the Roman Catholic Church under the dominating influence of Spain. The Netherlands were to play an important part in his design, partly because of their strategic position at the mouth of the Rhine and opposite the English coast, and partly because of the great wealth of the southern Netherlands with their prosperous trading cities and their great port of Antwerp.

It was unfortunate for Philip's projects that the Protestant religion in various forms had already penetrated into the Netherlands. His attempts to stamp it out, combined with an interfering economic policy, brought the country to the verge of revolt. At this, in 1567, he sent the Duke of Alva to impose an iron military rule on the recalcitrant people. But the Netherlanders found a leader

in one of their noblemen, the Prince of Orange, William of Nassau
—or William the Silent as he came to be called. Organizing a rebellion with heroic tenacity and against fearful odds, he succeeded in dislodging the Spaniards from the northern half of the country. He had hoped to liberate and to hold united the whole of the Netherlands, but after his assassination in 1584 it became clear that the rich southern provinces, which were Catholic in sympathy, would remain with Spain, while the northern regions alone would form the new and independent Dutch Republic.

Gradually this small new nation was recognized by surrounding European powers. It was a federated republic governed by elected representatives, although two sons of William the Silent in turn held the highest offices in the state, both civil and military. Prince Maurice, the elder son, was a soldier of formidable intelligence who fought the Spaniards to a standstill and made a twelve years' truce with them in 1609. He died in 1625, shortly after the resumption of the war. The rule of his brother Frederick Henry, which was later to be so fruitful and so glorious, began inauspiciously with the loss of the border fortress of Breda.

The capture of Breda was the last significant Spanish victory over the Dutch. Frederick Henry, the new Dutch leader, was not a military genius like his elder brother, but he had great tenacity and great patience, and he had inherited from his famous father, William the Silent, an inspiring capacity for remaining calm in the face of disaster. As a statesman he was to show himself, at least during his first and best years, just, tolerant, and wise; in external politics he was a persuasive and often subtle diplomat. He did not cause the Golden Age of Holland, but it is impossible to imagine it without his generous and reassuring presence in the background. Under his leadership the Dutch soon re-established equilibrium in the war with Spain and pushed doggedly on to final victory at the Peace of Münster in 1648. During all these years Spain was visibly a declining power, while the young Dutch Republic went from strength to strength.

From the very outset of the war of liberation, sea power had been of the first importance to the Dutch. There were two reasons for this: first, they had to prevent the Spanish fleet from feeding the battle front in the southern Netherlands with sea-borne reinforcements of men and arms and money; secondly, they had to keep open the channels of trade into their own country. They had built their prosperity on overseas trade and in particular on the herring industry; their fisheries were the basis of a great commerce in salt fish, a universal part of diet in an age when there was no canned food.

The Dutch now extended their trading ventures with increasing boldness, fiercely competing with other nations. Thus, early in the seventeenth century, Sir Walter Raleigh warned the English that they were losing ground in the northern waters. "We had a great trade in Russia seventy years," he asserted, "and about fourteen years past we sent store of goodly ships to trade in those parts, and three years past we sent out but four and this last year two or three; but to the contrary the Hollanders about twenty years since traded thither with two ships only, yet now they are increased to about thirty or forty, and one of their ships is as great as two of ours."

Dutch expansion was not confined to northern seas. Their ships boldly entered the enclosed waters of the Mediterranean and established commercial contact with Constantinople. With splendid daring they challenged the power of Spain on remoter seas in the West Indies, and sent out expeditions to find a northeastern or a northwestern passage to the treasures of the East. The survivors of one such expedition led by Willem Barents in 1595 came back with fearful stories of an Arctic winter spent on Novaya Zemlya. Henry Hudson, the English leader of another Dutch expedition in search of a northwest passage, sailed up the unknown majestic river which now bears his name and anchored off Manhattan island where soon the Dutch settlement of New Amsterdam would arise. Dutch navigators scattered their names over the map of the world; Cape Horn was named by Willem Schouten, who rounded it in 1616, after the little Dutch town of Hoorn, where he had been born. Abel Tasman, who in 1642 established the fact that Australia was an island, is commemorated in the name of Tasmania. But the energy and ambition of Dutch traders centered on the East Indies.

In 1595 Cornelis de Houtman sailed for the East Indies, returning two and a half years later from Java, to set all the church bells in Amsterdam ringing for joy of his arrival, laden with the spices of the East. It was the beginning of the Dutch East Indian empire. In 1602 the Dutch East India Company was founded, which competed ruthlessly with its English rival. Java, with its capital at Batavia, became the center of Dutch power in the East. They drove their English rivals out of the Malay Archipelago; they thrust the Portuguese out of Ceylon; they made themselves a foothold in Formosa. In energy and daring, in single-minded enterprise, they had not their equals; and the small country far off in

Europe grew rich and confident as Dutch seamen and Dutch merchants took toll of the whole world.

The young, energetic people were proud of their mounting achievements. Books were written about them, pictures painted. The journeys of explorers were celebrated in poetry and carefully recorded in prose. The profit and glory of Dutch merchants was the perennial subject for painters, commissioned to paint portraits that were often set against the background of some Eastern scene, or showed in the distance some splendid ship unloading at the quay. The Dutch East Indiamen were the largest vessels afloat, palatial monsters of the high seas, armed against pirates and storms.

The English were rivals for the herring fisheries and competitors in the East Indian trade, but the Spaniards were still the principal enemy. Themselves a great seafaring nation and pioneers in exploration, it was long before they could bring themselves to realize that the Dutch had outdistanced them. But in 1628 Piet Heyn, veteran Dutch admiral and daring seaman, who had long harried the Spaniards in the West Indies, intercepted the Spanish treasure fleet off Cuba and destroyed it in the Bay of Matanzas. The booty that he brought home to Holland from the wrecked and captured Spanish vessels amounted in silver ore and goods to the value of eleven and a half million Dutch florins; its effect on the Netherlands' prosperity may be gathered from the fact that in that year the shareholders of the Dutch West India Company, which had financed Heyn's expedition, received a dividend of 50 per cent.

Such a loss, financial as well as naval, was crippling to Spain. Eleven years later, in 1639, the Dutch admiral Martin Tromp almost wholly destroyed, off the English coast, a Spanish fleet of seventy-seven vessels, an armada bringing troops and arms to prosecute the war in the Netherlands. From this second blow the staggering Spanish fortunes never recovered.

Dutch merchants consolidated the position prepared for them by Dutch explorers and Dutch admirals. In 1629 the burghers of Amsterdam declared with pride: "Through our economic management and exertions we have sailed all other nations off the seas, drawn almost all trade from other lands hither and served the whole of Europe with our ships." The statement was hardly an exaggeration. Besides their ancient trade in fish and their new expansion to the Indies, the Dutch had made themselves the intermediaries and the carriers for all Europe. The banks of Amsterdam now financed private and public enterprise far beyond the borders of Holland; the granaries of Amsterdam received corn brought from other countries in Dutch vessels and redistributed it through western Europe. Even the Spanish government had to turn a blind eye to the Dutch grain ships in their ports, without which people would have starved.

Once Antwerp in the Spanish Netherlands had been the financial center of the Western world and the greatest port in northern Europe. But Amsterdam took her trade and her pre-eminence from her. As early as 1619 an English traveler wrote, not without anxious envy, that Amsterdam, once a small fishing village, had "come in a short revolution of time by a monstrous increase of commerce and navigation to be one of the greatest marts in Europe."

The citizens of the young, expanding city behaved with unusual vision. Instead of leaving its growth to chance, they evolved in 1612 one of the earliest and most enlightened town-planning schemes in Europe. The expansion of Amsterdam has truly been called a "triumph of communal co-operation," for the scheme that was laid down by a highly intelligent committee was obediently put into effect by succeeding generations of citizens. The plan was in essence simple: a series of concentric canals, the three *Grachten*, were to contain the city. They were planned spaciously, like three great horseshoes one inside the other, and it was believed that allowance had been made for the utmost development of the city. In fact the plan fulfilled the needs of Amsterdam for over two hundred years, and few town planners in our own time would hope for better success.

Although Amsterdam towered in importance over all the Dutch cities, all shared in the prosperity of the age and each had its proper civic pride. With the change of religion, the ancient Gothic churches of the older towns had been strenuously cleared of "idolatrous" images, but the structures were carefully preserved. The severely whitewashed interiors of these lofty buildings have been recorded by many a painter of the seventeenth century, often with a black-gowned Calvinist preacher in the pulpit and a full congregation of burghers and their wives intently listening.

The buildings of ancient convents and monasteries were also usually preserved. Some of them were transformed into the residences of the rich, like the convent at Delft where William the Silent made his home. Others were used as civic buildings; still others were turned into orphanages or homes for the aged. The Dutch cities prided themselves on the orderly if sometimes rather authoritative benevolence that kept their streets free of beggars. The occasional appearance of a beggar in street scenes painted by

Dutch artists suggests that they were not quite uniformly successful, but we have the contemporary evidence of travelers that it was a rare thing to see a beggar among the Dutch—and this at a time when most great cities teemed with them.

Deserted and orphan children were brought together into institutions and carefully educated to be respectable citizens. Old and disabled soldiers were regularly pensioned—a system that scarcely existed in any other country at this time. The aged poor were gathered together and decently cared for in almshouses. Frans Hals, the great painter, who fell on evil days, spent much of his time in later years in one of these at Haarlem, which today houses a museum containing the last pictures that he painted, portrait groups of the governors of the almshouse.

From energy and industry had come great wealth, and the

Indoor scenes of gentle and quiet domesticity were a specialty with Pieter de Hooch. He titled this canvas The Bedroom.

Dutch merchants, both in their civic and their private lives, showed an orderly discrimination in the uses to which they put their money. Although three great noblemen, the Princes of Orange, remained for many years at the head of the state, and the small, exclusive group of Dutch nobility preserved their existence and their identity as a class, the whole tone of the young Republic was that of the mercantile middle class. It was their wealth and vigor, their aspirations and prejudices which gave force and direction to every part of the national life.

How came it that this civilization of hard-headed, hard-working merchants, adventurers, industrialists, dairy farmers, and seamen inspired great literature, great thought, and even greater painting? What made this mercantile society, in the words of the modern Dutch historian Pieter Geyl, "so abundant, so free, so receptive?" The secret lies, paradoxically almost, in the Dutch religion. The Calvinists had formed the spearhead of the revolt against Spain, and they remained dominant in the young Republic. Calvinism is not a religion that greatly encourages freedom of speculation or, for that matter, aesthetic sensibility. But these people had fought for freedom of conscience for themselves and were therefore committed to it. The Calvinist Dutch might bitterly disapprove of other religious doctrines; they might curtail the civil and political power of those who held them, but they could not deny them the right to worship and believe as they chose. Moreover, quite apart from the principle of religious liberty for which they had fought, the Dutch could not, for practical reasons, do without the industry and skill of the religious minorities. There remained always within the Republic a considerable Roman Catholic minority who had never changed their faith; there was, especially in Amsterdam, a large and growing Jewish community; and Protestant refugees of many different sects continuously flooded in from all parts of Europe. The work and co-operation of all these were needed by the young Republic, and the existence of so many different communities within a small country naturally stimulated the circulation of ideas.

Religious conflict was by no means at an end. There was constant jealousy and fear of the Roman Catholic minority, and there was from time to time harsh conflict between Protestant groups which broke out in violence. A bitter struggle during the years of truce with Spain had ended only when Prince Maurice made himself virtually—for a space—dictator. But this very friction stimulated the growth of ideas and generated new energy. Indeed the

278

extraordinary vitality of Dutch culture at this epoch may well
have been an outcome of the tension between the new and the old,
the experimental and the conventional.

A mercantile community, to be successful, as the Dutch so
transcendently were at this time, must encourage not only self-
reliance and industry among its members but also originality and
enterprise. No one can accuse the Dutch merchants of the Golden
Age of being hidebound or conventional in their business operations. Here they showed courage and imagination. In politics, in
religion, in the arts, they might be—and probably most of them
were—extremely conventional. But in such a society, where courage, originality, and enterprise are encouraged because of their
value in business, there will always be a considerable number of
men and women in whom these same valuable qualities will be directed to quite different ends—to scientific enquiry, to philosophic
speculation, to art or literature. Some of these may come into conflict with the community; others will find a way of being accepted.
A vigorous mercantile community can thus provide the artist and
the thinker with that mixture of encouragement and frustration, of
opposition and of stimulation, in which many talents flower. The
Renaissance culture of the Italian cities had had something of this
in it; the pattern can be detected in such great and prosperous societies as England in the nineteenth century or the United States
in the twentieth. It was evident in seventeenth-century Holland.

The contrast and the challenge is seen at its clearest in the world
of learning. One of the first acts of William the Silent had been the
foundation of the first Dutch university, at Leiden in 1575, when
only a small part of the country had been liberated and the war
was still in a critical stage. In the ensuing fifty years, provinces had
vied with each other in the encouragement of learning, and universities had been founded at Groningen, Utrecht, and Harderwijk.
These universities were seats of learning where a fine tradition of
scholarship was steadily built up, but they were often the scene of
violent disputes between traditional teaching and new ideas. At
Utrecht the theories of Galileo were vehemently opposed, as were
also those of the French scientist and philosopher Descartes. The
professor of medicine was required to teach only such doctrine as
had been laid down by the ancients. Doubts were felt as to whether
the theory that the blood circulated in the body, as the Englishman Harvey had recently argued, could be reconciled with the
Scriptures. As late as 1642 the Senate of Utrecht passed a resolution against the new scientific teaching which was making converts

among the younger professors. "It is contrary to the ancient philosophy which the universities of the whole world have thus far taught with wise deliberation," they said, and added a warning that "there may be deduced from it by inexperienced youth several false and preposterous notions which conflict with the other sciences and faculties and above all with the orthodox religion."

Yet the country whose academic teachers passed this resolution counted among its citizens some of the greatest pioneers of modern science. Anton van Leeuwenhoek, combining immense technical dexterity with concentrated powers of observation, first greatly improved the magnifying powers of the microscope and then used it to penetrate secrets of nature. He was the first to describe accurately blood corpuscles and to discern bacteria. His contemporary, Jan Swammerdam, who also, in a way which seems to have been peculiarly Dutch, combined great technical skill with an inquiring and patient observation, studied the anatomy of invertebrates and was the first fully to observe (and most delicately to illustrate) the transformation of insects. He watched and recorded the process by which a caterpillar becomes a butterfly and the frog emerges from the tadpole. But both these men were, in the modern sense, amateurs; they worked outside the universities, discussing their ideas with like-minded friends and exchanging discoveries and information with other interested experimenters in different walks of life.

In spite of some academic opposition, the atmosphere of educated Dutch society was sympathetic and stimulating to men with new ideas. Whatever the pundits of Utrecht might say, it was in the congenial atmosphere of Holland that the greatest of all the new philosophers, the Frenchman René Descartes, lived his happiest years and wrote his *Discours de la Methode*, long to be regarded as the foundation of modern philosophy.

In the field of political philosophy the Dutch themselves can claim Hugo Grotius as one of the greatest pioneers of modern thought. His epoch-making book *De Jure Belli et Pacis* laid the foundations of international law. But he wrote it in exile, in France. Here was an odd paradox, that the Dutch Republic, which gave asylum to religious refugees and men of learning from all over Europe, forced one of its greatest thinkers to seek safety outside its borders. It was not, however, on account of his opinions that Grotius fled the country, but because he was one of the victims involved in the political crisis at the end of Prince Maurice's rule.

Dutch literature of the seventeenth century reflects the same conflicting tendencies. This young independent people had a language and a way of thought very much their own. But their past history had made them also conscious of a position in western Europe; they could not sever the links that still bound them to the southern Spanish Netherlands from which they had so recently separated themselves. The culture of the south was the international culture of late Renaissance Europe: its greatest painter was Peter Paul Rubens, its poets and writers belonged to the wide and rich tradition common to such princely and aristocratic lands as France, Spain, and contemporary Italy. But in the Dutch Republic—geographically so near, politically so different—international influences and the strong individual flavor of the new mercantile republic was strangely and often attractively mingled.

The most famous poets of the time present a study in contrasts. There was Constantijn Huygens, a man of wide culture and learning, a diplomat well versed in European society, whose poems have all the mannered subtlety of the cultivated poets of the earlier seventeenth century in England, in France, in Germany, or in Spain. He admired and translated John Donne with a rare skill. A younger man, Joost van den Vondel, has often been compared to Milton, not merely because one of his greatest works was the poetic drama *Lucifer*. He managed, with a ravishing fluency, to capture in Dutch (which is not the easiest of languages for poetry) the subtlety and ripeness of baroque culture.

In sharp contrast is the work of Jacob Cats, who celebrated in anecdotal, didactic verse the domestic joys and duties, the morality and prejudices of contemporary Dutch civilization. His popular fame was, and remained, enormous; his works were, next to the Bible, the literature best known to the Dutch people for centuries. He was the people's poet par excellence and was familiarly thought of as "Father Cats." But he owed his permanent position in literature to more remarkable qualities. He illuminated his conventional opinions with much genuine wisdom and with an understanding of men and women, in the daily problems of life, which is both humorous and humane.

The most famous center of Dutch literary life during the Golden Age was the castle of Muiden on the Zuider Zee where Pieter Corneliszoon Hooft gathered about him a remarkable group of friends who, in the pleasant atmosphere of his country house, exchanged ideas, discussed each other's writings, made music, and followed the new theories and the new discoveries that seemed to flower almost daily in the brave new world. Hooft himself wrote a famous history of the recent wars with Spain, a work conceived in the classical manner and based on the style of Tacitus. The circle included also Constantijn Huygens; occasionally Joost van den Vondel; the famous scholar Gerard Vossius; Laurens Reaal, soldier, seaman, and poet; Samuel Coster, who was both a physician and a dramatist; and the two sister poetesses, both women of exceptional charm, Anna and Maria Visscher.

Women were not excluded from the culture of the Dutch Golden Age. Indeed they could hardly have been, for it is one of the characteristics of a hard-working mercantile society that the woman is expected to show energy, industry, and intelligence in the management of her household, and sometimes to take a part in her husband's business. Moreover, a seafaring people, whose menfolk are often absent for long periods, will naturally delegate responsibility to their women. There was, of course, no question of equality; it is clear from the poems of Cats (and indeed from the whole domestic morality of Calvinism) that the woman's place was one of obedience to the man, but it was none the less a recognized and valuable place. The Dutch woman was not brought up to be a voiceless drudge nor, in a higher class of society, to be merely decorative. She was brought up to be an intelligent and valued, if junior, partner in a man's world.

It was natural therefore that a few women at least should make their mark in the world of learning and the arts. The most famous of them was Anna Maria van Schuurman, who was famous rather for the multiplicity of her talents than for her supreme excellence in any one field. She was an artist of distinction, a linguist, scholar, and theologian, who corresponded with some of the most learned men of her time. Among the painters, the most famous was Judith Leyster, one of whose most striking pictures, *The Lute Player*, was for a long time thought to be the work of Frans Hals.

When we think of the Golden Age of the Dutch Republic we think above all of the great painters. A wonderful series of canvases from many different hands have recorded both the outward face and the inward spirit of that great epoch. Such landscape painters as Philips de Koninck, Jacob van Ruisdael, Jan van Goyen, and Aart van der Neer have recorded the physical appearance of their country at this time. We can see, in every detail, the farmsteads with their red-tiled roofs, the water mills and the windmills, the wide flat fields over which the windy clouds make moving patterns of sun and shade, the winding canals, the neat little towns with their towers and spires seen across pastures where cattle graze. We can see the people who inhabited these fields and towns about their everyday work and their holiday amusements. In the foreground of Ruisdael's *View of Haàrlem* they are bleaching great strips of linen cloth in the sunny fields; Aelbert Cuyp and Paul Potter preferred to show them pasturing their fine dairy cattle. Jan van Goyen shows them sailing their canals or putting their ships out to sea; Wouwerman, when he is not painting battle scenes, has caught the atmosphere of salt and sand and wind on the dunes as the fishermen bring in their catch; Avercamp, Adriaen van der Venne, and Aart van der Neer liked to show them during the winter, skating and sleighing on their frozen canals.

Other painters preferred indoor scenes. Thanks to them we know more of the Dutch middle classes in their everyday setting than of any other people at this period. Gerard Terborch captures the

The pleasures of an inn, by Jan Steen. Steen, himself an innkeeper, was unexcelled at recording the lusty exuberance of the Dutch.

moment of concentration as young people make music in a comfortable, well-appointed room; Pieter de Hooch has shown them in the small gardens of their town houses, playing at skittles or taking a glass of wine in the quiet mellow afternoon; or, moving within doors, he catches the vista from some shadowed, tile-floored room where two young people sedately sit along the sun-streaked corridor with a distant glimpse of a serving maid or some gay, peeping child. Jan Steen, equally at home in the fresh air or the congested interior, has shown roistering parties of country folk dancing in the courtyard of an inn, or enjoying the fun of the fair, or family parties celebrating a christening or perhaps the feast of Saint Nicholas in some four-square, cheerfully overcrowded room. Certain characters in his pictures come in again and again—the kindly Granny, the funny, ugly little girl, the naughty grimacing boy. These are surely his own family, seen with love and humor, and the rooms must be those of his own home, for when he was not a painter he was a jolly innkeeper.

These painters of popular scenes flourished in response to a demand for a new kind of picture. In earlier times and in other countries painters had worked for the Church, for princes, or for wealthy private patrons. They had painted great religious subjects for altarpieces or had decorated the walls of palaces. But, apart from portraits and occasional traveling altarpieces painted for diplomats and princes, the demand for smaller paintings, for easel paintings, had been light. But the new Dutch middle class wanted homely paintings to decorate the walls of their comfortable rooms. They wanted secular paintings because they were predominantly Protestant, and they valued above all lifelike representations of their countryside, their domestic life, and the objects that gave them pleasure—great baskets of fruit and flowers or an arrangement of crystal goblets on a precious piece of oriental carpet. The demand for them made these paintings into an investment; especially good examples changed hands for high prices, and even quite humble Dutch burghers and Dutch farmers thought it not only a pleasant thing in itself to buy paintings, but a good speculation. John Evelyn, the English diarist, thus describes a Dutch picture market at Rotterdam in 1641:

"We arrived late at Rotterdam where was their annual mart or fair, so furnished with pictures (especially landscapes and drolleries) that I was amazed. Some I bought and sent into England. The reason for this store of pictures and their cheapness proceeds from their want of land to employ their stock, so that it is an ordinary thing to find a common farmer lay out two or three thousand pounds in this commodity. Their houses are full of them, and they vend them at the fairs to very great gain."

There was a rising demand for portraits too, as the Dutch burghers gained in wealth and confidence and liked to hang on their walls paintings of themselves, their wives and children that captured not only a likeness but also fitly represented the social standing, the prosperity, and distinction of the sitter. The clothes are usually somber, but the quality of the stuff is carefully shown; black silk facings shine against the deeper richness of black velvet—no easy trick for a painter to catch the precise texture of the different materials. A gleaming jewel, a gold chain, the snowy contrast of a fine muslin ruff or a lace collar—these are the principal ornaments, and for the artist often the only points of color and excitement that he can use to emphasize his composition. Dutch portrait painters acquired an extraordinary forcefulness in the treatment of the human face and hands, and an extraordinary skill in working out a striking design with small points of color and relief.

An easier task confronted the artist who was required to paint one of the group paintings, which were also immensely in demand. Companies of merchants, learned societies, and above all—for this was a country still at war—the officers of the local volunteers wished to be painted in groups. So there came into being the innumerable group portraits of citizen-officers, wearing the broad, gold-fringed, many-colored sashes which at that time were the designating marks of military men. The only essential was that the face of each man should be clearly shown.

Rembrandt gave offense by breaking this rule. Carried away by his own more profound and subtle vision of the play of light and shade, he painted in *The Sortie of the Banning Cocq Company* (familiarly and quite incorrectly known as *The Night Watch*) one of the greatest of his pictures, and certainly the most memorable of all the group portraits of this epoch. But it is easy to understand why some of the sitters, whose forms and faces are lost in shadow, were far from pleased with the result.

Rembrandt was for a time a fashionable and successful portrait painter, but he stands apart from the portrait painters and genre painters who supplied the new and eager demands of the Dutch. He has the quality of genius which (like that of Shakespeare in another sphere) is outside historic time and place. But this can and should be said: Rembrandt could have achieved the fulfillment of his genius probably nowhere else so well as in seventeenth-century

In paintings like A Woman Weighing Gold, *Jan Vermeer raised the seventeenth-century Dutch genius for genre art to new heights.*

Holland. Amsterdam with its world-wide trade provided him with exciting and infinite visual material; his book was life, and he read men and learned in the end to set down what he had read with a sad and silent wisdom that has never been equaled. In Amsterdam his penetrating talent could draw on a multitude of different kinds of men and women—the philosopher, the merchant, the soldier, the rich young girl, the grizzled seaman, the kitchen maid, or the withdrawn faces of rabbis.

For a time he was successful, but genius so individual and so strong can rarely retain popular favor. He went beyond his public and fell into disfavor. But he was never utterly neglected. He always retained a small group of discriminating admirers and of patrons who valued and bought his pictures. It is the great merit of a society like that of seventeenth-century Holland—so competitive and so various—that it has room for small groups, literary and artistic cliques, which can sustain and encourage work outside the grasp of the general public.

It would not be strictly true to say that Rembrandt reveals the inner spirit of the Dutch at this time. He is a painter of the spirit, but his message is at the same time so individual and so universal that it would be a belittlement to attach it merely to the Dutch Golden Age. But no epoch, however fruitful, can be held to be truly great unless it has produced one giant of universal stature, one genius who transcends time and place. For the Golden Age of the Dutch Republic that giant is Rembrandt.

One other painter of this time has a claim to rank among the greatest—a painter whose achievement, unlike that of Rembrandt, belongs in time and space and by every outward convention to Holland in the seventeenth century and to no other epoch or place in the world. That painter is Jan Vermeer of Delft. He depicted with absolute faithfulness the domestic scenes and simple views that were so dear to Dutch collectors. A girl offers a glass of wine to a visitor; a housewife sits sewing in her doorway; a youthful party make music at the virginals; a young woman is discovered reading a love letter. The broom is propped against the wall, the paved floor has been mopped clean, the sun throws onto the dazzlingly white wall the harsh shadows of the heavy picture frames, picks up the sheen of a satin skirt, lingers in the soft glow of a pearl earring. It is the world of Gerard Terborch, of Jan Steen, and Pieter de Hooch. But it is also—and who can say why?—a moment stopped out of time. Here is an incident of no importance, a fragment from the lives of unknown people held forever, not just as a picture but as a reality. With the other Dutch genre painters we know we are looking at a picture; with Jan Vermeer we are experiencing a living moment.

With him, therefore, we come nearest to the inner essence of the Dutch seventeenth century. The zest for liberation, the adventurousness, the energy, and the wealth of this remarkable people do not explain all. Politically they achieved freedom; materially they achieved wealth; their Golden Age was built on these things, but they are not the spirit and the secret of its greatness. What else must there have been? Does the secret lie in this intensity of *living,* this concentration of the spirit, which Vermeer has so perfectly and so indefinably captured within the narrow limits of his few surviving paintings?

287

PICTURE CREDITS

72 73 74 75 76 9 8 7 6 5 4 3